D1047070

Early praise for *The Purpose Effect*

As the sense of meaning in the corporate world continues to plummet, the shortage of clear and comprehensive thinking on solutions has become acute. Dan Pontefract rides to the rescue with *The Purpose Effect,* providing a well-argued and detailed framework for organizations and their people to find and maintain their purpose "sweet spot."

—Roger L. Martin, author and Institute Director,
Martin Prosperity Institute, Rotman School of Management

The Purpose Effect helps individuals and leaders connect the dots between the personal, professional, and organizational. Dan Pontefract makes a strong case that we shouldn't check our core values in life at the office door.

—Adam Grant, Wharton professor and *New York Times*
bestselling author of *Give and Take* and *Originals*

A compelling thesis on how purpose can drive not only personal fulfillment but also lead to more stable, cohesive and higher performing organizations. *The Purpose Effect* is a must-read for any who doubt the impact of purpose on organizational stability and performance.

—Paul Polman, Chief Executive Officer, Unilever

Purpose has never been more important in the world. If the workplace is truly going to be 100% human, it has to start with purpose, for individuals and for the organisation. Dan Pontefract takes you on a journey on how to make this a reality for yourself and your organisation.

— Jean Oelwang, President and Trustee, Virgin Unite

We are at a momentous inflection point. Income inequality, plummeting levels of trust in major institutions, the disillusionment of a generation of young people and a sense that for many, the future is going to be less secure and predictable than the past are leading to a deep hunger for fresh ideas for a new social compact. *The Purpose Effect* presents a marvelous and optimistic approach to achieving this. For many who are discouraged by the emptiness of organizational life, this readable, practical guide is an antidote to disengagement and cynicism at work and in society. I am delighted to see such a powerful guide to how each of us can proactively take charge of making sure that our lives have meaning.

— Rita Gunther McGrath, Associate Professor,
Columbia Business School and author of *The End Of Competitive Advantage*

Hollywood and popular literature would lead you to believe that big business and a meaningful life don't mix. Not so, says Dan Pontefract. When we align our purpose with that of our job and our organization, we can have, as Studs Terkel said, "astonishment rather than torpor…life rather than a Monday through Friday sort of dying." Read *The Purpose Effect* to find your astonishment.

— Karie Willyerd, author of The *2020 Workplace* and *Stretch*,
Workplace Futurist, SAP SuccessFactors

Dan Pontefract brings us back to the principles of purpose. *The Purpose Effect* helps professionals and leaders from all sectors know how to connect the dots between purpose and positive results.

— Don Tapscott, author, CEO of The Tapscott Group Inc., and
Inaugural Fellow, Martin Prosperity Institute, Rotman School of Management

In our quest to grow our careers, advance and develop our skills, we often forget the importance of purpose. *The Purpose Effect* is a wonderful book that reminds us how important it is to look within, and find purpose in our jobs, careers and organizations.

—Josh Bersin, HR Industry Analyst,
Principal and Founder, Bersin by Deloitte

Purpose mobilizes people in a way that profits alone never will. Dan Pontefract's *The Purpose Effect* shows why and how, lifting the discussion of this crucial ingredient to a whole new level of clarity.

—Herminia Ibarra, The Cora Chaired Professor of
Leadership and Learning, INSEAD and author of
If You Act Like A Leader You Will Think Like A Leader

Dan Pontefract raises the discussion of purpose to the next level using his three-category model with the "sweet spot," looking at it holistically and its impact on individuals, organizations and society as a whole. This book is loaded with examples that take it from what might seem as a nice-to-have, to a must-have in order to maximize impact, engagement and contribution.

—Tony Bingham, President and Chief Executive Officer,
Association for Talent Development

Building on the insights into organizational culture that he developed in *FLAT ARMY*, Dan Pontefract takes us on a journey that explores one of the most fundamental questions of the ages: how do we make our lives matter? Through sharing his personal experiences and those of many others, Dan makes a compelling case for the need to align our personal values with those of the organizations where we choose to work and the roles we perform. The result is not only personal fulfilment, but also superior organizational performance and societal progress.

—Saul Klein, Dean & Lansdowne Professor of International Business at the
Peter B. Gustavson School of Business, University of Victoria

Individuals spend a significant majority of their adult lives at work. Looking in the mirror at the end of a day, month and year should result in recognition that the time investment has been worthwhile at a very human level. This requires intrinsic attention to purpose and meaning from each of us, individually, and as teams and communities. In *The Purpose Effect* Dan Pontefract shares years of wisdom for how to cultivate this "sweet spot" leading to more individual and organizational satisfaction and success.

—Karen Kocher, Chief Learning Officer, Cigna

Dan Pontefract provides a powerful framework to make work deeply fulfilling and productive for the most valuable members of the workforce, those that are purpose-oriented.

—Aaron Hurst, Chief Executive Officer, Imperative and author of *The Purpose Economy*

Engagement research is clear: people want to work for a purpose, not just a paycheck. *The Purpose Effect* should be required reading for anyone who wants to find and develop meaning in their life, their role and throughout their company. A great read for anyone who is looking to get the most from their career and life.

—Kevin Kruse, *New York Times* bestselling author of *Employee Engagement 2.0*

The Purpose Effect should become a go-to resource for all leaders who want to drive a purposeful and meaningful organizational culture. The ever-changing workplace demands direction for how to encourage people to live out their purpose; this book explains how to do so in a way that positively impacts the individual, workplace and overall organization.

— Meghan M. Biro, Founder and CEO, TalentCulture

The separation of personal purpose from our professional lives limits our perception of success. In examining the benefits of uniting personal and professional with organizational purpose, Dan Pontefract has built a three-legged machine around the principles of purpose.

—Faisal Hoque, founder of SHADOKA and author of *Everything Connects* and *Survive to Thrive*

The separation of personal purpose from our professional lives limits our perception of success. For leaders who want to understand how employee purpose impacts an organization, *The Purpose Effect* stands alone as a guiding instrument.

—Jeff Booth, Co-Founder, President and CEO of BuildDirect

Dan Pontefract's *The Purpose Effect* is a challenge to both the worker and the leader to find the winning trifecta—a combination of a personal sense of purpose, an organizational purpose and a role purpose.

—Dee Ann Turner, VP, Chick-fil-A and author of *It's My Pleasure*

With *The Purpose Effect*, Dan Pontefract addresses a key organizational and human challenge for today's leaders. As Peter Drucker noted already in his early writings on management, the purpose and meaning that organizations convey are not only essential for economic performance but represent a key contribution to the coherence of society.

—Richard Straub, President of Peter Drucker Society Europe
and Associate Director of EFMD

Thankfully, momentum is building against the "maximize shareholder value" mindset that has undermined the long-term health of so many companies and done so much damage to society. Dan Pontefract's *The Purpose Effect* is sure to become an important part of this movement, for it makes abundantly clear that corporations—and all of their team members—are far happier and perform better when they remember that what they do affects customers, colleagues, the community and owners alike. As Dan shows, profit is actually higher, and certainly more sustainable, when it's linked with purpose.

— Rick Wartzman, Senior Advisor, The Drucker Institute

While educators are driven by passion, until we intentionally outline why we do our work, we won't achieve our goals for every student in every school. *The Purpose Effect* offers a compelling rationale to define our purpose in ways that will increase our effectiveness both individually and collectively, and to hold ourselves accountable for what really matters.

— Stephanie Hirsh, Executive Director of Learning Forward

As robotics, artificial intelligence and cheap computing power drive us toward a large disruption in the world of work, it is time to think of the question, why do we work? *The Purpose Effect* tells us how to discover the answer in today's context. The sweet spot lies at the intersection of one's own purpose with the purpose of the organization and the purpose of the role we have.

—Abhijit Bhaduri, author and Chief Learning Officer, Wipro

Good things happen when people are connected with purpose. In *The Purpose Effect*, Dan Pontefract challenges both leaders and individuals to find their purpose and use their workplace to live it out.

—David Burkus, author of *Under New Management* and
Associate Professor of Management at Oral Roberts University

The Purpose Effect Scorecard is possibly the most valuable tool for any business leader picking up Dan Pontefract's insightful book. Start with the end in mind:

1. Know what you are going to measure to shift your organisation's results;
2. Decide what numbers you want to see on that scorecard; and
3. Follow his advice to connect your organisation's purpose with your employees' purpose and role purpose to get there.

— Annalie Killian, partner at Alchemy,
Creative Director at Spark Labs and Founder of Amplify Festival

Brilliant, practical, inspiring. Higher Calling meets Daily To-Dos and creates your awesome Sweet Spot. In *The Purpose Effect*, Dan Pontefract has delivered that sweet spot to you, simply, clearly, deliciously. Get this book now and lead, live and work on purpose, every day!

—Bill Jensen, author of *Future Strong* and *Disrupt!*

The Purpose Effect is the reminder to everyone in your organization that good things happen when we work with purpose. Dan Pontefract's challenge to all of us: determine your purpose and then watch how society can flourish.

—Peter Johnston, author of *Negotiating with Giants*

THE
PURPOSE
EFFECT

BUILDING MEANING IN
YOURSELF, YOUR **ROLE,**
AND YOUR **ORGANIZATION**

DAN PONTEFRACT

Copyright © 2016 by Dan Pontefract.

Published in Boise, Idaho by Elevate. A division of Elevate Publishing.

For more information please go to www.elevatepub.com or email us at info@elevatepub.com. 1-800-208-3216

All rights reserved. No part of this publication may be reproduced, distributed or transmitted in any form or by any means, including photocopying, recording, digital scanning, or other electronic or mechanical methods without the prior written permission of the publisher, except in the case of brief quotations embodied in critical reviews and certain other noncommercial uses permitted by copyright law.

For permission requests, please contact Elevate Publishing at info@elevatepub.com

Editorial Work: AnnaMarie McHargue
Cover Design: Aaron Snethen
Interior Design: Kiran Spees

This book may be purchased in bulk for educational, business, organizational or promotional use. To do so, contact Elevate Publishing at info@elevatepub.com

ISBN-10: 1937498891

ISBN-13: 978-1937498894

Library of Congress Control Number: 2015956307

For Claire, Cole and Cate,

You are three shining beacons of tenderness, curiosity and hope.
May the entirety of your lives be filled with meaning and purpose,
through your chosen calling.
"Love is life. All, everything that I understand,
I only understand because I love."

Love always, *Daddio*

DESIDERATA

Go placidly amid the noise and haste, and remember what peace there may be in silence.

As far as possible without surrender be on good terms with all persons.

Speak your truth quietly and clearly; and listen to others, even the dull and ignorant; they too have their story.

Avoid loud and aggressive persons, they are vexations to the spirit.

If you compare yourself with others, you may become vain and bitter;

for always there will be greater and lesser persons than yourself.

Enjoy your achievements as well as your plans.

Keep interested in your career, however humble; it is a real possession in the changing fortunes of time.

Exercise caution in your business affairs; for the world is full of trickery.

But let this not blind you to what virtue there is; many persons strive for high ideals;

and everywhere life is full of heroism.

Be yourself.

Especially, do not feign affection.

Neither be critical about love; for in the face of all aridity and disenchantment it is as perennial as the grass.

Take kindly the counsel of the years, gracefully surrendering the things of youth.

Nurture strength of spirit to shield you in sudden misfortune. But do not distress yourself with imaginings.

Many fears are born of fatigue and loneliness. Beyond a wholesome discipline, be gentle with yourself.

You are a child of the universe, no less than the trees and the stars;

you have a right to be here.

And whether or not it is clear to you, no doubt the universe is unfolding as it should.

Therefore be at peace with God, whatever you conceive Him to be,

and whatever your labors and aspirations, in the noisy confusion of life keep peace with your soul.

With all its sham, drudgery and broken dreams, it is still a beautiful world. Be careful. Strive to be happy.[1]

Max Ehrmann 1927

CONTENTS

Acknowledgments xvii

Foreword xxi

Introduction 1

Part I

Chapter 1: The Purpose of Purpose 15

Chapter 2: Moral Purpose 35

Part II

Chapter 3: Not On Purpose 51

Chapter 4: Purpose Mismatch 67

Part III

Chapter 5: Creating a Personal Sense of Purpose 83

Chapter 6: Developing Organizational Purpose 101

Chapter 7: Establishing Role-Based Purpose 129

Part IV

Chapter 8: Communitas—A Community of Purpose 151

Chapter 9: Sweet Spot Guidance 175

About the Author 207

Index 209

References 223

ACKNOWLEDGMENTS

In the Trenches . . .

This book was nearly a disaster, a personally calamitous act like no other. The original manuscript was 93,000 words, rather dark and missing an integral component. Just prior to printing 200 copies of the galley, I actually said, "Stop The Press" to Mark Russell, CEO of Elevate Publishing. "Whatever it takes, Dan," he said to me over the phone. It was cool to say those words out loud—stop the press—but equally humiliating. The unadulterated support provided by Mark was the type of relationship I was hoping for in a publisher. *The Purpose Effect* is a much different book than the one I originally wrote, and it is because of six key people, and a healthy supply of scotch. I cannot thank these people enough. This book came to be mostly because of their guidance, input and support. O sherpa, where art thou? To Mark Colgate, for helping to set me straight. (You were spot on in your early feedback.) To Roger L. Martin, for indeed setting me straight. (I am indebted to your advice and assistance.) To Richard Martin, for setting it straight. (Every author would be far better off working with you.) To Anna McHargue, for keeping me straight. (Thanks for your sage counsel and tone reminders.) To Mark Russell, for accepting my strait. (Your commitment to me is most appreciated.) To Don Loney, for always straightening my strait. (Clarinet players pop up in the weirdest spots.)

To the entire team at Elevate: What can I say? While thinking about and writing (and then re-writing) this book, in parallel, I divorced the publisher that published my first book, *FLAT ARMY*. What a difference! You are a caring, open and very responsive group of people. You are very much like the publishing office that brought me to print in 2013. Sadly, corporate megalomaniacs shuttered their office and displaced everyone. When I was punted to another office, they wanted nothing to do with me. Orphaned, lonely and disillusioned, I was looking for someone like you. Thanks for all that you have done, and will continue to do in the future. Thank you Mark Russell, Anna McHargue, Bobby Kuber, Aaron Snethen, Todd Carman, Emily Border, Leslie Hertling, Kim Sutherlin and everyone else.

Thank you, Nilofer Merchant, for the foreword, and a budding relationship.

In Work . . .

I am forever indebted to those who helped both this book and my ongoing personal pursuit of purpose come to fruition. Thank you, in no particular order, to John Helliwell, Joel Bakan, Tim MacDonald, Helena Clayton, Martin Seligman, Richard Straub, Herminia Ibarra, Brian Scudamore, Bridget Hilton, Joe Huff, David Autor, Brenda Rigny, Kim Graham-Nye, Jason Graham-Nye, Karl Moore, Connie O'Halloran, Brian Church, Mana Ionescu, Mary Hewitt, Hazel Po, John Hagel, Bryan Acker, Lynette Van Steinburg, Paul Bleier, Megan Smith, Dan Price, Mike Desjardins, Elango Elangovan, Céline Schillinger, Kelsy Trigg, Jill Schnarr, Steven Hill, Martin Perelmuter, Kenneth Mikkelsen, Robert Morris, Henry Mintzberg, Rick Wartzman, Janice Williams, Amy Wrzesniewski, Daniel Pink, Jennifer Aaker, Bas van Abel, Saul Klein, Chuck Luttrell, Lorna Shapiro, Ken Takagaki, Phil Noelting, John McNaughton, Sanjee Singla, Adam Grant, Michael Bungay Stanier, Praveen Singh, Debra Criveau, Aaron Hurst, Andrew Marks, Aaron Johannes, Sarah Wright, Rosabeth Moss Kanter, Charles Handy, Stephen Denning, Lisa Brummel, Jon Husband, William Lazonick, Otto Scharmer, Linds Redding, Cory Bouck, Michael Papay, Darren Entwistle, Josh Blair, Donna McNicol, Andrew Turner, Jeffrey Puritt, Dan Klein, Tim Kastelle, Josh Bersin, Craig Dowden, Linda Duxbury, Sameer Patel, Carolyn Beal, Gordon Downie, Ryan Honeyman, Brian Reid, Steven Hill, Alexandra Samuel, Deb Arnold, Alison van Buuren, Marcia Conner, Chuck Hamilton, John Ambrose, Karie Wilyerd, Shawn Hunter, Euan Semple, Bruce Duthie, Jocelyn Berard, Stephen Lamb, Bill Jensen, Harold Jarche, Rawn Shah, Anne Marie McEwan, Charles Jennings, Deborah Wickens, Sara Roberts and of course, the folks at Evernote. Undoubtedly I have missed someone. For that, I am profusely apologetic. Parts of the book were written at the Penny Farthing Pub and at the Oak

Bay Beach Hotel, in particular Kate's Café. I blame your double chocolate chip cookies for the weight gain. Just saying.

In Contact . . .

I am a privileged individual who does not take for granted the hundreds of people I get to meet in person and over the interwebs. Thank you for your emails, retweets, texts, voicemails, likes, whatever that thing on Twitter is now, handshakes, claps, letter (there was that one), smiles, emojis, kiss (there was that one), selfies, comments, shares and hugs. I try my darnedest to respond to every query, quandary or inquiry, but if I have missed you—like a true Canadian—I am sorry. Next beer is on me.

. . . And In Love

As always, my love for family completes my personal purpose. Love ya, Mia, Roy, Nicole, Alana, Natasha, Adam, Michelle, Zoe, Rich, Kara, Suzanne, Chris, Madeleine, Tyler, Debbie, Diane, Ron, Jane, Lawrence and the reason I smile every day...Claire, Cole and Cate. Gautama Buddha wrote, "Your purpose in life is to find your purpose and give your whole heart and soul to it." How lucky am I to devote my love—indeed my whole heart and soul—into the three of you. I love you to the moon and back. No, to Pluto. No, to Endor. No, to Dagobah. Ok, I'll stop. Finally, thank you to Denise, the one who has shared so many highs (and a few lows) with me over 20 years of marriage. (20 years! We made it!) Not entirely sure what life would be like without you, so let's sign up for another 20 years and see what happens. It seems to be working just fine. I know you wonder "when" I actually write books, but your unwavering support is unquestionably the reason they get written in the first place. In this case two books for the price of one! Thanks for your patience, encouragement and above all, your spidey sense to pour scotch at 10:00 p.m. every now and then when I needed a Rabbit Room inspiration. I'll always give you an A+. "We'll be Friends Forever, won't we, Pooh?' asked Piglet. 'Even longer,' Pooh answered." Thanks, Pooh. I'll be here even longer, too.

FOREWORD

Purpose is not a new idea. People have discussed the idea of purpose since the time of the ancient Greeks.

In modern times, purpose has been discussed by the best. Peter Drucker wrote about the role of purpose in *Theory of the Business* back in the 1970s. Simon Sinek's book popularized it with his *Start With Why*. Martha Beck shared finding personal purpose in her book, *Finding Your Own North Star*, while Rick Warren guided readers to discover it in their spiritual life in his best-seller *The Purpose Driven Life*.

So, purpose isn't new to any discipline. But you know what *is* new?

Expecting and hoping to be purposeful. We want purpose to apply to our lives, not as the decorative frosting on top—a nice to have—but instead the abundant yeast that creates growth. We want to live with a sense of purpose in our personal life and then, we want to bring our purpose to our work. And, we want the organization for which we work to likewise be purposeful. We imagine that when this happens, we will benefit, our organization will benefit and society will benefit. It's a big wish.

So why do we keep talking about it? Because embodying your purpose in life, in work and at work is hard to do. It's easy in theory, but then reality hits and all those nice intentions go out the window.

But purpose matters more than ever, especially in business. Purpose has moved from a "nice to have" to a strategic business imperative. An organization's purpose is not the icing on the cake, but the cake itself. It is core to what matters. It is central to making a difference in society.

For nearly 20 years, the marketplace has shown us that organizations once holding an advantage are either gone or on the verge of extinction. Experts have called this shift from the Industrial Era to the Social Era radical, even tectonic.

Today, connected individuals can do what once only large centralized organizations could. Across every part of the value chain, connected people can create, build, ship and compete with the largest of entities.

But the key principle is "connected humans." Some people hear the word "connected" and read it as "platforms," suggesting that the technology is the central part. They are wrong. A great deal of management mindsets lead us in the wrong direction by discounting the value of team members with their inherently unique capabilities and potential.

Purpose—not platforms—is what enables all creative endeavors. Purpose is what empowers people to do great things, both in life and at work.

Dan writes about "the sweet spot," the axis on which talented people gather together to create value through an alignment between three types of purpose: personal, organizational and role. This central argument is critical, something that successfully expands upon the works of others.

Purpose brings out the best in people, and the best people. Purpose is a better motivator than money. Money, while necessary, motivates neither the best people nor the best in people. Purpose does.

When people know the purpose of an organization, they don't need to check in or get permission to take the next step; they can just do it. When the organization is demonstrating purpose, the likelihood of employees going above and beyond the call of duty greatly increases. When people share in purpose, they will bring their all to the group's efforts. When organizations stand for something, it brings coherence to everything, and a real advantage to what they offer.

Purpose can *and* does aid society.

You know the concept of purpose is important. Dan's book, *The Purpose Effect*, will help turn the concept into reality for you, your role and your organization.

Nilofer Merchant
2015

INTRODUCTION

On the fifth floor of a nondescript Amsterdam building lies Fairphone. It is the world's first socially responsible and sustainable company to design, manufacture and sell mobile phones. Like most companies, Fairphone aims to make a profit. But less common is that the company refuses to do so at the expense of its purpose. As its name suggests, Fairphone operates on the principle that a philosophy of fairness can inform its production and sales. Fairness, balance and accountability to all stakeholders—including its employees—sit at the center of the organization's purpose.

When I walked into Fairphone headquarters, employees were busy coding, engaging one another in conversation, talking on their phones and making tea in its open-plan office. The scene reminded me of many other high-tech start-up firms I have visited in the past. It reminded me of places I have worked at, too. Whiteboards were chock-full of ideas and various scribbles. The hum of activity was palpable. There were huddles of people working together. Plates of pastries were scattered across the kitchen bar. However, people were not working at Fairphone for the free food or for the discounted bus pass.

Bas van Abel is the Founder and CEO of Fairphone. He is an individual who clearly wants to change the world. In particular, Bas sees the world needing to evolve from what he calls its "pernicious and unsustainable ways." His perspective is both reactive and inclusive: "We are part of everything. None of us at Fairphone feels as though the financial system is connected to who we are, and as a result, we all need to collaboratively think differently and act differently, too." The "we" he refers to is not only Fairphone and its employees, but society itself.

Bas has built a business based on one simple point: We are all part of the ecosystem. As Haydn Shaughnessy argues in *Shift: A User's Guide to the New Economy*, it is organizations that participate in an ecosystem of interaction and innovation that will help achieve mutual gains. More importantly, the ecosystem way of thinking is the manner in which future generations may prosper. At Fairphone, society is part of the ecosystem. The core of the organization's purpose is to build a product that delivers value to all stakeholders that make up the entire ecosystem. As Bas claims, "Fairphone goes beyond being a company." He believes Fairphone—and all organizations, for that matter—is an important part of the change needed in today's model of economics.

Fairphone's purpose is to manufacture mobile phones that are ethical. The phones are made from conflict-free minerals assembled by firms who also ensure fair wages for the factory workers. The 40 employees who work directly at Fairphone in Amsterdam think of themselves as caretakers of the Earth. They make a mobile phone but do so ensuring they keep the greater good of society in mind.

Operating as an independent social enterprise since 2013, Fairphone seeks to achieve a balance between its organizational purpose and the need for profit. Like any private company, Fairphone requires increased revenues and positive profit margins in order not only to grow the business but simply to stay *in* business. Everyone involved in Fairphone subscribes to the overarching purpose; nevertheless, all have bills to pay, too. The company is unwilling, though, to allow for imbalance: Organizational purpose cannot be sacrificed in favor of the quest for profit.

Interestingly, Fairphone decided at an early stage not to take on any investors or venture capitalists. Likewise, there are no plans for any capital-backed investment. "Going the private investment route is very short-sighted," Bas explains. "Our success is defined by creating impact with proportional growth. Purpose does not mean you're doing something special. It's the idealism of a more holistic view that isn't focused specifically on private gains."

Bas believes the company will grow, but not at the expense of its organizational purpose to serve the ecosystem. He chose to start a business in the commercial space—and the mobile phone industry specifically—mostly because he is someone who loves to learn. In fact, loving to learn is part of Bas's personal definition of purpose. We all have personal priorities and goals. Bas places a tremendous amount of value in learning, so much so that he considers it one of his personal priorities. Think of it as one of his core operating principles. If Bas is not learning, he is not fulfilled and therefore he is not meeting his own personal sense of purpose.

Starting Fairphone helped satisfy Bas's personal need to learn and it cemented his quest to create a more sustainable mobile phone. For example, he teamed up with the United Nations in the Congo to learn how the company might source materials and minerals for the phone more ethically. This partnership has allowed him to learn, and to continue fueling Fairphone's purpose. When he began working with local leaders in the Congo, he used this connection as a way to acquire knowledge about the local working conditions—as well as how materials were being sourced by suppliers of the iPhone and Android devices—in order to improve Fairphone's procurement and production processes.

Bas's experiences with Fairphone have given him further insight into the value of purpose and the efficacy of new practices. "The only way a 'purpose-with-profit' model will work is if everyone believes it. How can you create a new economic model of thinking to achieve a profit with purpose? All the time at Fairphone we're trying to show that purpose can *balance* with profit. Mistakes are made at Fairphone, but we don't think binary. It's not people; rather, it's the systems of stock exchanges and financial models that are the problem. It's the long-term view that we take. The better question is *how can one challenge the status quo*, and that's what Fairphone keeps doing."

He concludes our discussion with an expansive observation: "The purpose of Fairphone goes beyond being a company. All of us at Fairphone are looking at the world in a different way. We can only do that as being a part of a bigger thing. We are part of that change toward a greater purpose, and I'm so proud."

After departing, it dawned on me that Bas's personal sense of purpose was being fulfilled at least partially through Fairphone. The personal values, attributes, interests and priorities that are important to Bas are being met through Fairphone's organizational purpose and the role he serves at the company. He wants to learn and change the world, and he gets to do that at Fairphone. Furthermore, Bas has developed a culture and hired people at Fairphone that supports the intersection of three different types of purpose: personal, organizational and role.

He believes an organization's purpose is to serve society and that includes its employees. Fairphone has dedicated its mission to carry this out in the form of making a more ethical mobile phone. Not only is Bas personally engaged and seemingly delighted to work in a role that permits him the opportunity to operate with a purpose mindset, but he also is an individual who is passionate, innovative and committed to a meaningful and engaging workplace that serves all stakeholders.

Could it be that Bas, Fairphone and its employees are exhibiting the three key principles of what I call *The Purpose Effect*?

The Opportunity for Purpose

Since 1994, I have enjoyed the good fortune of working with people and teams in both corporate and academic settings. Throughout my career, whether working internally with thousands of peers, interviewing various leaders and employees across the globe or consulting with organizations who seek counsel and guidance on their own internal culture and operating practices, I have noticed the emergence of a unique pattern.

The Purpose Effect is a three-way relationship between an individual's personal sense of purpose in life, the organization's purpose and a person's purpose in their role at work. When all three aspects of purpose are properly defined, are well aligned and function in partnership with one another, then the employee, the organization and society mutually benefit. When they are not, it can lead to significant damage in society and in the organization. *The Purpose Effect* is the pattern I have exposed.

If an organization exhibits a high degree of purpose in its mission and objectives—taking a stand to benefit society—there is a good possibility that employees will more easily demonstrate purpose in their roles at work, likely aiding and adding to their own personal sense of purpose in life as well. It is no coincidence that the organization, society *and* the employee greatly benefit when this occurs.

If an individual joins an organization that is in direct conflict with their personal sense of purpose, there is a strong likelihood they will develop a workplace mindset that is negative, ambivalent, even melancholic. If the role an individual performs provides the opportunity to demonstrate purpose—in alignment with both a personal sense of purpose and that of the organization—there is a very good chance of increased engagement, even fulfillment.

Think of it as a three-legged barstool. If one of the legs is broken or uneven, either an individual ends up crashing to the ground or there is a perpetual wobble, prompting a feeling of uneasiness, of disequilibrium. Such a lack of balance in the workplace can result in personal disengagement, disbandment of a team, or in the direst instance, the end of the organization itself. Those who lack direction in these situations, simply go through the motions, longing for the day when their opinions and ideas mattered, helpless as senior leaders pursue an organizational purpose that has no meaning for them personally. Any lack of alignment between the three categories of purpose—the barstool legs—can have devastating consequences at both an individual and a collective level.

The Purpose Effect requires balance, harmony and ultimately alignment between a person's life, the organization where they are employed and their role at work. When this alignment is present, there are strength and unity between the three categories. When such strength and unity are prevalent, they result in psychological and emotional employee commitment. That is, when an employee feels part of something bigger at work and it aligns with their personal sense of purpose, they perform better. The organization also benefits. Deloitte reported purpose-first types of organizations "have 30 percent higher levels of innovation and 40 percent higher levels of retention, and they tend to be first or second in their market segment."[1]

What Exactly Is *The Purpose Effect*?

The Purpose Effect chronicles my thesis and findings. This book draws on research, interviews and first-hand leadership experience, establishing a potentially positive and reciprocal connection between three distinct categories of purpose:

- Personal purpose

- Organizational purpose

- Role purpose

If all three categories of purpose can come to fruition—if there is a positive interconnection between the three distinct definitions of purpose—the benefits should be felt by employees, teams, the organization, customers, owners and, perhaps most importantly, society as a whole. We can refer to this balanced state as the *"sweet spot."* This includes the *ecosystem* that Bas van Abel referred to at Fairphone and is made up of *all* stakeholders. For it is the stakeholders whom an organization ought to serve, not those who solely seek increases in power, bureaucracy, economic rents or greed. Indeed, *The Purpose Effect* is a mission to put "Stakeholders First." The stakeholders I am referring to are customers (the group an organization serves), employees (the team members who carry out an organization's mission and objectives), society (our planet and the communities in which we live) and, if applicable, owners/shareholders (those due a fair and just return for their investment).

This book, therefore, is aimed at both leaders *and* employees who wish to achieve a purpose mindset on a personal level, for the organization where they are employed and in their role at work, too. They do so, I hope, in order to create meaning. This book is targeted at those individuals who seek to arrive at the aforementioned sweet spot regardless of their title or level in the organization where they work. *The Purpose Effect* is for anyone interested in becoming more purpose-driven. It is important to note that it takes courage to create the sweet spot. Individuals *and* the organization must demonstrate a degree of fearlessness and prowess if purpose is ever to be simultaneously recognized in the three categories. Courage comes first by establishing your "why."

In 2011, author Simon Sinek taught us to "Start With Why" in the book of the same title. "Leaders start with WHY we need to do things,"[2] writes Sinek. The same observation can be applied to our working selves. Why do we work, why do we work at a particular organization and why are we motivated to work? Indeed, the question of "why" can be applied to the self, too. Why do I enjoy one thing over another? Why am I interested in this facet over the other? Why do I dislike doing things a certain way? The organization (through its senior leaders) must also ask why it is in business. Why is the organization operating the way it does? Why does it serve all stakeholders, or perhaps why does it not? For both the individual and the organization, it really does start with "why." Both parties must have the courage to define their "why." Simon was right.

Bas van Abel seemed to embody an individual who defined his and Fairphone's "why." He found the sweet spot for himself, his co-workers and eventually the broader Fairphone family. Like Bas, the employees of Fairphone are demonstrating purpose in their roles. The organization has instilled a powerful ethos, an open culture. It is the Fairphone employees who have subsequently demonstrated a purpose mindset. The end result is an organization that is achieving its objectives, priorities and mission. The Fairphone workforce believes that there is purpose both in their lives *and* in their roles. Of course, stakeholders are benefiting from the motivated and engaged employees at Fairphone, and its ethically produced phone is benefiting society. We might even go so far as to suggest that any of the Fairphone stakeholders are sitting rather comfortably on their purpose stool enjoying the level ground of the sweet spot. So what exactly is *The Purpose Effect*? I have crystalized it down to one simple sentence:

> *The Purpose Effect* results in a higher calling, where individuals *and* organizations seek to improve society to benefit all stakeholders.

For *The Purpose Effect* to materialize, however, not only must the question of "why" be answered for the individual and the organization, the three categories of purpose—personal, organizational and role—must be defined, aligned and enacted. When this has been accomplished, a "sweet spot" will materialize for both individuals and the organization. Each category that makes up *The Purpose Effect* is defined as follows:

Personal Purpose: *What motivates someone in life; their "why."* An individual's values, experience and beliefs inform personal decisions and actions.

Organizational Purpose: *Why the organization exists.* An organization's principles, ethics and culture inform its ways of operating.

Role Purpose: *Why a role exists in the organization.* To achieve its goals and objectives, an organization establishes a variety of roles to support its mission.

A unique Venn diagram focusing on personal, organizational and role purpose outlines my thesis below:

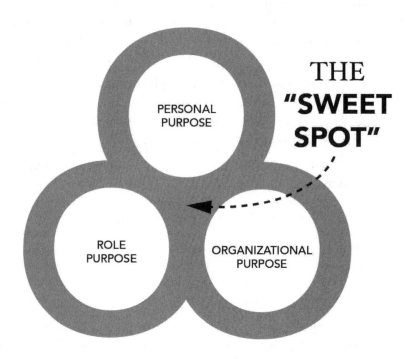

The Book in Brief

The ultimate question is how both an individual *and* the organization might achieve their own respective "sweet spot." Each of us possesses a personal purpose, but we also have to work in order to pay for groceries, a night out at the cinema, donations to a charity or clothes for the children. An individual will experience imbalance if their personal purpose is misaligned with that of the organization, as well as the role they fulfill in service of it. By the same token, an organization can experience imbalance if its purpose is misaligned with the expectations of the society it serves, starting with its own employees. To attain the sweet spot—either individually or organizationally—balance and alignment are essential.

Purpose, and a multi-faceted approach to it, is not new. Greek philosophers openly discussed the meaning of life centuries ago. More recently, David Hieatt diagrammed the notion of purpose in his book *Do Purpose*. Here the focus is on an individual's specific quest for meaning in life through their *love*, their *skill*, and the *zeitgeist*. The area where the three circles overlap he labels *most alive*;[3] a notion of fulfillment that resonates with our own concept of the *sweet spot*. In *The Good Life*, social researcher Hugh Mackay suggested a Venn diagram made up of *listening attentively*, *apologizing sincerely* and *forgiving generously* as the instrument to instill meaning in our lives.[4] Even the comedy troupe Monty Python, in their 1983 movie, *The Meaning of Life*, got into the definition of purpose, poking fun at birth, learning, fighting and death. This book continues the conversation, building on the foundations laid by previous works and research.

The Purpose Effect is written to help both leaders *and* followers. These individuals make up our organizations. Far too many Corporate Social Responsibility (CSR) statements and annual reports claim, "Our employees are our most important asset." Is that what we are? Assets? We are not assets. We are not human capital. We are not a headcount.

We are team members. We are co-workers. We are colleagues. We are both leaders *and* followers. It matters not what level you reside on the corporate hierarchy. We are on the same team that is defining and enacting purpose. It is my aim to surface insights, theories and methods to attain personal, organizational and role-based purpose. I intend to help team members realize they are not an asset, rather the key link to improving society. I intend to help leaders see the importance of purpose in the lives of employees, and for the betterment of society. Indeed, team members are an organization's most important *advantage*.

The Purpose Effect endorses the practices of visionary and purpose-first leaders such as Sir Richard Branson. Much has been written about Branson's Virgin empire and his business acumen, but at the root of the Virgin success story lies its team members, encouraged to innovate while riding high on a wave of purpose for its many stakeholders. That is what makes Virgin and Branson so successful. Innovation may be the seed, but purpose is the pollen that spreads success across the Virgin empire.

The Purpose Effect is a book that highlights truly courageous leaders. People like Paul Polman, CEO of Unilever, who vowed to ensure society is not left behind while his organization redefines the meaning of capitalism against the throes of entrenched economic systems and thinking. It pays homage to people like Howard Schultz, CEO of Starbucks, who once wrote, "Work should be personal. For all of us. Not just for the artist and entrepreneur. Work should have meaning for the accountant, the construction worker, the technologist, the manager and the clerk."[5]

The book, however, mainly surfaces stories and examples from organizations, leaders and individuals you may not know at all. It focuses on their purpose journeys, changes they instituted, organizational practices they implemented and the results they achieved.

This includes people like Mana Ionescu who left a six-figure digital marketing job to start a business that allows her personal sense of purpose, her role and her organization's to shine. Michael Bungay Stanier wants to "infect a billion people with the possibility virus." We will find out why. Mary Hewitt spent 15 years seeking and struggling to establish her own personal sense of purpose in concert with various roles and organizations. Did she ever find it? In Australia there is a couple—the Graham-Nyes—who took it upon themselves to start a diaper company because they felt a higher calling to serve society and the environment better. We will meet Tim McDonald who left an organization and a leader spilling over with purpose—*The Huffington Post* and Arianna Huffington—because his own personal sense of purpose needed to be fueled even more. Céline Schillinger took on her CEO, and in return, redefined her role purpose. Market Basket, LSTN, Earls, Johnsonville Sausage, Etsy, 1-800-Got-Junk and King Arthur Flour are examples of firms trying to get the quest for organizational purpose straight. There are other individuals and organizations we will hear from as well that helped to shape *The Purpose Effect*.

I also take pride in featuring the evolution of TELUS, my own workplace. TELUS is a $12 billion telecommunications firm that believes everyone at the company is a leader of purpose. The organization enables its 43,000 global team members to continuously put its customers first—the omnipresent purpose of the organization—in any of its actions and decisions. We will discover how all of its stakeholders—society, team members, community, customers and shareholders—have benefited.

The book is broken down into the following sections:

I. Moral Purpose

Between 1994 and 2016 I have been fortunate to have found (and help create) the sweet spot on several occasions in my working life. There have been a few points in my career, however, where things did not feel as purposeful as I wanted. Whether related to personal, organizational or role purpose, this section details my own experiences, what I have learned, and how it helped shape my thinking with respect to the overall thesis of *The Purpose Effect*. This is the focus of Chapter 2. It seeks to establish moral authority. At a minimum it provides a moral compass of my past experiences within the three categories of purpose.

II. Not On Purpose

There is much to share in terms of evidence, history and observations about current organizational and leadership practices. This will help the reader understand why purpose is such a difficult aspect to master in any three— let alone all three—categories of purpose. There are five key symptoms that prevent *The Purpose Effect* from materializing: remuneration, profit, role, power and performance. Chapters 3 and 4 help illustrate why purpose has become a difficult concept to implement, and to master.

III. The Three Categories of Purpose

The central arc to *The Purpose Effect* is when personal, organizational and role purpose categories are in alignment. Chapters 5, 6 and 7 outline the specific details of the three categories of purpose. I provide research and stories from both individuals and organizations that have contemplated and accomplished the three parts of the model. Additional emphasis is applied to the unique relationship between an organization's purpose and a team member's role.

IV. Communitas and Sweet Spot Guidance

I turned to Wikipedia—arguably society's best definition of a community— to help define *communitas* or "an unstructured state in which all members of a community are equal, allowing them to share a common experience." In other words, perhaps communitas is the state at which the three categories of purpose intersect to create the sweet spot. As such, Chapters 8 and 9 outline what this ought to look like, and it highlights several tips for both individuals and organizations to achieve the sweet spot.

In Summary

I have written *The Purpose Effect* as a supportive tool to help team members connect the dots between personal, organizational and role purpose and to emphasize accompanying actions that can create multiple benefits for an organization *and* its stakeholders. Over the course of my working life, I have found that individuals *and* organizations that manage to create the sweet spot are the truly enlightened ones of this world. It takes courage, but it is possible.

As Gonzalo said to Prospero in Shakespeare's *The Tempest*, "All torment, trouble, wonder and amazement Inhabits here. Some heavenly power guide us, Out of this fearful country!" Let this book potentially be a guide to affect purpose, to better our society.

I hope you enjoy the journey.

SECTION I

CHAPTER ONE
THE PURPOSE OF PURPOSE

When a man does not know what harbor he is making for,
no wind is the right wind.[1]
Lucius Annaeus Seneca

Life shrinks or expands according to one's courage.[2]
Anaïs Nin

In their influential book, *In Search of Excellence*, Tom Peters and Robert Waterman wrote, "Companies that develop a philosophy and live the philosophy that involves everyone within the organization with the overall success of the company will become better for it."[3] When paired together to enact change, it is the influential open partnership of employees *and* leaders that will ensure the three categories of purpose can come to fruition.

As we progress through the book, however, we will discover that purpose—be it personal, organizational or role—does not materialize out of thin air. An individual ought not to wait for purpose to magically appear. Purpose is often a partnership between the three intersecting categories of personal, organization and role. While it can deliver the sweet spot for the individual, if everything aligns, the organization also can benefit. But the relationship between employee and leader is key. The quest for purpose in any of the three categories fails miserably if this particular relationship is broken.

In his book, *Give and Take*, author and academic Adam Grant wrote, "People often end up working on tasks that aren't perfectly aligned with their interests and skills. A powerful way to give is to help others work on tasks that are more interesting, meaningful, or developmental."[4] *The Purpose Effect* will help leaders recognize the importance of an employee's sense of personal and role purpose, as well as helping to establish purpose at an organizational level. Purpose is hard work. It takes a team. It takes individual effort. Put simply, purpose is not a one-way street of responsibility.

Take for instance, Paul Bleier. He was working at a large consulting firm, but something began to gnaw at him. Paul sensed he was treating his role merely as a job, simply collecting a paycheck, putting in the hours, performing transactional tasks and not exactly thriving at work. In the consulting role, he learned what he could, but he recognized that his personal sense of purpose was not being fulfilled. Paul self-discovered that his personal purpose included being innovative, sociable and enabling others to grow; attributes that were not being utilized or appreciated at his place of work.

He also learned that his company would not be supportive of those attributes and desires that fueled his personal sense of purpose. Ultimately, there was a misalignment between his workplace role, his personal purpose and the organization's purpose. The firm that employed him was focused mostly on its profitability and billable hours count. This is not a bad thing, per se, however a higher organizational purpose was missing and it ran counter to Paul's personal purpose.

When he decided to leave the consulting firm, he eventually joined TELUS as an organizational development consultant, tasked with various aspects of employee engagement. In his role, Paul could be working with teams on collaborative leadership concepts, guiding individuals on career development, or partnering with leaders on various engagement strategies. When he arrived, not only was his sense of relief palpable, but his zeal, energy and creativity were abundant. He was not only productive, his spirit was infectious.

Paul was not just full of purpose in his role, he was glowing, and his stakeholders were happy. His purpose matched that of the organization's purpose, an organization that was galvanized around a customer-first ethos, an open leadership culture and a spirit of community giving. He was able to match his personal sense of purpose, values and attributes with the organization's purpose and his consulting role. I know this because Paul reported directly to me when he arrived.

"I have found that the beautiful thing about personal purpose," Paul informed me one day, "is that it's fluid and can change over time to align with your career stage and aspirations." Paul believed that purpose misalignment is difficult for people to handle. He believed if individuals recognize the early warning signs and take initiative to do something about it, it can thwart any potential for personal or workplace blues. "For me, finding a new organization that more closely aligned to my innovative interests while offering more autonomy to practice new ideas and forge deeper relationships was the key. I learned that when you move away from a victim mindset of 'why is this happening to me' and instead take the time to really understand what inspires and motivates you at work—both you and the organization will reap the rewards."

Paul's view was from the perspective of an employee. He sought out the change himself. He possessed the courage to create and reach the sweet spot. It can be difficult for an organization, however, to attain a purposeful mission or culture by abdicating responsibility for change. Purpose in a role and purpose in the organization both require hard work. It most certainly will not materialize if leaders continue to utilize many of today's ineffective organizational practices. Paul sought out an organization that aligned with his personal sense of purpose, and he ended up achieving role-based purpose in a matter of months. If an organization does not involve its employees to generate a purposeful culture—does not empower or trust them to "do good" in their role—misalignment will continue and stakeholders will suffer.

Members of the Team

This is not a story of "us versus them," of employees versus leaders, of Paul pitted against his former company. *The Purpose Effect* is not the unilateral responsibility of leaders, nor should employees be solely accountable themselves. In fact, whether you lead people or not, employees at any level in the organization are both leaders *and* followers. Whatever the scenario, all employees are in fact leaders fulfilling personal, role-based and organizational objectives. While each of us has crafted our own personal values, interests, dislikes, priorities and objectives in our life, we all have tasks that are part of our role at work, things we have to get done.

In our roles, we each serve the interests (and requirements) of the organization, too. Thus, we are leading our lives, and performing our roles, in concert with the organization that employs us. Paul Bleier contributed to the purpose of TELUS and created a purpose mindset in his role at work, fulfilling part of his personal sense of purpose. The same can be said for Bas van Abel of Fairphone. Both of these gentlemen *and* their organizations are operating in the "sweet spot."

As followers, employees who join a firm become part of and influence an existing system of organizational processes, decisions and personalities. We all have a boss of some sort. My trip to San Francisco and the accompanying expense report have to be approved by someone. The CEO reports into the board who in turn possesses the responsibility to hire or fire that same organization's most senior leader. A politician is often elected by constituents, whom she ultimately serves. A call center agent leads her customers to answers and solves many problems while reporting to a team manager. So, too, we must follow rules and processes inside and outside our places of work. There are rules to follow in order to earn a driver's license, just as there are rules to drive the car itself. For *The Purpose Effect* to be enacted, all people at whatever level of the organizational chart must accept they are both followers and leaders at work, and in life.

For the remainder of the book, I will refer to such people using the term *team member* rather than *employee*, which I find somewhat derogatory, and, in fact, even dehumanizing. *Employee* is suggestive of a head to be counted, another asset to be logged on a spreadsheet. The notion of a *team member* is something I have learned while working at TELUS. The Chief Executive Officer of the company, Darren Entwistle, does not refer to himself as CEO but instead as a "member of the TELUS team." Like me, Darren is a team member.

It is the same for everyone. We are all part of the team. Be it private, not-for-profit or public sector—whether full-time or part-time—I believe everyone has the right to feel as though they are an important part of the team. I believe the term is far more inclusive, more engaging. Such a term unites us. *Team member* also removes the impersonality and subjugation implied by *employee*. Perhaps most importantly, *team member* recognizes the potential we all carry within us to both lead and follow, looking past the formality of hierarchical structures and job titles.

As team members, we should begin to think of ourselves as both leader *and* follower. So, too, we ought to be both a dreamer *and* a doer. We must dream about an idea or an outcome, but we must also make it happen. Therefore, all of us are leaders *and* followers; dreamers and doers. Omnificent. On purpose. We are all *team members.*

A question, then, for all team members to ponder is whether any of us should continue waiting for purpose to magically happen. We might dream of a higher calling or purpose, but we must possess the courage to achieve it, too. *The Purpose Effect* requires bilateral action. It requires a new way of thinking about the relationship between an individual and an organizational definition of purpose. The resulting manner in which team members perform in their roles is understood in the context of this relationship. It also requires, however, a definitive course of action to ensure the sweet spot is achieved.

We should become what Danish philosopher Søren Kierkegaard referred to as a continual fluid process. "An existing individual is constantly in the process of becoming; the actual existing subjective thinker constantly reproduces the existential situation in his thoughts and translates all his thinking into terms of process."[5] But too often, we remain static, forever solely the dreamer or the follower. It remains a "what might have been" mindset whether as individuals or for the organization as a whole.

As psychotherapist Carl Rogers put it, "To some it appears that to be what one is, is to remain static. They see such a purpose or value as synonymous with being fixed or unchanging."[6] But Rogers, like Kierkegaard, believed humans ought to be both the leader and the follower; the dreamer and the doer. "To be what one is," he wrote, "is to enter fully into being a process. Change is facilitated, probably maximized, when one is willing to be what he truly is. It is only as he can become more of himself, can be more of what he has denied in himself, that there is any prospect of change."[7] Therefore, for purpose to manifest in ourselves, our organizations and in our roles, we must heed Kierkegaard's advice, which is, "To be that self which one truly is."[8]

This book encourages individuals to become a fluid process of insight *and* action in the quest to create the "sweet spot." *The Purpose Effect* is possible, but it requires a different way of both thinking and acting, especially in the three areas that make up *The Purpose Effect:* personal, organizational and role.

Personal Purpose

An individual who seeks a personal sense of purpose in life will be one who is constantly developing, defining and deciding their values, priorities, attributes and general ways of conducting themselves in their activities. It is a perpetual cycle of self-discovery. For personal purpose to be identified—to reach their why—the questions of what, who and how ought to be continually asked by the individual. For someone to reach "their" personal purpose, they first must ask themselves how they plan to develop, define and decide their purpose in life. Consider these questions for each:

- **Develop.** *What* is the individual doing to grow and establish their personal values, priorities and attributes?

- **Define.** *Who* is the individual trying to become in life?

- **Decide.** *How* will the individual operate when balancing the realities of life with the opportunity for growth?

As these questions are repeatedly explored and answered throughout one's life, clarity of self comes into focus. If the answers can align with an individual's role at work and in parallel with the organization where they are employed, the individual is potentially on a path toward their own sweet spot of *The Purpose Effect.*

Organizational Purpose

Roger L. Martin is the Academic Director of the Martin Prosperity Institute and former Dean of the Rotman School of Management at the University of Toronto. In his book, *Fixing the Game,* he outlines a series of issues preventing the organization from truly benefiting society. Roger argues that organizations should be placing "customers at the center of the firm and focus on delighting them."[9]

I am extending Roger's argument to introduce a model that organizations could follow to achieve such a state, called the Good DEEDS. I argue that the purpose of an organization ought to be to "provide service to benefit all intended stakeholders."[10] With a workforce that has discovered a sense of purpose in life—complemented by purpose in their role at work—the sweet spot for the organization can be achieved if the Good DEEDS concept is implemented. The Good DEEDS idea can be defined as follows:

- **Delight your customers**. An organization ought to commit to working with and for the customer—continuously dedicated to delighting them while improving value—always remembering why an organization exists in the first place.

- **Engage your team members**. To improve value and service with customers, team members must feel as though there is purpose in their work—that they are engaged and flourishing in their role as part of a team—while possessing the opportunity to imagine, incubate, initiate, innovate, interact and influence.

- **(Be) Ethical within society**. Ethics is an organization's integrity. It is the bridge of trust between customer and team member. How is the firm taking responsibility for publicly setting targets (looking out for the interests of all stakeholders in society) through financially, environmentally, socially and educationally improved means?

- **Deliver fair practices**. An organization's results are reflected by significantly improved people practices. If team members are able to work in an environment devoid of the existing and systemic operational inanities that are prevalent in today's organization, it will deliver both fairer and markedly improved business results in a new purpose-first organizational mindset.

- **Serve all stakeholders**. Recognizing that no organization is an island unto itself, the firm or group will deliver its results to all relevant stakeholders, realizing its responsibility as an integral partner in society's ecosystem that affects customers, team members, the community and owners alike.

Role Purpose

Roles are created by the organization to achieve its mission and goals. Roles make up the whole of the organization. If there are no roles, there is no organization. From the perspective of the team member, roles can be of varying tenures, too.

Some individuals remain in a position for life (whether fulfilled or disengaged) whereas others are interested in very short stints or short-term contracts. Roles can come and go due to factors such as contraction, expansion or the introduction of new technologies like automation or artificial intelligence. Regardless, when an individual is performing in their role at work for the organization and themselves, one of three different mindsets will likely be exhibited:

- **Job Mindset**. Performing transactional duties in return for compensation and not much else.

- **Career Mindset**. Focused on increasing one's career girth by advancing salary, title, power, team size and/or span of control.

- **Purpose Mindset**. Passionate, innovative and committed to a meaningful and engaging workplace that serves and benefits all stakeholders.

An individual's role-based mindset, therefore, is the result of whether their personal purpose is in alignment with the organization's purpose, as well as with the duties required to perform in the role itself. Often a job or career mindset is a result of misalignment between personal, organizational and role purpose. For the sweet spot to be attained, I contend individuals ought to operate with a purpose mindset in their role for a majority of the time.

There are moments, however, when either the job or the career mindset might crop up as part of a role. It is to be expected. No one will ever demonstrate purpose in their role 100 percent of the time. There will always be parts of a role—or actions one must take—that are disliked. However, if the majority of time is spent on either the job and/or career mindsets, chances for *The Purpose Effect* to materialize and the sweet spot to manifest become unlikely. Once an individual is able to spend the bulk of time in their role occupying a purpose mindset, the sweet spot has a greater chance of being generated for all stakeholders.

Throughout the book, I will examine each of the three categories of purpose, concluding with examples and scenarios when each of the points are working together in harmony.

FLAT ARMY meets *The Purpose Effect*

In 2013, I published a book titled, *FLAT ARMY: Creating a Connected and*

Engaged Organization. The manuscript centered on the concept of "closed leadership" and "organizational disengagement." In fact, the book posited that far too many individuals in an organization are dissatisfied in their roles at work due to a general lack of open and collaborative leadership. This state of team member disenfranchisement is partially caused by leaders who are both controlling and commanding. Backed by research and first-hand experience, the book did offer some hope. I hypothesized an antidote based on methods and tools I previously deployed (and witnessed) at organizations where I have worked, in addition to research and interviews I previously conducted. The solution that surfaced to contest such a deleterious situation with respect to workplace culture was represented by five interlocking models of team-member engagement:

- Connected Leader Attributes

- Collaborative Leader Action Model

- Participative Leader Framework

- Pervasive Learning

- Collaboration Technologies

If the culture of an organization is open, connected, collaborative, participative and demonstrates general reciprocity, more often than not I have found it will become an engaged organization. When the culture of an organization is harmonious—when team members feel as though their opinion and contributions matter—a causal relationship between increased team member commitment and bottom-line improvements becomes a likely outcome. *FLAT ARMY* was an organizational culture change book.

For an organization to create value with its customers, and so the firm might become innovative and prosperous in the long term, it should possess an engaged workforce. This point, I would suggest, is rather irrefutable based on the mounds of evidence surfaced by consulting firms such as Gallup and Aon Hewitt. An engaged organization ultimately leads to multiple business benefits. We will continue to investigate this thesis in Chapters 3 and 4.

But for an organization to truly delight its customers—to create an environment where team members feel there is a purpose to their role that benefits society and solidifies their own personal purpose—I would like to argue that there is a link between purpose *and* culture. The concept of purpose is the basis of this book. How can one's personal sense of purpose connect with their workplace role and with that of the organization's overarching purpose? *FLAT ARMY* was based on organizational culture. In it I argued that the narrowing of the gap between team members and leadership resulted in a more collaborative operating environment. Improved levels of engagement and connection help the organization achieve its goals and objectives, ultimately improving various results and metrics.

If the purpose of the organization and its team members is aligned—and the organization is operating in an open, collaborative and harmonious culture—it delivers the one-two punch of societal and organizational benefits. *The Purpose Effect* is, therefore, a companion to my first book, *FLAT ARMY*. It connects the dots between purpose and culture, and it solidifies the outcomes of an engaged organization, improving personal and organizational results. I have found purpose to be a close partner of culture. You do not have to read *FLAT ARMY* first (or at all), but I want the reader to recognize the link I have surfaced between these two facets: purpose and culture.

But what exactly *is* purpose?

What Is Purpose?

In his posthumous 2004 book, *Pathways to Bliss*, Joseph Campbell provides us with an appropriate introduction to the concept of purpose. I have found Campbell to have been a brilliant philosopher and writer. His was a world that embodied altruism and giving. Campbell was arguably someone who knew how to demonstrate purpose and meaning in what was obviously his true calling: writing.

> What I think is that a good life is one hero journey after another. Over and over again, you are called to the realm of adventure, you are called to new horizons. Each time, there is the same problem: Do I dare? And then if you do dare, the dangers are there, and the help also, and the fulfillment

or the fiasco. There's always the possibility of a fiasco. But there's also the possibility of bliss.[11]

Purpose . . . it is a word that offers the "possibility of bliss." While purpose in the workplace is imperative, leaders are potentially overlooking its significance to the overarching health of our civilization. My experience and research suggest purpose ought to be the objective, but it is the misalignment of the personal, role and organizational categories of purpose that ensures the journey toward purpose never begins.

Which begs a few questions:

- What is the true purpose of an organization?

- Is a for-profit or private organization merely a vehicle for economic rents, profit hoarding, unethical levels of greed and a fixation on increasing the share price?

- Is the private organization's primary responsibility a fiduciary obligation to maximize shareholder value or profit margins?

- Have well-rewarded leaders of organizations rejected the interests of all other stakeholders and the common good to selfishly fill their own bank accounts and satisfy their hedonic impulses?

There are additional questions, which may relate specifically to a public sector or not-for-profit organization as well as a private firm:

- Is the purpose of an organization and its leaders to uphold power and positional rank?

- Is one of the goals for leaders to "command or control" team members?

- Is the organization's structure burdened by rigid operational systems created by cabinet shuffles, organizational changes, stonewalling tactics or abdication of leadership responsibility?

Organizations of any sort that are replete with heavily bureaucratic processes and hierarchically driven management styles may continue to exist simply because it is easier. In fact, mantras such as: "But this is how we've always done it," might be invoked as the de facto rationale. If this is the case, what is the true purpose of the organization?

One academic who has been sounding alarm bells aligned with this hypothesis is Otto Scharmer. He is a Senior Lecturer at MIT and the founding chair of the Presencing Institute, an awareness-based, action-research community that creates social technologies, builds capacities and generates holding spaces for profound societal renewal. Scharmer has long argued that organizations and their leaders need to shift from "ego to eco." In other words, he believes the organization at large has morphed into empire building instead of generating well-being for all. In the book he co-wrote with Katrin Kaufer, *Leading From the Emerging Future: From Ego-System to Eco-System Economies*, the authors argue that there are eight systemic disconnects that are aiding and abetting the current situation of purposeless organizations. One of the problems they surface is particularly interesting:

> [There is] a disconnect between institutional leadership and people. This disconnect results in a leadership void that shows up in the widely shared sense that we are collectively creating results that nobody wants. This collective condition of felt helplessness and disempowerment is a hallmark of our system-wide leadership void (or bubble) today.[12]

Purpose might be reflected by a team member who yearns for a greater sense of understanding, autonomy and even duties in the role they fulfill. It could be an individual's "calling"[13] as another academic, Dr. A.R. (Elango) Elangovan of the University of Victoria suggests.

Perhaps purpose is the combination of a calling and being able to do "good work." The Work Foundation, an independent charity founded in 2002 and part of Lancaster University, influences, advises and consults with organizations on a better form of capitalism, promoting, as their motto states, "Good work for all."[14]

Is that what we need in the workforce? Good work for all? Perhaps we may look to Greek philosopher Aristotle for assistance. He believed and taught that human beings were driven by purpose, autonomy and the natural desire to seek out and understand the truth. A person's ideals manifest when they are pursuing and then attaining a life of purpose, ultimately the end state of human well-being. This end state is sometimes referred to as eudaemonia, the Greek word for human flourishing.

Elango and his colleagues indicated a calling "is a course of action in pursuit of pro-social intentions embodying the convergence of an individual's sense of what he or she would like to do, should do, and actually does."[15] During an interview, I asked Elango why purpose is so important to one's role at work. He responded that "having a purpose to our work is convergent with our sense of who we truly are and what we stand for in life." Elango believes the authenticity that is rooted in such clarity of purpose in work motivates team members to greater effort and contributions. Perhaps this is a clue toward our definition of purpose.

A Culture of Purpose

Earlier I suggested there is a relationship between an organization's culture and purpose. Deloitte LLP has unearthed evidence suggesting a culture of purpose in the organization directly creates confidence, short- and long-term growth as well as an improved internal culture *and* financial benefits. Based on their research, Deloitte's Chairman of the Board, Punit Renjen, believes "an organization's culture of purpose answers the critical questions of who we are and why we exist through a set of carefully articulated core beliefs."[16] He contends an organization that instills a sense of purpose—permeating all stakeholders, including team members, customers and society—not only builds business confidence, but fosters a thriving business community.

The firm investigated the concept they coined, "top drivers of employee confidence." For those workers who felt a very strong sense of purpose in their organization, respondents indicated a commitment to delivering top-quality products and services was the overarching driver of confidence. For those team members and organizations that lacked purpose, the leading driver of confidence was a fixation on financial results, specifically the bottom line. Furthermore, as it relates to team member engagement, in those organizations where individuals felt a high level of purpose, 73 percent of the workforce indicated they were fully engaged whereas in organizations devoid of purpose, only 23 percent felt the same.

Finally—and consistent with the benefits of a purpose-driven organization—82 percent of respondents from the Deloitte research who felt the strongest sense of purpose were far more optimistic about their own future prospects and the "ability to stay ahead of industry disruptions" than those (42 percent) who did not. Tellingly, 79 percent of the purpose crowd believed in the organization's long-term prospects to outperform the competition versus 47 percent of those who had no sense of purpose in their place of work.[17]

It is not solely Deloitte who has surfaced interesting data points. When studying sustainability factors—arguably what should be a key part of an organization's purpose—McKinsey & Company warned organizations that they "should integrate environmental, social and governance issues into their business model—and act on them."[18] Another firm, the Economist Intelligence Unit (EIU), purported large businesses benefit (including positive productivity gains) when they are able to improve purpose and engagement in the workforce. When individuals are engaged, stated the EIU, the engagement leads to "improved customer satisfaction, increased productivity, and reduced employee turnover and absenteeism."[19]

Even Goldman Sachs—the global investment banking firm partially responsible for the bankruptcy of AIG in 2008's financial crisis[20]—had the wherewithal to create the GS Sustain Focus List in 2007. This covers a variety of companies it ranks based on environmental, social and governance records. According to Goldman Sachs, since the list's inception in 2007 through to the end of 2013, the so-called GS Sustain Focus List has outperformed the MSCI All Country World Index by over 43 percent.[21] MSCI, formerly Morgan Stanley Capital International, is used by many financial firms to benchmark global stock investments and funds.

If there is indeed a relationship between culture and purpose—and it leads to improved organizational results—what exactly is the purpose of work?

The Purpose of Work

Famed advertising mogul, George Lois, once said, "Most people work at keeping their job, rather than doing a good job. If you're the former, you're leading a meaningless life. If you're the latter, keep up the good work."[22] To pay the bills, most of us have to work. The question we might pose, however, is whether work is merely a job or, with it, the possibility of a meaningful experience. Depending on your situation, work is either loved, liked, tolerated, loathed or treated with ambivalence. For certain, though, it is a guaranteed topic of discussion at any social gathering you attend. When attending any kind of dinner party, for example, how many times have you asked or have been asked the question, "So, how is work?"

Management expert Peter Drucker once said of the link between life and work: "To make a living is no longer enough. Work also has to make a life."[23] When work can in fact make a life, we know we are resting confidently in the sweet spot between personal, organizational and role purpose. But for a large portion of today's team members, work seems to act as a stressor, the consequence of not finding one's purpose in their role. Perhaps disengagement of team members stems from a lack of purpose in the organization itself. I asked several people for their definition of work. Some interesting examples surfaced:

Best thing in the world if you can't wait for the weekend to finish. Worst thing in the world if you say, "I don't like Mondays."
—SAP Global Operations Director, John McNaughton, UK

Engaging tasks that provide returns, such as monetary compensation, personal growth and meaning.
—99Tests Founder & CEO, Praveen Singh, India

A purpose-driven series of mental and physical activities during which the collective learns and shares their learning with others.
—Founder, IndaloGenesis, Richard Martin, UK

Minds collaborating for the same purposeful result.
—Harry Krantz Co. LLC Purchasing Manager,
Debra Criveau, USA

To achieve something of substance.
—OspreyData Co-Founder, Andrew Marks, USA

It is evident from such responses that the concepts of meaning, purpose, achieving, engaging and collaborating comprise the patches for an intriguing quilt of definitions. What does your own quilt say about work? What does your definition of work say about you? Do you define work—both the place you are employed and the profession that makes up your trade—with words like *flourishing, meaning, well-being, balance, community, giver* and *purposeful*? Are you viewed as someone who cares about the purpose of the organization? Does your organization bring purpose and meaning to all stakeholders in its operating mandate and mission?

Or, perhaps, you think of work as a quest to climb the career ladder, judging success by the improvement of your title, remuneration level and the number of direct reports you are in charge of. Is work the quest to assume greater power? As American journalist Robert Quillen once wrote, "By working faithfully eight hours a day you may eventually get to be boss and work 12 hours a day."[24] Is your purpose solely to become *the boss*?

Maybe you view work merely as a paycheck: a means to an end. Maybe work is solely a job leading to a state of individualism. In 1831, French historian Alexis de Tocqueville referred to this state as, "a calm and considered feeling which disposes each citizen to isolate himself from the mass of his fellows and withdraw into the circle of family and friends; with this little society formed to his taste, he gladly leaves the greater society to look after itself."[25] If the organization's purpose creates isolation, loneliness or a sense of individualism, will a team member ever achieve purpose in their role? What about in their life?

Perhaps work is the fixation on profit. If you are a private company, profit is important and necessary. Without profit there is no business. But the question a company needs to ask itself is whether or not it is solely focused on profit (or shareholder return, in some cases) rather than serving the interests of all stakeholders. Recall Fairphone's example: As a private company, it seeks to make a profit but not at the expense of its overarching purpose.

If you are working in a not-for-profit or public sector organization, are you operating in harmony with the board, regulators or fellow team members? Take for instance the United States government. Each year, the United States Office of Personnel Management aggregates employee engagement results from over 48,000 offices, across 82 federal agencies. In 2014, almost 400,000 workers participated in what is known as the Federal Employee Viewpoint Survey, or FEVS. Since 2010, job satisfaction is down eight percentage points to 64 percent. With almost three million workers in government, that's roughly one million people who are dissatisfied in their roles at work. Other data points demonstrate continued "wear and tear" on engagement levels of employees. Only 52 percent of workers, for example, believe their management does an effective job at encouraging communication and collaboration. That correlates to only 55 percent of all U.S. government employees being satisfied with the organization they work for itself.[26]

Judging from global employee engagement surveys—where levels of internal employee engagement continue to remain anemic—well over three-quarters of those employed on the planet do not find meaning in their work. Some of this blame falls squarely on the individual, for certain, but organizations devoid of true purpose and senior leaders fixated on power or profit do nothing to help the current plight of the purpose of work.

At its root, work is a means by which we get paid to partially satisfy what Abraham Maslow defined in 1960 as the Hierarchy of Needs.[27] In particular, when we are paid for performing at work, we can utilize the funds we are remunerated with to satisfy such physiological and safety needs. It can also include personal requirements such as financial, economics, property, goods, food, drink, well-being and health.

But the workplace is not solely a place to be paid, is it? Some argue that team members merely rent their skills to an organization in return for compensation. Might the other three components of Maslow's thesis (belongingness, esteem and self-actualization) be incorporated into the way work ought to be conducted? Perhaps this is when a team member reaches the sweet spot. Perhaps "purpose at work" occurs at a state of what we may refer to as workplace actualization.

If work is to make a life, as Peter Drucker suggested, the purpose of the organization might need to shift to include a greater degree of meaning. If this occurs, perhaps more team members will be able to feel a sense of purpose in their roles as well. If this occurs, I would like to argue that work can also then make a life. Perhaps at this point there may be a link between self-actualization and workplace actualization. Is this the *purpose* to purpose?

Affecting Purpose

The etymology of purpose is important to understand. Circa 1300, the Old French word *porpos* and the Anglo-French word *purpos* combined with *porposer* to give us *purpose*. Whether as an "intention, aim and goal" or "to put forth," purpose can denote a state of being—a noun—or it creates action as a transitive verb. There might be a *purpose* to attending a meeting or you may be seeking *purpose* in the meeting itself.

Aaron Hurst, author of *The Purpose Economy*, captured the importance of purpose in the workplace when he wrote, "Much like technology a few decades ago, purpose has now become a business imperative. In today's world, running an organization without an intentional emphasis on purpose for employees and customers is like running an organization in the early 1990s and failing to implement technology."[28] I asked Aaron why he felt it still seems so difficult for senior leaders in today's organizations to establish a "Purpose Economy," to embed a purpose culture at work. His response highlighted necessary ingredients:

> Creating a successful organization in the Purpose Economy requires two types of leadership. You need authentic leaders who are able to model purpose and vulnerability and you need leaders who have the courage to look beyond short-term results.[29]

Indeed, purpose will never envelop an organization by quarter's end. For an organization to become purposeful, it requires time and effort. The long game ought to be considered. Richard Ellsworth, author of *Leading with Purpose*, claimed, "The highest level of individual development and the greatest happiness are derived from serving ends beyond the self—ends that employees value, that enable them to feel they are 'making a difference,' and consequently that bring increased meaning to their lives through work."[30] Can the majority of for-profit organizations and leaders argue that their firm is not being run as though the overarching goal is to extract value in favor of profits and/or power? Can not-for-profit or public sector institutions honestly state their mission is to serve the community and the team members it employs?

Arguably there are too many leaders forgetting it is the team members of any type of organization that are the frontline to its customers and society. We need more of the leaders and organizations that Aaron mentioned. We need more team members believing they are "making a difference," as Richard outlined. We also need team members to take action for their own sense of purpose, in their role and in the organization. We cannot wait for purpose to materialize on its own.

In 1970, on the topic of corporate purpose, Peter Drucker observed that purpose, "must lie outside the business itself. In fact, it must lie in society since business enterprise is an organ of society. There is only one valid definition of business purpose: to create a customer."[31] Almost 30 years later, he went on to write that there is a link between an organization's purpose, its operations and the way it treats the workers. Drucker wrote:

> We will have to redefine the purpose of the employing orga-nization and of its management as both, satisfying the legal owners, such as shareholders, and satisfying the owners of the human capital that gives the organization its wealth-pro-ducing power, that is, satisfying the knowledge workers. For increasingly the ability of organizations—and not only of busi-nesses—to survive will come to depend on their "compara-tive advantage" in making the knowledge worker productive. And the ability to attract and hold the best of the knowledge workers is the first and most fundamental precondition.[32]

Charles Handy, another sage on the topic of management, once wrote, "Let us be clear, profits—and good profits—are always essential, and not just in business. But the myth dies hard, the myth that profit is the purpose." He also commented in *Harvard Business Review*, "The purpose of a business is to make a profit so that the business can do something more or better. That 'something' becomes the real justification for the business."[33]

If we were to define how to serve the customer collaboratively as a part of community, society and the environment, levels of employee disengagement, workplace dissatisfaction and customer unhappiness might disappear. Perhaps this is part of the relationship between culture and purpose. Building purpose in the work (for everyone) is a journey. The state at which the sweet spot is created might actually mitigate one of Drucker's issues: "Business purpose and business mission are so rarely given adequate thought is perhaps the most important cause of business frustration and failure."[34]

Abraham Lincoln once wrote, "Every man is proud of what he does well; and no man is proud of what he does not do well. With the former, his heart is in his work; and he will do twice as much of it with less fatigue. The latter performs a little imperfectly, looks at it in disgust, turns from it, and imag-ines himself exceedingly tired. The little he has done, comes to nothing, for want of finishing."[35] How many individuals in today's organizations are empowered, as Lincoln suggested, to put their hearts in their role and to go above the call of duty at work?

How many team members truly feel a sense of both accomplishment and purpose? How many of the leaders and followers believe there is a purpose in their place of work, one positively affecting all stakeholders in society? How many team members have defined their own sense of personal purpose, yet end up working in contradiction to that definition?

How can *The Purpose Effect* actually come to fruition?

In the next chapter, I will share my personal experiences with purpose, on a personal, organizational and role level, hoping to shed some light on my interpretation of the sweet spot.

CHAPTER TWO
MORAL PURPOSE

To improve is to change, so to be perfect is to have changed often.[1]
Winston Churchill

I prefer to be true to myself, even at the hazard of incurring the ridicule of others, rather than to be false, and to incur my own abhorrence.[2]
Frederick Douglass

The Purpose Effect is not merely a theory. It is established in groundwork, proven by and solidified through additional interviews, site visits and external research. I have personally experienced this model throughout my entire working life. I also have been in a position to assist others—individuals and organizations—create the sweet spot of *The Purpose Effect*. We learn as we do. I share my story here, therefore, not only to reflect the authenticity of the model but to share personal experiences and lessons learned for the benefit of others.

First, let me go back to the early 1980s. Growing up I wanted to be a doctor. Many kids do. When I reached the age of 17 in 1988, an injury to my right knee required surgery, putting an end to my dream. After falling unconscious when the sixth vial of blood was removed from my body during a "pre-op procedure," it seemed the thought of blood and being a doctor was not a good mix for me long term. As my dad reminded me, it was perhaps not in the best interest of future patients either.

After the surgery, I went through a rather painful six months of physiotherapy. As a brooding teenager, these were dark days. Three times a week

I schlepped my body onto a public bus for a 45-minute ride to a renowned rehabilitation clinic where I received treatment on my leg. The experience strengthened my intention to help other people during my adult life. Instead of being a doctor, I committed myself to becoming a physiotherapist. No blood in those clinics, I said to myself repeatedly.

As high school concluded in the spring of 1990 and important decisions were being made by thousands of graduating students on their choice of post-secondary education, I had another epiphany. Albeit noble and important work, a physiotherapist helps clients get back to previous levels of health prior to an injury or surgery. A physiotherapist's role was not necessarily meant to improve someone's ability to go past their original status quo; it was to get as close to the previous state of health as was possible. The staff helped mend my knee, but it was not as though I became faster at the end of the six months of therapy.

I was fortunate to be admitted into several physiotherapy programs at the university level, but my epiphany had a significant bearing on my life and my work history. This epiphany is the reason that I can write a book like *FLAT ARMY* or this one, *The Purpose Effect*. It was during the summer of 1990 when I turned down all offers of attending a physiotherapy university program in favor of pursuing a Bachelor of Education degree. As I considered my personal sense of purpose, I did not want simply to help people get back to a previously attained state of healthiness. I wanted to help people overachieve, to accomplish great things in their life. It was at this moment in time—as a naïve but insistent 19-year-old student—that I chose a profession in which I could help others to excel.

I graduated in 1994 as a high school teacher, but my entire working tenure in the field amounted to less than three years of cumulative service. Having defined my personal sense of purpose—my values, interests, goals and priorities—as someone who wanted to help others while being able to continuously learn and innovate, I recognized early on in my high school teaching career that my personal sense of purpose was misaligned with the organization that employed me and the role I occupied. What to do?

What motivates me in my life is the chance to innovate, learn and assist others to achieve great things. I thought this might be accomplished in a high school organization, in a role as a high school teacher. I was wrong. The organization I was a part of possessed an ambivalent if not apathetic culture. There were several people who demonstrated purpose in their role, but far too many were simply in it for the vacations and the paycheck. This environment affected both my personal sense of purpose, and somewhat obviously, the role I was occupying. I quickly fell into a job mindset at work. I felt as though I was performing transactional duties in return for compensation and not much else.

My personal sense of purpose was going unfulfilled. The attitude of staff members and the organization in general was stifling my growth, my learning and my innovating mindset. The organization tried desperately to portray a purposeful working environment—it was, after all, a high school—but politics and bad processes got in the way of achieving my personal values *and* goals. I felt I had to take matters into my own hands.

It was perhaps the first time I could put *The Purpose Effect* into action. I certainly was not calling it *The Purpose Effect* in 1997, but in hindsight, that is exactly what it was. I was not feeling fulfilled. I was disengaged at work. I needed to revisit my personal purpose in order to work out what might be next. If I could not help the organization change its ways, perhaps it was time to move on. After a year of reflection and additional schooling, I found myself in 1998 at the British Columbia Institute of Technology (BCIT) as a Program Head. I made the switch to higher education. Maybe this role at this time—and this organization—could help balance my take on *The Purpose Effect*.

It was the first time I entered into a role where all facets of the sweet spot—personal, organizational and role—seemed to quickly come into alignment. The institution and the faculty provided the opportunity to start up a business unit, and with that came the chance to help shape and reinforce the organization's purpose. The larger entity I was employed by—BCIT—was a hub of engagement and purpose. It delivered value to the students and there were benefits across multiple stakeholders. The institution was constantly innovating, encouraging faculty and personnel to revolutionize education, take risks and to make the student experience as practical and outstanding as possible. It was always thinking how it could positively affect society.

One group of educators and administrators, for example, sought to create an aviation and aerospace campus. The team involved managed to get actual airplanes donated for students to work on. A partnership with Lufthansa Technical Training (LTT) was also formulated. This reinforced the innovative and practical mindset that emanated from the organization's purpose. It created a number of jobs for graduates as well.

With my personal purpose intact and the organization in good stead, I found the role I held in higher education allowed me the chance to fulfill my values and interests: to learn, to innovate, to prosper and to help others truly grow and develop. In the department and in programs that I helped launch, we worked with the broader community in British Columbia to develop websites, systems and technology solutions to aid not-for-profit, public sector and for-profit organizations. There were always obstacles to overcome, but for me, the sweet spot was evident between the three categories of purpose. The department (and BCIT in general) was also demonstrating the sweet spot, with an engaged workforce, profitable returns, and most importantly benefits that were accruing across all stakeholders including the thousands of students partaking in various education programs.

After five years of being part of a truly purposeful scenario, I felt it was time to continue my learning and innovating values elsewhere. I wanted to continue to develop, define and decide what I was about, who I was and how I was going to operate in my life. I was not disappointed or disengaged with BCIT. On the contrary, I sought out a position away from academia and education in which to continue my purpose journey. I challenged myself to find another sweet spot. I decided to enter the corporate world.

The High-Tech Years

While my time in higher education helped me teach (and understand) the intricacies between learning and technology, it has been my time in the corporate world where I have refined the link between purpose, culture, engagement, technology, business results and leadership development. Between 2002 and 2008, I was the head of UBI, the University of Business Intelligence. It was a corporate university that I first founded and led at Crystal Decisions and later, Business Objects. These companies created business intelligence software. The team of over 100 in UBI served employees, partners and customers with various learning, knowledge, implementation and leadership needs. Business Objects acquired Crystal Decisions, but UBI continued on with the audience size substantially growing after the deal closed in 2003.

I was fortunate to be on the UBI team and part of the Business Objects company because both demonstrated quite effectively how organizations can be purpose-driven. For example, Business Objects possessed a team dedicated to community investment and philanthropy, unheard of in high-tech companies at the time. Various teams would often donate time in the community, it becoming a staple of the organizational culture. Software was often gifted to schools and not-for-profit organizations, and the UBI team would find ways to donate instructional time or eLearning modules as part of the practice. The employee engagement scores at UBI measured in the high 80s while customer feedback and opinion were equally high. Although the UBI team was spread across 12 time zones in seven different countries, the culture and operating norm was as though team members were not only in the same room, everyone was proactive, harmonious and collaborative with one another.

During my tenure at UBI, my personal values and interests were being fully met. UBI existed to deliver various educational and learning services to a range of audiences. We operated to make a profit, but we also focused on the community. We also looked after one another. The level of camaraderie and togetherness was simply magical. UBI and its parent companies existed to deliver value to all stakeholders: the community, customers, partners, owners and team members. Its operating culture was one that was open, collaborative and harmonious. In terms of my role, it existed to serve the mission of Business Objects (and UBI), but it also permitted me the latitude to continuously innovate, learn and assist others. Again, the three categories of purpose were in complete alignment and thus both the organization and I were demonstrating the sweet spot.

In the blink of an eye, things changed dramatically for me *and* the organization. By the summer of 2007, giants in the high-tech space—Oracle, IBM, SAP and Microsoft—were circling like turkey vultures do when spotting a field of mice to acquire business intelligence companies like Cognos, MicroStrategy and Business Objects.

SAP—an enterprise resource planning company based in Waldorf, Germany—announced its intention to acquire Business Objects in October of 2007. Over the next nine months I flew from Vancouver to Germany and the Bay Area of California numerous times to help with the integration of Business Objects into SAP. The meetings between the two organizations were cordial, but it was evident from the outset that things in the future were going to be different. I was not so naïve as to think everything was going to remain the same, but the tone in those discussions was perhaps more one-sided in favor of "the SAP way" than I had anticipated or hoped for.

I was beginning to question whether SAP possessed the same type of organizational purpose as Business Objects. At the time, it seemed to be a company fixated on profit and revenues, not the holistic purpose that I was used to for the previous five years at both Crystal Decisions and Business Objects. I was also beginning to query whether the sense of purpose I possessed in my role at Business Objects would continue at SAP. Would the sweet spot turn sour? Would the team (and organization) that once was, be engulfed by a very motivated and power-hungry SAP? Would I be given the opportunity to help shape (or reshape) the culture and purpose of SAP, like I had done at BCIT and Business Objects?

It was early on in the integration process between the two organizations, however, when the leader whom I reported into, Dan Klein, took me aside during one of my trips to San Jose, California, and jostled my understanding of workplace purpose. Dan had been my leader and vice president since the summer of 2003, and he was always looking out for my future, and for my best interests. He would ask personal questions in our 1-1 meetings like how our children were doing. He would frequently discuss with me ways to continue learning, developing, innovating and building up my leadership skills; my personal purpose values and priorities were well understood by Dan. He often suggested conferences and other external learning opportunities for me to attend. He always gave me a long leash to innovate. Dan truly was interested in my workplace mindset, but he was equally concerned for me as a human being. He helped me continue honing my personal and role-based purpose.

When he took me aside that day, Dan had a different message about my career. "I want you to contemplate something that I know you haven't thought about. I want you to think long and hard about leaving SAP this year when the integration completes." I was stunned. How could the senior leader I was trusting to help our team get through the integration suggest I leave? Was he unaware how much I loved my role, my team and the work we were doing? Did he not want me to stick around to continue building on what we had already accomplished? Was I no longer good enough?

In fact, Dan saw something that I could not at the time. His guidance as a career coach ensured that I retained my sense of purpose. He put the individual before the company, encouraging me to continue developing and firing my professional interests. This was a great example of leadership, of assisting someone else with *The Purpose Effect*. Dan wanted me to continue demonstrating my sense of purpose in what Reid Hoffman of LinkedIn refers to as a "tour of duty"[3] at another organization, one that could benefit from my passion and personality and values. He did not want to see me lapse into a job mindset where I was there only for the paycheck.

On a trip back from Germany several months after our initial discussion in 2008, I made a decision on the plane to follow Dan's advice. I was going to leave SAP and my work family of the previous six years. The conclusion I had reached was entirely selfish, but it ensured I was true to the purpose that I had built with respect to my personal and professional life. Dan was disappointed to lose a team member when I told him, but grateful I heeded his advice. In terms of my professional life, it has been, up until this point, the hardest decision I have ever made. Why?

I was leaving behind six years of absolute workplace bliss. The UBI team and Business Objects as a whole had arguably established a near-perfect way in which to achieve business results through an engaged and purpose-driven ethos. While I was grateful to have achieved the sweet spot (again), I knew that blissful state could no longer continue. I was resigned to the fact that Dan was right. It was time to seek out another opportunity for *The Purpose Effect* to ideally be achieved.

The Telecommunications Years

Since late 2008, I've witnessed, helped lead and participated firsthand in *The Purpose Effect* at TELUS, Canada's fastest-growing national telecommunications company. I may be biased, but it is a story I am proud to share, one that helps demonstrate the overarching thesis to *The Purpose Effect*.

To be fair, it was not always the case. In the summer of 2008, team member engagement at TELUS sat at 53 percent; customer satisfaction and corresponding likelihood to recommend scores were low, too. Team member opinions about innovation or business process improvement were rarely sought. It was an office-only culture where employee results were measured by whether or not their leader saw them seated at their desk. Community outreach and sustainability practices were forming, but not well established.

I joined TELUS in the Fall of 2008 based on several conversations and meetings with team members and senior leaders who were already working at the company. While there was much to do in terms of becoming a purpose-driven organization—and roughly half of the organization were either not engaged or disengaged in their roles—it was evident to me this was an organization seeking to create not only a "great place to work," it wanted as many of its team members as possible to be operating in the sweet spot.

The leader who insisted on the development of an organizational ethos of purpose was Darren Entwistle, who became CEO of TELUS in 2000. Darren not only believes shareholder value is an outcome of a healthy corporate culture and a customer-first ethos, his unwavering commitment to serve communities and citizens in need is noteworthy.

Through the efforts of all 43,000 team members, including Darren, things began to change dramatically at TELUS circa 2010. Purpose was beginning to be instilled at an organizational level and in all workplace roles. A sense of pride began to kick in for team members, and the organization began to flourish.

There were a number of key programs and initiatives that helped reshape the culture, as well as organizational and role-related purpose.

Customers First

An enterprise-wide initiative identified customer experience as the key differentiator and long-term measure of success at the company. TELUS devised a strategy that embedded a renewed sense of commitment and dedication to customer service excellence among its global team members. The company ensured the corporate vision, strategic imperatives and corporate priorities were meaningful at each level within the organization and that each team member could clearly see how the majority of their work impacted customer service and satisfaction.

TELUS Leadership Philosophy (TLP)

The TLP became an enterprise-wide, open and collaborative leadership framework that engendered consistent behaviors and practices for performing, managing and leading across the entire TELUS team. The launch of the TLP marked a shift from leadership based on a team member's position in the organization to one where all team members were encouraged to take the lead. This increased empowerment gave team members a sense of purpose while providing the added fuel to go above and beyond the call of duty each and every day.

Community Investment

TELUS also began to differentiate itself in the hearts and minds of the customers it serves. Shifting toward becoming a socially responsible organization, TELUS delivered a message that in order for it to do well in business, it must do good in the communities it serves. TELUS recognized it wanted to do better as an organization. In short, it instituted a "we give where we live" mindset across its team members, further fueling its redefined organizational purpose that it was not merely an organization fixated solely on increased shareholder return.

Recognition

A culture of recognition became an important part of the culture at TELUS. As Darren said to me, "Strong and innovative leadership means fostering a culture of appreciation and recognizing the behavior rather than just the outcome. It is important to recognize the *how* and emphasize it above the *what*." All team members are encouraged to utilize Bravo, a recognition platform that was first implemented in 2008. It can reward team members with points, enabling them to redeem their points to purchase a wide variety of items and/or gift certificates with local and national vendors.

Flexible Work Styles

The Work Styles program gave TELUS team members the flexibility to work when and where they were most effective so they could focus on supporting TELUS customers in the most effective manner. Even in a time when other organizations were asking their own team members to come back into the office, TELUS continued to advocate and advance a flexible form of working for its team members.

Pervasive Learning

A new learning model redefined all forms of learning as equal parts formal, informal and social. Senior leaders were re-educated on the benefits of this new way of learning and were encouraged to support the model wholeheartedly. Team members began utilizing the model in both in-role development and next-role aspirations. Collaborative technologies were implemented across the organization, aiding the purpose mindset of team members' roles and the organization itself.

It was a long process of change. But the outcome has been rewarding, both for me—as a team member and leader in the organization—and for other team members and the company on the whole. Between 2010 and 2015, employee engagement rose from 57 percent to a world-leading 87 percent while customer satisfaction in the consumer space rose by 1800 basis points.[4]

As a result of its "we give where we live" community investment ethos, TELUS has donated approximately $250 million since 2010 to various charities and foundations. In 2014, the company contributed 2.6 percent of pre-tax profits to all forms of giving.[5] The investments did not even include the more than 600,000 hours of time TELUS team members volunteered in the communities they served in that same year. If you go back even farther, since 2000, the company, its team members and alumni have donated close to $400 million and six million hours of volunteer time.[6] That is as much time and money as Verizon contributes, a giant American telecommunications firm with almost five times the number of employees as TELUS. In fact, TELUS is so invested in the communities it serves, the company received the Association of Fundraising Professionals' Freeman Philanthropic Services Award for Outstanding Corporation. It was the first Canadian company to receive this international distinction.

The organizational purpose of TELUS (the shift to putting customers first, backed by a commitment to improve team member engagement) became part attitude, part mantra, part behavior and part action. It led to increases in every business segment of customer satisfaction. Customer complaints, as measured by Canada's Commissioner for Complaints for Telecommunications Services (CCTS), dropped by over 66 percent over a four-year period to an all-time low of only 466 consumer complaints in 2015. This represented a mere 4.7 percent of all complaints received by the CCTS against all telecommunications providers in Canada, even though complaints in the industry itself were up by over 40 percent since 2011.[7]

How does a purpose-filled organization—and its team members—benefit the bottom line? Absenteeism is down at TELUS by over 15 percent and the company witnessed 17 consecutive quarters of ARPU (average revenue per user)[8] increases with their various mobile phone services. Were shareholders happy? Indeed. Shareholder return of more than 200 percent since 2010 has been realized and the TELUS stock rose from $13.79 on September 18, 2008 to close the year in 2014 at the $42 mark, a 300 percent gain over the span.

Since Darren came on board, TELUS has been the global leader among all telecom service providers with a total shareholder return of 338 percent, outpacing the number two incumbent by 82 percentage points.[9] By any scorecard measurement, this is an incredible feat to accomplish and unique amongst North American public companies. By investing in and committing to a customer-first philosophy—in parallel with an improved corporate culture and community mindset—another one of the outcomes became increased shareholder value. The key point, however, is that it was never instituted as the primary goal of the company. For example, 60 percent of the TELUS corporate scorecard is aligned directly to the achievement of customer commitments and team member engagement, not stock market price, dividends or shareholder returns.

But what is interesting about Darren's leadership and the culture at TELUS is that total shareholder return is not the end game. Shareholder return was and still is a by-product of its focus on both team members and customers. The purpose of TELUS shifted, as did the sense of workplace purpose for most team members, but improved financial metrics was not the reason for making the shift. One day over a conversation, Darren said to me, "Increased shareholder return is an outcome of a thriving, customers-first culture." He went on to observe, "Ultimately, our culture is our only sustainable competitive advantage. One important component to the culture of TELUS, however, is our efforts in the community. I believe that in order to do well in business, we must also do good things in our communities. If we foster a symbiotic relationship between our company, our team and the health of our communities, everybody wins."

Having this personal level of proximity to a truly pervasive example of organizational purpose—while witnessing the transformation of both the company and its people toward a purpose mindset—has left an indelible mark on me as a human being. It is not always perfect, and there are great, healthy debates internally at TELUS—not dissimilar to Google as surfaced by Laszlo Bock, head of people operations, in his book, *Work Rules! Why Google's Rules Will Work for You*—but it is an example of an organization that aims to delight its customers while addressing the interests of all its stakeholders: team members, shareholders, customers and the community at large.

Jeffrey Puritt, President of TELUS International—a wholly owned subsidiary to TELUS that provides global contact centers and business process outsourcing services to global clients—provides another perspective. Puritt is a firm believer in an organizational model that balances purpose with profit. "Corporations, in what's been termed capitalism 2.0," Jeffrey suggested to me, "will be called upon to distribute their earnings in support of shared values, inclusive wealth and social equity." He believes purpose is a fundamental aspect to business. Without hesitation, Jeffrey concludes that there is a link between purpose, culture, engagement and humanity. He believes that culture, "embodies the values and beliefs of an entire workforce—providing the impetus to rally people around causes simply because it's who they are as a company."

Jeffrey was adamant that an interdependent relationship between companies and communities can exist, where both parties might benefit tremendously from the virtuous cycle of corporate philanthropy. He remarked, "As companies invest in local communities, like TELUS has done, those communities thrive, ultimately producing better educated, more skilled citizens, who in turn can and want to contribute more to supporting the success of those companies." He suggested companies will begin to become much more intentional about their corporate cultures, where purpose will play a much larger role, even to the point where it is a daily expression of who they are and why they exist as a business. "Social purpose and corporate social responsibility won't be an afterthought to financial and business performance discussions in the future," he claimed. "CSR won't be an unrelated, secondary conversation; rather, social purpose will be a fundamental part of day-to-day business."

Persistent Purpose

Back in 2008 when I started my TELUS career, the organization was mired in average results. I had left SAP in pursuit of another purposeful organization so that I could remain in harmony with my own personal sense of purpose. By 2015, TELUS was not only achieving above-average results in its business and team member metrics; it was helping to substantially improve the communities in which it operated. Almost 90 percent of the organization is engaged, the purpose of the organization is multifaceted and team members are—for the most part—thriving in their roles. Shareholders are reaping the benefits as well. I look back now on the organization's evolution with pride and humility. Led by the incontrovertible leadership of Darren

Entwistle who urged everyone to put society, communities, team members *and* customers first, I feel fortunate to have personally been a part of yet another example of attaining the sweet spot.

I am no longer responsible for the leadership development, learning or collaboration practices at TELUS. Instead, I launched an external future-of-work consulting firm in 2014 called TELUS Transformation Office (TTO). The team aims to help other organizations, leaders and team members with their quest to achieve a purpose mindset alongside a more engaged and open culture. In my role as Chief Envisioner, I possess the opportunity to fulfill my personal values (learning and innovating) in a role and organization that affords the three categories of purpose to intersect. My role allows me to help other individuals and organizations achieve great things. To suggest I am fortunate and appreciative of my situation is indeed an understatement.

I am not a doctor, nor am I a physiotherapist. I am no longer a high school teacher. My personal experiences since 1990 regarding the intersection of personal, organizational and role purpose have, in part, led me to surface the contents and overarching thesis of this book, *The Purpose Effect*. I have worked directly with many team members, leaders and organizations to hone and refine the model. I have spoken with and interviewed many people to revise and test the three categories of purpose. The rest of the book, however, foregoes further autobiographical examples. It focuses on the three components of *The Purpose Effect*: personal, organizational and role purpose through other avenues and sources of investigation, research and analysis.

But to achieve the sweet spot—whether you are an individual or an organization—is hard work and requires a high degree of persistence. Greek philosopher Heraclitus once wrote, "Protracted and patient effort is needed to develop good character."[10] In my negative experiences I was forced to draw upon a well of patience and persistence in order to attain (and regain) the sweet spot.

Self-determination, my various direct leaders and the organizations where I worked helped achieve it. But not everyone is able to attain the sweet spot. In fact, many do not. This demands a closer examination in Part II of this book before we explore what can be done about it in Parts III and IV.

SECTION II

CHAPTER THREE
NOT ON PURPOSE

I know of nothing more despicable and pathetic than a man who devotes all the hours of the waking day to the making of money for money's sake.[1]
John Rockefeller

Fish see the bait, but not the hook; men see the profit, but not the peril.[2]
Chinese Proverb

It started out as many of my new relationships begin these days—online, via social media.

When I virtually bumped into Janice Williams, she was a 35-year-old mother of two young children, married to Darren for five years. She worked in Victoria for a ministry in the Government of British Columbia and had done so for the previous 10 years. At one point in 2014, Janice began retweeting a few of my tweets on Twitter, so I decided to check out her profile. It read:

> Economist, mother, blogger and advocate for patient rights in maternity care—including the rights to informed choice and timely access to care. Tweets are my own.

I became very curious. Economist? Healthcare? Janice provided a link to her blog, which cleared things up for me. Her bio stated she was "keenly interested in making birth better for women in British Columbia by supporting and fighting for the right to informed consent, patient autonomy, and timely access to medical care." I figured it out. By day, she was an economist in the health sector of a provincial government, but by night, she was an advocate of improving birth practices.

The same day I visited her personal site, Janice coincidentally posted a blog entry titled, *"And in 25 Years?"* She wrote:

> In 25 years, I'll be 60 and if I stay where I'm at, or even just some- where else within government, I'll have a full pension, my chil- dren will be grown, the house paid for. And maybe, if I was still the person I was six years ago, I'd be content. But, I am not that woman.
>
> My work-outside-of-work has been a refuge, a life raft in an otherwise turbulent sea. Indeed, my work-outside-of-work has sustained me during some of my most difficult times and has chal- lenged me to think in new ways about healthcare and the health system. It is meaningful and can and has affected change.
>
> It is rather ironic then, that the work that has reminded me of how much I care about healthcare—about the system—is the same work that makes my work-at-work an exercise in tedium and toil.
>
> It is a shame that the work-outside-of-work does not come with a paycheck . . . because in 25 years, although I would not have a pension, I could have done some great things, things that matter and things that have meaning. Perhaps, after 25 years, I would have lived a life worth living.

Recall Peter Drucker's words: "To make a living is no longer enough. Work also has to make a life." Janice's post was highlighting an imbalance between her work and the rest of her life; the experience of millions of today's workers.

The Purpose Effect aims not simply to make a living, but to make a life. It results in a higher calling for team members so they are permitted the chance to improve society and the stakeholders they serve. *The Purpose Effect* is also the opportunity for an organization to redefine itself, plac- ing purpose on par with profit and its strategic objectives. Janice was at a crossroads. Although she felt purpose in her life, the organization she worked for *and* the role she occupied were largely devoid of such purpose. At first blush, after reading her blog post, it seemed her vision of purpose was established on a personal level, while her organization and role left something to be desired.

I met up with Janice a few times to find out more, to offer assistance and in particular to ask questions about the relationship between life, work and purpose. Through those meetings, she struck me as someone who had successfully defined her own personal sense of purpose, but she might not have been working in a role with a purpose mindset or in an organization that matched. Like many other individuals I have interviewed, worked with or coached, Janice seemed to be undergoing a form of adversity.

"Upon returning from maternity leave," Janice said to me over one of those coffees, "the culture of the ministry had changed considerably. It had become much more hierarchical. There was fear around the use of data, and most data had become locked down." As an economist trying to use data to make logical, evidence-based decisions and predictions to improve the healthcare sector, this was an obvious issue to Janice. "There seemed to be a shift away from promoting 'Evidence Informed Decision Making,'" she continued, "toward 'Decision Based Evidence Making.' Not only was there this change in leadership and organizational culture, I was being under-utilized and I began feeling uncomfortable exhibiting openness at work. In fact, I found myself in a personal conflict regarding 'who I am in life' versus 'who I need to be at work.'"

Janice's story is interesting, but so, too, is the organization that she worked for. *The Purpose Effect* is not a one-way street of cause and effect. Recall, to achieve the sweet spot, all three categories of purpose (personal, organization and role) ought to intersect. Consequently, there are many symptoms, obstacles and dilemmas at team member *and* organizational levels that can cause purpose to remain misaligned.

The aim of the following two chapters is to highlight those indicators so we can proceed to Section III where we will discuss in depth the three categories of purpose that ideally intersect to deliver *The Purpose Effect*.

The Continuing Story of Engagement

Engaged team members fuel sustainable success in an organization. Purpose and culture are a bit like fraternal twins. If the concept of purpose is solid and balanced—if the organization also portrays an open and collaborative culture—stakeholders ought to see improved results. But there remain far too many Janices in the working world and not enough Paul Bleiers, Bas van Abels or organizations like Fairphone and those we will be introduced to later in the book. Ultimately, this lack of engagement *and* purpose could be inhibiting an organization's future stability and growth.

Research proves there is a causal relationship between a highly engaged organization with marked improvements in customer satisfaction, innovation, productivity and community initiatives. In the case of private organizations, stock price, shareholder value, profitability and revenues also increase. This causal relationship between culture, purpose and bottom line benefits was outlined in a 1998 *Harvard Business Review* article, "The Employee-Customer-Profit Chain at Sears."

Sears was trapped in an "old command-and-control culture [that] was too parental and didn't value people enough" and it showed. The company suffered an annual net loss problem of $3.9 billion. By adapting the nature of their organization through the creation of a "great place to work, shop and invest" culture, Sears markedly increased employee and customer satisfaction, as well as garnering $200 million in additional annual revenues.[3] Sears is an example of demonstrating causality between an engaged, purpose-driven workforce and improved business results. TELUS is arguably another. In the previous chapter I indicated employee engagement at TELUS increased from 53 percent to 87 percent. Since 2010 it also has achieved greater than 200 percent total shareholder return. Both organizations demonstrate causality between an engaged workforce and improved business metrics.

The University of Pennsylvania found that organizations with high levels of employee satisfaction perform much better than those without. The researchers indicated that "firms with high levels of employee satisfaction generate superior long-horizon returns, even when controlling for industry factor risk, or a broad set of observable characteristics." They also discovered companies with highly engaged team members "earned an annual four-factor alpha of 3.5 percent,"[4] which in layman's terms, is a 3.5 percent difference in the stock price. The research ultimately demonstrated causality between high organizational engagement and increased shareholder returns. Indeed, the benefits seem to be felt across sectors. The University of Warwick, for example, discovered that employees in any sector (public, not-for-profit and private) who were classified as "flourishing at work" were actually 12 percent more productive than those who were not, generating all sorts of additional organizational benefits.[5]

Over the course of a 10-year period, involving the analysis of more than 111,000 surveys, Queen's University unearthed several bottom-line benefits to an engaged workforce, including:

- 26 percent less turnover

- 100 percent more unsolicited employment applications

- 20 percent less absenteeism

- 15 percent greater team member productivity

- 30 percent greater customer satisfaction levels

In the case of publicly traded companies, Queen's also found there to be a 65 percent increase in the share price in organizations considered engaged versus those that were not.[6]

The Opener Institute for People and Performance is an organization founded at the University of Oxford that helps its clients with productivity, performance and engagement. It collaborated with the *Wall Street Journal* to survey over 9,000 people worldwide. Their findings suggest that individuals who consider themselves to be engaged at work are twice as productive, stay five times longer in their job, are six times more energized and take 10 times fewer sick days than those who are not. Interestingly, they also report that those same workers help their peers 33 percent more than their least engaged peers do.[7]

These data demonstrate both the organization *and* the team member benefits when the categories of culture and purpose are aligned. When the culture and purpose of an organization are those in which the team member feels engaged and can exhibit their own sense of role-based purpose, it is possible for all intended stakeholders to benefit. The research surfaced by academics and consulting firms—as well as the examples of Sears and TELUS—is enlightening, but there is unfortunate evidence to suggest that disengagement and a lack of purpose are still a main feature of organizations today.

Perhaps there are far more Janice Williamses in our midst than is healthy. It is this state of disengagement that should be concerning to both team members *and* the organization's senior leaders. Yet far too little has changed even with studies such as that offered by Deloitte. The firm issued a report in 2015 that found "87 percent of organizations cite culture and engagement as one of their top challenges" and 50 percent identifying the problem as "very important."[8] But is anything being done about it?

The Conference Board found that only 47 percent of Americans were satisfied in their jobs, a number that has not dramatically improved since the late 1990s. In fact, the opposite is occurring. In 1987, job satisfaction in America actually stood at 61 percent, the high-water mark since job satisfaction became a metric, but it has been getting progressively worse since. The authors remarked, "Widespread job dissatisfaction negatively affects employee behavior and retention, which can impact enterprise-level success."[9] Perhaps nothing *is* being done about culture and purpose.

According to Gallup, the percentage of United States workers actively disengaged or not engaged stood at 67 percent in December of 2015. Gallup defines engagement as the point at which workers are "psychologically committed to their jobs and likely to be making positive contributions to their organizations."[10] In fact, since 2000, the percent of United States workers who consider themselves engaged at work has not materially changed. It remains stuck in and around the 30 percent mark.

Things are actually worse from a global perspective. Gallup indicates 87 percent of team members across the planet are not at a level that would be defined as engaged. If you read further into the research, 52 percent of all global team members report that they are "checked out at work." According to Gallup, one out of every two individuals at work simply does not care.[11] Apathy is more dominant than not.

If research proves an engaged workforce leads to improved organizational results—yet it also suggests the vast majority of team members and organizations remain far from being engaged at work and devoid of workplace purpose—what are those symptoms? If research suggests an organization that possesses a purpose that intentionally and willingly serves all stakeholders through an open and collaborative operating environment, what obstacles get in the way of doing so?

Over the years, I have discovered and witnessed that there are many issues that disturb and actually prevent *The Purpose Effect* from materializing. There are many reasons why team members and organizations are "*Not On Purpose.*" There are five concerns in particular, however, that seem to rise to the top, causing the most damage to team members, leaders and the organization. Those factors are:

- Remuneration

- Profit

- Role

- Performance

- Power

The remainder of this chapter discusses the first two symptoms, and the next chapter delves into the latter three indicators. Both chapters highlight how these symptoms prevent *The Purpose Effect* from ever being achieved.

Remuneration

If there was one sublime piece of advice I received when under the tutelage of Lorna Shapiro, Associate Dean at the British Columbia Institute of Technology during the late 1990s, it was this: "There are three things people hate being messed around with: parking spots, offices and pay." As I have witnessed over the years, the last one is fundamental.

The Easterlin Paradox, named for Richard Easterlin's argument in a 1974 essay, taught us that increasing levels of pay over time does not equate to increased levels of happiness.[12] It is not possible to buy one's way to *The Purpose Effect*. For example, United States gross national product per capita has grown 300 percent since 1960, yet average engagement in America has remained the same.

That is, Americans have more money to spend, on average, yet their level of contentment has flatlined. While we all want to be appropriately compensated, pay raises alone are not going to curb this workplace malady any time soon.

Reporting the outcome of a Princeton University study for the Center of Health and Wellbeing, Daniel Kahneman and Angus Deaton observed that emotional well-being can rise to a certain level in relation to earnings, "but there is no further progress beyond an annual income of ~$75,000."[13] In response to the study, Dan Price, founder and CEO of Gravity Payments, determined to put theory into action in early 2015. By announcing to the 120-person organization that over a three-year period, those making below the threshold would have their salary bumped up to $70,000, Dan signaled his intentions to be true to his company's motto: "Take care of your employees, and they'll take care of your customers."[14] Some have challenged his motive, but Dan is adamant to stay the course.

When I asked him why he thought this good deed was necessary, he said, "As a leader, there's a moral imperative to do the best you can for those you're leading. Setting a living minimum wage allows people to unleash their passion, continue to push the boundaries of service and further our mission to make credit card processing fair for independent businesses." Dan believes Gravity team members are the most passionate people he knows. As such, he wanted to ensure all of them became adequately compensated.

Tellingly, Dan indicated that team members at the company "are willing to cancel Friday night dates to help a merchant in need, working for a purpose, not profit." Dan thinks the new $70,000 minimum wage will provide the team with the resources to live a happier life without financial distraction or worry. "It helps turn their job into an extension of their values," he said, "rather than a place they go to make ends meet."[15]

Another factor that might help accentuate a lack of purpose is the widening gap in pay between senior-level executives and the average worker. According to the non-partisan Economic Policy Institute, between the years 1978 and 2014, CEO pay in the United States increased by approximately 1,000 percent. The wages of non-executive workers, on the other hand, have only increased by 10 percent.[16]

It makes infinite sense that there ought to be a gap in wages between the CEO and the average worker's salary, but should it be 300 times, as was the case at the end of 2014? In 1965, the compensation ratio between a CEO and the average salary was 20-1. Even Peter Drucker, writing in the *Wall Street Journal* in 1977, observed that a 25-1 ratio should be the target difference.[17] It is near impossible, however, for team members not to read the business section of a newspaper or website—or watch any mainstream media news footage—and wonder why executives earn so much money in comparison to their own wages.

Stock options and stock awards are certainly a factor in private or publicly traded companies, but even public sector firms can be forced to take action around pay issues for the betterment of its goals and mission. One such company is BC Ferries—an arms-length crown corporation—a firm that is established and regulated by a provincial government providing ferry services across a multitude of routes in British Columbia. Its CEO's annual compensation was $915,000 in 2012 but, after public and worker backlash when the figure was released, the firm's board lowered it to $500,730 in 2014.[18]

But I will suggest further that innovation apathy in the organization becomes a pervasive problem because of such discrepancy. Who wants to innovate when top-level brass becomes the sole group that is compensated for growth? Perhaps this is why closed-minded behavior and idea hoarding characterize many disengaged organizations. If objectives are set for the individual—as opposed to the team—it becomes a competitive quest to outdo your peer rather than working together for the overarching benefit of the stakeholders that everyone ought to be serving.

In *FLAT ARMY*, I explored the meaning of the term *collaboration*:

> As many words do, the word collaborate originates from Latin—in this case, from *collaborare*, which means "to work with." The prefix *col* means "with" and, of course, *labore* is familiar to us as "to work" or, in today's lexicon, "to labor." Thus, to collaborate is to work with.[19]

Imagine a team where members work to improve their collaboration skills instead of their competition skills, working with one another to establish goals and achieve outcomes. Instead, though, our workers are plagued both with the preoccupation of more pay as well as the "compete versus collaborate" mindset. A lack of purpose stems not only from gaps in pay, or fixations on increased amounts of remuneration, but also on the consumerism mindset that has enveloped parts of the Western world.

On the topic of pay and consumerism, economist John Maynard Keynes wrote in 1930, "Now it is true that the needs of human beings may seem to be insatiable. But they fall into two classes—those needs which are absolute in the sense that we feel them whatever the situation of our fellow human beings may be, and those which are relative in the sense that we feel them only if their satisfaction lifts us above, makes us feel superior to, our fellows."[20] This money-induced, consumerism mindset is a form of "keeping up with the Joneses." As author Richard Layard remarked, "People are concerned about their relative income and not simply about its absolute level. They want to keep up with the Joneses or if possible to outdo them."[21]

The IMF found as households accumulate more debt, the deeper the subsequent slump the economy can take. Furthermore, as they studied the Great Recession (the economic meltdown that occurred between 2008 and 2012), they found "housing busts preceded by larger run-ups in gross household debt—mortgages, personal loans, and credit card debt—are associated with significantly larger contractions in economic activity."[22] We might argue that the pursuit of possessions has clouded some people from reaching a personal sense of purpose. Author Charles Handy chimed in on the subject stating, "Maybe consumerism is the cancer of today's society."[23] Maybe it is.

Consider consumer debt. In the United States, each adult now possesses approximately 3.7 credit cards[24] and is responsible for $15,799 of consumer debt.[25] The total credit card debt in United States alone is $2.43 trillion.[26] In 1989, combined credit card debt sat at roughly $211 billion. Put differently, credit card debt rose by $2.2 trillion in roughly 20 years. It is even worse in Canada where each adult is responsible for $27,131 of consumer debt.[27] What about the UK? Total credit card debt in the UK has increased by £25 billion since 2001 and shows no signs of slowing.[28]

Not surprisingly, personal savings rates likewise have decreased in the United States from 12 percent in 1982 to just under one percent, while household debt as a percentage of GDP has risen from just over 45 percent to 80 percent over the past 50 years. Similar levels can be found in other Western countries. In the United Kingdom, household debt as a percentage of GDP currently sits at 98 percent. In Singapore it sits at 77 percent, and in South Korea it is 88 percent.[29] The problem therefore is not an isolated one to America.

It could be that Scottish economist Adam Smith was far more prescient than scholars and economists give him credit for in his 1776 treatise, *The Wealth of Nations*. On the topic of useful production versus empty consumption, he wrote: "Consumption is the sole end and purpose of all production; and the interest of the producer ought to be attended to only so far as it may be necessary for promoting that of the consumer. The maxim is so perfectly self-evident that it would be absurd to attempt to prove it."[30]

To put things into perspective with *The Purpose Effect*, let me recall a coaching exchange I once experienced with a colleague. We had met several times over the previous year, discussing his career and future possibilities. On this particular day, sensing the chance to be far more direct, I asked a rather blunt question: "Are you interested in a progressive role, one with purpose, or are you simply looking to make more money?" The reply was illuminating: "I've got to pay off my credit cards and then I need to buy a house. We want to start a family and we need a second car. Can you help me? I need to make more money, and I need to do it fast." This particular individual was not so much interested in a role with purpose—or working in an organization that demonstrated purpose across its stakeholders—as he was desperately seeking an increased amount of money from a paycheck to fuel his lifestyle desires.

In summary, money, widening compensation gaps and the relationship to increased consumerism (as well as household debt) are likely contributors to misaligned purpose. At a minimum, everyone should be aware of these types of indicators.

Profit

Charles Handy stated, "The principal purpose of a company is not to make a profit—full stop. It is to make a profit in order to continue to do things or make things, and to do so even better and more abundantly."[31] There may be some deep-rooted issues in today's private organizations concerning the relationship between purpose and profit. Although this "Not On Purpose" issue is primarily focused on the private organization, rest assured there are facets that can be applied to the public sector and not-for-profit organizations, too.

Theodore Roosevelt is someone we can still learn from today, particularly as it relates to a firm's fixation on profit for the sake of profit. Roosevelt was President of the United States between 1901 and 1909, serving America as its 26th Commander in Chief. At the turn of the 20th century, as America was beginning to usurp the United Kingdom as the dominant superpower, society was well on its way to shifting from agrarian to manufacturing modes of economic prosperity. Leaders such as Roosevelt possessed a keen sense of the future. Roosevelt clearly described in his State of the Union speech of 1902 the potential for a bifurcation of profit from purpose, due in part to the large gap in citizen wealth that had manifested over the previous 30 years.

> Our aim is not to do away with corporations; on the contrary, these big aggregations are an inevitable development of modern industrialism, and the effort to destroy them would

61

be futile unless accomplished in ways that would work the utmost mischief to the entire body politic. We can do nothing of good in the way of regulating and supervising these corporations until we fix clearly in our minds that we are not attacking the corporations, but endeavoring to do away with any evil in them. We are not hostile to them; we are merely determined that they shall be so handled as to sub-serve the public good. We draw the line against misconduct, not against wealth.[32]

Roosevelt recognized that the corporation was here to stay, but that it required both guidance and good governance if it were to achieve profit and purpose for the good of all stakeholders. Roosevelt argued that corporations were, in fact, creatures of the state and should therefore be forced to serve a more purposeful intent for the public. The previous 30 years or so had clearly created a divisive wedge in society between the haves and have-nots.

Roosevelt—clearly onto something—was providing us with a clue. Perhaps the misconduct witnessed by some of today's corporations—putting profit, greed and power ahead of purpose and not on relative equal terms—comes from a lack of better processes, guidelines and laws.

Professor of Law at the University of British Columbia, Joel Bakan, seems to think so. In his book, and subsequent documentary, *The Corporation: The Pathological Pursuit of Profit and Power* in 2003, Joel explained, "For in a world where anything or anyone can be owned, manipulated, and exploited for profit, everything and everyone will eventually be."[33] I read the book many years ago and watched the documentary, so I figured it was time to directly reach out to him to see if his thoughts might have changed more than a decade since *The Corporation* debuted in print and film formats. I suppose I wanted to see if he was continuing to channel his inner Roosevelt.

According to Joel, things have not changed all that much in society or inside the corporation. When I met with him over a coffee and asked if corporations were beginning to demonstrate different or improved behaviors than what he put forward when he wrote *The Corporation*, he said, "Despite the very clear and encouraging changes we see in corporate consciousness over the last decade, including new practices and expectations, the corporation itself as an institution has remained the same."

Joel believes the doctrine known as the "best interest of the corporation principle" remains firmly entrenched in the corporation. This principle is a legally binding agreement of managers, directors and owners of the company to continue prioritizing financial interests above all other decisions and concerns. He contends it is a deeply rooted principle and has been at the core of the corporation's success over several decades in raising investment capital and thus fueling job creation and innovation—all good things, he states—but there remains a problem and it is not the people, rather the institution of the corporation itself.

"The 'best interest of the corporation principle' effectively bars leaders from pursuing the best interests of society," he said. For Joel, the corporation remains fixated on profit and greed. As is evident from the financial crisis of 2008 onwards, and the continued devotion to both maximizing shareholder value and extracting profits from a company in order to "game the system," he believes, "the corporation needs to entrench sustainability into core business plans and that the corporation of the future will recognize that sustainability is not enough, and that more is needed." That "more" he refers to are public laws and regulations that demand and incentivize sustainability rather than hoping and trusting corporations to embrace it voluntarily. But why do things remain the same?

Milton Friedman, noted economist and statistician, wrote in 1962, "There is one and only one social responsibility of business—to use its resources and engage in activities designed to increase its profits."[34] Over a period of time, this doctrine has become the principle habit of most corporate leaders in the Western world, evidenced by his role as adviser to Ronald Reagan during his presidency in the 1980s.

It has become "the way" to run a business, particularly so after an article of his was published in *The New York Times Magazine* in 1970 titled, "The Social Responsibility of Business Is to Increase Its Profits." Arguably, this became the launch point for today's profit and greed-focused missions. The most telling passage of his essay in the magazine reads:

In a free enterprise, private-property system, a corporate executive is an employee of the owners of the business. He has direct responsibility to his employers. That responsibility is to conduct the business in accordance with their desires, which generally will be to make as much money as possible

> while conforming to the basic rules of the society, both those embodied in law and those embodied in ethical custom.[35]

Friedman's opposition to the concept of egalitarianism—at the time, a by-product concept of socialism and welfarism theories—was unfortunate. The socioeconomic benefits of an engaged and flourishing organization are arguably irrefutable. Maybe Friedman missed his chance to place purpose on the same pedestal as profit. Perhaps he overlooked the opportunity to redefine capitalism, one that included social, community, intellectual, environmental and societal well-being alongside financial.

Since Friedman's article appeared in 1970, the results have been arguably devastating for society in general, particularly if society sticks with the current definitions of organizational success. It can affect the public sector, too. The U.S. Government shutdown in early October 2013—where roughly 800,000 federal employees became furloughed for an indefinite period of time and another 1.3 million employees had to show up for work, but didn't know if they were going to be paid—is an example of leaders in the public sector forgetting about society's well-being in favor of partisan politicking, and arguably their own profit. Recall Janice Williams who was struggling with the difference between her personal self and the team member she was displaying while working in a government ministry that did not know how to unleash her role purpose, let alone profit from it.

In his 2005 paper entitled, "Has Financial Development Made the World Riskier?" former Economic Counselor and Director of Research at the IMF, Raghuram G. Rajan, chillingly foresaw the financial collapse that would follow three years later. He wrote, "If firms today are implicitly selling various kinds of default insurance to goose up returns, what happens if catastrophe strikes? Will they start defaulting on obligations to policyholders and pensioners precisely when such protection is most needed?"

Rajan was spot on. Much of the financial meltdown that began in the fall of 2008 was predicated on an unhealthy appetite of greed by investors, insurance brokers and executives of banking institutions. So, too, a zombie-like penchant for risk combined with a blatant disregard for societal well-being was rampant. It was profit for the sake of profit. Interestingly, financial incentives—particularly those aimed at the investors—were his biggest worry. He wrote, "Changes in the financial sector have altered managerial incentives, which in turn have altered the nature of risks undertaken by the system."[36]

As we now know, those incredible incentive packages of investors, brokers and executives made millions for a few, but put thousands out of work simultaneously. This lack of organizational purpose—this disregard for society itself—led to a loss of 8.8 million jobs in the United States,[37] over 900,000 in the United Kingdom[38] and nearly 450,000 in Canada.[39] According to The World Bank, over 25 million migrant workers in China were laid off directly because of the financial crisis.[40]

If the investors, brokers and executives of financial institutions were able to get away with millions of dollars in compensation—in return for pushing society to the brink of financial ruin—do we find it eerily similar that investors, brokers, executives and lobbyists continue to wreak havoc by a form of induced stock market volatility for purposes of gaming the system to create individual wealth?

On the topic of shareholder gains and the current state of Wall Street, William Lazonick, an economist, noticed this dilemma and in a 2014 *Harvard Business Review* article, wrote, "Corporate profitability is not translating into widespread economic prosperity. Trillions of dollars that could have been spent on innovation and job creation in the U.S. economy over the past three decades have instead been used to buy back shares for what is effectively stock-price manipulation."[41]

Has the myopic quest for profit (if not profiteering) become a symptom of failure—a failure to create *The Purpose Effect*?

Next, let us investigate even further evidence—the concepts of power, performance and role—that also work to prevent the sweet spot from ever being realized.

CHAPTER FOUR
PURPOSE MISMATCH

"Continuous effort—not strength or intelligence—
is the key to unlocking our potential."[1]
Liane Cordes

"Power consists in one's capacity to link his will with the purpose of others,
to lead by reason and a gift of cooperation."[2]
Woodrow Wilson

In October of 2012, at the age of 52 years, Linds Redding of Auckland, New Zealand died of inoperable esophageal cancer. Prior to his battle, he was the owner and operator of a small animation and art studio called The Department of Motion Graphics. The firm specialized in "designing and crafting unique, high-quality motion graphics and animation solutions."[3] Prior to starting the business, Linds worked at large advertising agencies such as BBDO and Saatchi & Saatchi as an art director. His entire 30-year career had been spent serving the advertising industry in one way or another.

In March of 2012—taking stock of his life, career and the inevitability of his own death—Linds wrote a 3,000-word essay on his blog entitled, "A Short Lesson In Perspective." He started by focusing on what he referred to as "The Overnight Test." When working on an advertising project, he and his colleagues would spend hours coming up with ideas, pinning each of them to a board for viewing. The next day—and not at the moment of ideation—the team would decide which options to put forward to a client.

In his post, Linds lamented the modern corporation's quest for profit maximization and regretted that the patience required by "The Overnight Test" was rarely to be witnessed at such organizations. "The Overnight Test only works if you can afford to wait overnight," wrote Linds.

But his essay went deeper. The chilling, reflective feedback did not solely focus on the profit-only mindset of the corporation. He set his sights on the people who do the work in the organizations, too—including himself.

"My old life looks, and feels, very different from the outside," he began. "It turns out I didn't actually like my old life nearly as much as I thought I did." Linds was dying. Perhaps it was this state of contemplativeness that urged him to write about his career. It was a career he was not all that happy with. "I think I've come to the conclusion that the whole thing was a bit of a con. A scam. An elaborate hoax," he opines. Linds believed his entire education and experience actually set himself up for an "epic act of self-deceit."

"Countless late nights and weekends, holidays, birthdays, school recitals and anniversary dinners were willingly sacrificed at the altar of some intangible but infinitely worthy higher cause," he recounted. "It would all be worth it in the long run."

But this myopia and fixation on the role, his performance and the rigidity that accompanied his behavior was like a career Ponzi scheme. He had convinced himself that sacrificing time from his life to work for the glory of his career and firms was dutiful. It was necessary. In hindsight, Linds believed, "It wasn't really important. Or of any consequence at all really. How could it be? We were just shifting product."

Toward the conclusion of the essay, Linds asks, "So was it worth it?" His answer cut to the heart of the matter. "Well, of course not. It turns out it was just advertising. There was no higher calling."

Eventually, Linds wonders if his 30-year professional existence was a sham. He closes the post by writing, "As a life, it all seemed like such a good idea at the time. I'm not really sure <my life> passes The Overnight Test."[4]

The story of Linds Redding ought to be a wake-up call for both individuals *and* the organization. Individuals who believe their purpose in life is solely tied to their role at work may be in for a rude awakening when a life event or organizational downsizing incident occurs. Our roles and careers are important, but they should not be considered the sole identifying factors that define us. When an organization creates an operating culture rife with power, a lack of caring or unethical behaviors, it becomes an accomplice in disengagement. The organization becomes a contributing factor in the creation of unfulfilled lives. No one deserves to die feeling their work was a sham. That is, the organization can be thought of as partially culpable for scenarios like that of Linds Redding.

This chapter focuses on three additional symptoms that prevent *The Purpose Effect* from ever materializing. They are role, power and performance. The first issue we will tackle is role.

Role

Paul J. Zak, a neuroeconomist at Claremont Graduate University, is the author of *The Moral Molecule*. He developed a theory known as Ofactor. Paul's model centered on organizational design and suggests a team member's level of joy in their role has a causal and direct relationship to both trust and purpose. In simpler terms, "Trust x Purpose = Joy." The "O" of Ofactor pays homage to oxytocin, what Paul believes (and proves in his research) is the chemical foundation for trusting others. He writes, "Trust can be raised by implementing policies explicitly designed to empower and engage employees." Paul indicates if levels of trust are raised in an organization such that team members feel as though they are allowed to "do good" in their roles, they then possess the "incentives and resources to perform better, boosting organizational performance."[5]

Maybe team members *are* on a constant quest to achieve joy in their roles. But that quest often comes up against various inhibitors and conflicting attitudes or behaviors regarding what type of responsibility or autonomy the individual has in the role itself. In 1957, Stanford University researcher Leon Festinger coined the term "cognitive dissonance," referring to a human being's search to achieve internal balance, harmony and consistency among the conflicts and factors that get in the way.[6] Cognitive dissonance may sound more academic than trying to achieve joy in their role at work, but what it may boil down to is a team member's general sense of worth in their role. If there is no worth, it may be the result of a lack of alignment between personal, organizational and role purpose. It may sour the chance for the sweet spot.

Without purpose, trust or joy in a team member's role and with cognitive dissonance perpetually lurking, a team member has to feel value and worth in their role for *The Purpose Effect* to materialize. In fact, UK-based Kalixa

Pro found that 49 percent of all workers were so unhappy in their role that they believed their career choice was a mistake. A further 24 percent were so disillusioned that they admitted to describing themselves as poor workers.[7]

Sanjee Singla, an entrepreneur based in Washington, D.C., did not feel value in his roles as an investment banker and financial modeler. He decided to take matters into his own hands instead of hoping for purpose to surface magically or to fall from the sky.

Sanjee calls himself a "serial creative," an individual who happily can work on almost anything, in almost any field, so long as he is creating something of real, lasting value. He is well educated, too, earning a Master's degree in Management Science and Engineering along with a Bachelor's degree in Economics from Stanford University. The various roles he held after graduating, however, were not doing much to help him achieve *The Purpose Effect*. What happens to many people in Sanjee's shoes is that they remain in their role and misery begins to compound. This is especially true when the direct leader of team members like Sanjee are ill-equipped to nurture environments or roles where worth and value are appreciated. All of this aids the alarming statistics of continued worker disengagement, dissatisfaction and disaffection.

But Sanjee was not about to become a statistic. During an interview he said, "I find the idea of being responsible for some change in the world truly captivating: the idea of closing my eyes 10 years from now and smiling at the fact that people are being helped directly because of what I have built." He wanted to ensure there was value to his role, whatever that may be. "I don't want to be separated from the excitement," he continued, "of that creation and execution as most employees are at larger companies; nor do I want to spend my life advising others on what to do with their great achievements. This captivation I'm talking about is compelling and one I believe is worth a career's effort."

It was Sanjee's recognition that a purposeful role was not going to materialize if he continued working in these soulless jobs and operating environments. "I believe the emphasis now is for people to navigate themselves by making good, disciplined, mature decisions," he said. "Part of this means being well adjusted, having self-esteem, showing temperance and working on projects that add something good to the world. As long as we live among unclear pathways, people have to educate and invest in themselves to become mature actors."

After carefully thinking about what brings him a sense of purpose, joy and value, Sanjee left the traditional form of working, and started a company called Apply.co. He helps other individuals with their job-seeking wishes in addition to assisting organizations with their hiring needs. He concluded our interview by suggesting, "People need to strive to become the best version of themselves."[8]

Disengagement will continue to be a problem if a team member's role at work does not contain opportunities to create value or if they are not recognized for their efforts. Further, if a leader does not choose to create a trusting environment—one where team members might achieve purpose in their role and a sense of value while working—it is possible cognitive dissonance will overpower and the three categories of purpose might never align.

Power

In his book, *Power: Why Some People Have It—and Others Don't*, author and Stanford University professor, Jeffrey Pfeffer writes the following:

> Not being able to control one's environment produces feelings of helplessness and stress, and feeling stressed or "out of control" can harm your health. So being in a position with low power and status is indeed hazardous to your health, and conversely, having power and the control that comes with it prolongs life.[9]

Pfeffer's thesis is provocative.

Some individuals will demonstrate both blind strength and deceptively forceful elements of power while trying to accomplish goals and objectives. It is the workplace equivalent of the "political arena," first observed by Henry Mintzberg, management author and McGill University professor. The more power an individual obtains, the more power they are able to wield. The more strength an individual acquires, the farther they can flex their muscles.

An analogy might be government. Take for example a Democrat in a Republican-controlled House of Representatives or a conservative in a liberal majority parliament. It is nearly impossible to change laws or institute new programs because you do not possess the power in which to do so.

Through his years of consulting and teaching, Pfeffer argues that team members in today's organizations have an unrealistic expectation (and thus understanding) of what makes people more successful than others. Power, as Pfeffer states, is extremely helpful, but if the individual thinks life in the workplace is supposed to be fair all the time—a "just-world phenomenon" myth as he defines it—then it leaves the team member with a false representation of how one's career can truly prosper.

Throughout my career and life, I have seen the pitfalls of power. As an example, let me share a story about the establishment of sales quotas. The individuals' names and organization have been removed to protect identities.

Imagine you are a sales executive covering a particular territory selling a unique but popular software product, and as the new fiscal year draws closer, you are handed an annual target for the next year. Nothing new here. The target has been created at the vice president level. It is handed down to the regional vice president, who in turn sends it down to the territory director, who in turn passes it on to you, the sales account executive. Right or wrong, any sales team will confirm that this is often the process.

Here is the rub: In this particular example, the target is unattainable. Why? The unique yet popular software product you are selling is already in the hands of 90 percent of the customer territory you serve. Even if you managed to convince the remaining 10 percent of the customer base to switch over and purchase the software product, you would only ever achieve 50 percent of your quota. Despite querying the target with senior management, it remains in place, unattainable, with the prospect of annual sales-based commission out of reach. This story demonstrates how rigid, power-based hierarchical thinking can have a detrimental impact on an individual's personal *and* role-based purpose.

The individual in question has since moved on to a different high-tech company headquartered in Silicon Valley. He enjoyed his role and team at his former organization, but this illustration of power forced him to move on, to feel less like a number on a headcount spreadsheet. His personal sense of purpose was being compromised in a role he used to enjoy through an organization that actually used to demonstrate purpose. It is this breakdown in the relationship between organization-role-self that can cause high-performing team members to flee for more purposeful pastures.

We can also learn a few lessons from the corporate ashes of Nortel, a telecommunications and data networking equipment manufacturer head-quartered in Canada that speaks to the relationship of rigidity to power. At its peak in 2000, Nortel employed more than 94,000 employees world-wide, was the ninth most valuable company in the world at over $300 billion and held more than one-third of the total value of the S&P/TSX stock exchanges.[10] In other words, it was a very successful company if those are the generally accepted measures. If we fast-forward a few years, Nortel never convalesced and ultimately withered away.

As is the case within some organizations that go belly-up, a rigid operating culture took root in the management ranks of Nortel. A blindness and inability to reshape its purpose were arguably its undoing. Researchers from the University of Ottawa spent three years interviewing numerous ex-employees, partners, customers, analysts and members of the media. They discovered evidence of arrogance, rigidity and a lack of resilience, particularly at the senior leadership level. The researchers wrote:

> Nortel's rigid culture played a defining role in the company's inability to react to industry changes. Respondents suggested that this lack of adaptability was partially based on the company's history as a leader in the market.

They further identified a fixation on power and disrespect of budgeting as a root cause of the company's extinction. By increasing divisional power among its various lines of business, Nortel effectively became an organization that had "increased internal politics and fruitless competition."[11] Perhaps the upper echelons of senior management shifted the organization's purpose to become one fixated on rigidity, fiefdoms and silos, instead of one that thrives on innovation, collaboration and engagement.

There were other factors that led to the demise of Nortel, including a dramatically changing business environment that the company never adjusted to, poorly conceived management ideas, misaligned corporate strategy and executives' penchant for status quo thinking. The highly engaged culture that was once Nortel turned into one of infighting and rigidity.

The lead researcher of the report, Jonathan Calof, said, "Nortel employees had a loyalty to the company and to customers that is hard to match." Calof found ex-Nortel workers really longed for its original culture and environment, that those people were "the most positive factor captured in our study" and that "their commitment, energy, determination and personal sacrifices resulted in incredible competencies and technologies that still permeate."[12] What was once an organization thriving on purpose—enabled by a workforce equally demonstrating role purpose—was decimated by power, control and corporate blindness.

From the July 1979 issue of *Harvard Business Review*, academic Rosabeth Moss Kanter summarizes what becomes of leaders in an organization when their power and tendency for rigidity are enhanced by title and position:

> What grows with organizational position in hierarchical levels is not necessarily the power to accomplish—productive power—but the power to punish, to prevent, to sell off, to reduce, to fire, all without appropriate concern for consequences. It is that kind of power—oppressive power—that we often say corrupts.[13]

Ask yourself if much has changed since 1979. Power can be addictive. Power can lead to a sense of entitlement. Power can lead to a persistent demonstration of rigidity. As pointed out by both Pfeffer and Kanter, power can be used in an organization to get things done, but it can have destructive consequences to a team member's self or role-based purpose, not to mention the organization's existence.

When power is used to mistreat or minimize team members, should it be a surprise that the individual becomes disaffected or disengaged? We might argue that any abuse of power will run counter to an individual's personal sense of purpose. If that team member feels as though power is being used to thwart role progression or other forms of development, it is likely a sense of purpose in the role itself diminishes, possibly even disappears entirely. If power is found as part of an organization's ethos—used to bully partners or disrespect customer wishes, for example—there is a good possibility society loses out. Just ask the 94,000 former employees of Nortel.

Paradoxically, power and the pursuit of control can be both an inhibitor and a supporter of organizational and role-based purpose. In fact, some organizations give off the appearance of disengagement simply because their leaders swing too far in favor of demonstrative power and control, or because their leaders become too fixated on profit or bureaucracy. But when a leader and her organization can strike a proper balance between the power one holds by virtue of being the "leader" and the concept of a higher purpose, it is creating an environment where purpose is at least plausible for the three categories of *The Purpose Effect*. Even the "Iron Lady" herself—Margaret Thatcher, Prime Minister of the United Kingdom between 1979 and 1990—once remarked, "Power is like being a lady . . . if you have to tell people you are, you aren't."[14]

Performance

Elton Mayo was an Australian organizational theorist who spent considerable time at Harvard Business School. His theories and applications of human resources management were highly influential. Mayo felt workers were more productive when their work output was associated with natural team member groupings where the natural social aspects of work (communication, networking, mentoring, sharing, etc.) should take precedence over the institutionalized nature of existing organizational structures (i.e., silos and hoarding). His ideas were antithetical to the command-and-control management practices of individuals like Frederick Taylor, Henri Fayol and Richard Daft. But for all of his good intentions, Mayo's actions and research helped lead us to our present-day performance development process. His work against power, ironic as it seems today, helped give birth to what is known as the performance management review process. It helped create an era of performance isolationism that has arguably led to a lack of organizational and role-based purpose.

Mayo's influence on performance management came as a result of the Hawthorne Studies—research conducted in the 1920s and 1930s at the Hawthorne Works plant of Western Electric in Cicero, Illinois—which led to better insights into productivity, motivating behaviors and how management should be treating workers in an organization. Unknowingly, his research eventually gave rise to the 1950 Performance Rating Act in America, where federal workers in the U.S. were mandated to undergo annual performance reviews. If you were a federal worker, your newly minted annual performance review classified you as outstanding, satisfactory or unsatisfactory. The power and thus control of team member performance were now clearly in play. Other countries followed suit. The Western world was hooked on annual performance reviews.[15]

By 1962, the U.S. introduced the Salary Reform Act—the first step toward pay-for-performance tactics—and through the 1970s and 1980s, performance management reviews, ratings and rankings as well as MBOs (Management by Objectives) established a tightened grip on management's thinking. This vision caught on and today performance management practices include the once-a-year review, stack ranking, and Likert-style ratings. It turns out most team members loathe the idea.

The Society for Human Resource Management (SHRM) reported only 5 percent of individuals who participate in performance management practices in any type of organization were satisfied with the process and the outcome. Sibson Consulting found similar results, indicating only 5 percent of respondents graded it with the highest level on a 5-point scale.[16] The firm also found that almost 60 percent of all HR managers actually disliked their own performance management practices.

In many organizations, the annual performance review itself doesn't necessarily assist the team member; it is a built-in process that assists the firm with the dissemination of salary bumps, rewards, additional perquisites or even excuses to initiate termination processes. The performance review can be used to weed out the disengaged or apathetic. While that may be a good thing in some cases, think of the example it sets for others. The manager must comply with the organization's rules, and therefore he or she adheres to this systemic and embedded process of whack-a-mole. In their book, *Get Rid of the Performance Review!: How Companies Can Stop Intimidating, Start Managing and Focus on What Really Matters*, authors Samuel Culbert and Lawrence Rout corroborate my point: "Mainstream management is embedded in, and relies on, a culture of domination and the performance review is the biggest hammer management has."[17]

The question we must ask is whether the existing system of the performance management process aids or hinders *The Purpose Effect* from ever becoming possible. Will a team member ever feel purpose in their role if the once-a-year "performance review" is hovering over their head?

In private companies, financial rewards—restricted stock units, stock options and other related monetary gifts—are often suggestively dangled in front of team members as recognition and performance carrots, interwoven with the annual performance management review process. Although it could be construed as a form of appreciation for certain members of the organization, it often results in the opposite intended effect. The manager is provided a pool of long-term incentives (LTIs) as a means in which to reward those team members who have demonstrated superb performance.

There is never enough to go around. Fairness is thrown out the window. Thus an arbitrary model of performance comes into play. The manager must carefully think about her next steps.

What will various team members think when the awards are allotted? Everyone is aware there are LTIs to be distributed, but the manager must devise a system so as not to upset the apple cart too much. Give too many LTIs to one person or not enough to another and it might uproot any existing goodwill found on the team, causing the manager to seem out of touch, should word get out. Worse she could be thrust into either doing more work or having to find new replacements because the "star performers" have become incensed that they did not receive enough LTIs, and they then decide to leave. All team members talk, so it is not as though this is some form of NASA secret either. When everyone finds out how the LTIs were allotted, disaffection creeps in. We might argue that there is not much good that can come of this process over the long term.

Every manager has to report to their manager the allotment of LTIs. To be safe, a manager might ensure the scores (and LTI allotments) follow organizational norms. Plotting workers onto the bell curve of performance becomes the next step. Spreading out the scores unevenly is definitely career limiting. Give too many LTIs to an individual the vice president is not fond of (and a higher score) and one might question whether their own promotion will ever manifest. The process stems from an antiquated system and method in which team members are graded. At times it is akin to high school.

Whether with central tendency—where everyone receives a rating that is average, placed in the middle of the bell curve—or through unreasonable performance standards that penalize team members who in fact achieve above the norm, the performance review is one of the most loathed processes in any organization, whether public sector, not-for-profit or for-profit. Any potential for intrinsic personal achievement, motivation or confidence becomes difficult.

Globoforce, a Massachusetts-based consulting firm, found 51 percent of respondents believe the performance development process is not an accurate measure of the work they accomplish. Over half of all workers think the way in which they are being measured at work is hypocritical. Furthermore, team members are skeptical of the process itself. For example, 24 percent actually feared the annual review. Worse, only 25 percent of workers received one or more performance reviews a year.[18] Put another way, 75 percent of individuals receive one or zero performance reviews a year and, when they do, visits to the dentist for a Lidocaine-free root canal may seem like a better experience.

Research firm i4cp found similar yet arguably poorer results. In their report, *Keys to Performance Management*, only 55 percent of respondents stated existing performance development processes had a positive impact on their organizations. What is worse is that only 28 percent believed their organizations were actually effective at performance management itself.[19]

Some organizations have taken a different direction. Microsoft, Adobe, Motorola and Kelly Services have all scrapped most or all of the performance management process. Of significance, perhaps, is Accenture. This 330,000-person global organization with close to $32 billion in annual revenues decided to revise 90 percent of its existing performance management practices. Their CEO, Pierre Nanterme, proclaimed in 2015, "It's not what we need. We are not sure that spending all that time on performance management has been yielding a great outcome." What the organization recognized is that performance management is not only an annual activity. It also realized team members should not be mapped against an arbitrary bell curve of output or performance. Nanterme nailed it when he said the following:

> Performance is an ongoing activity. It's every day, after any client interaction or business interaction or corporate interaction. It's much more fluid. People want to know on an ongoing basis, am I doing right? Am I moving in the right direction? Do you think I'm progressing? Nobody's going to wait for an annual cycle to get that feedback.[20]

The ultimate question to ask is whether the performance management process that is currently utilized in your organization is one that helps achieve *The Purpose Effect*. Or, is it a major factor that causes team members and perhaps the organization's operating ethos to remain wobbly.

In Summary

Trillions of words and legions of books have been written about the problems inherent inside the organization and with leadership in general.

This chapter (and the previous one) highlighted five specific harms—remuneration, profit, role, power and performance—that continue to prevent the sweet spot from ever being achieved in *The Purpose Effect* model, whether for team members or the organization itself. Undoubtedly there are other issues that can pop up, but I will leave it to other books and articles to fill in any of these perceived holes.

The next section of the book unpacks each of the three categories of purpose: personal, organizational and role. It offers examples of how we can mitigate against the five issues explored in Section II, and points the way to achieving the sweet spot.

SECTION III

CHAPTER FIVE

CREATING A PERSONAL SENSE OF PURPOSE

Beware lest you lose the substance by grasping at the shadow.[1]
Aesop

First say to yourself what you would be; and then do what you have to do.[2]
Epictetus

It is a shame we cannot travel back in time and observe the Greeks who occupied ancient Athens. We might spend our days walking, listening, learning and even giving speeches in the Agora—the marketplace of commerce and intellectual exchange. Philosophers and leaders like Plato, Socrates, Heraclitus or Pythagoras, were alleged to have bandied about the maxim "Know Thyself" on many an occasion. Self-understanding—knowing oneself—is essential to this. It leads us to surface a critical point. Personal purpose is the perpetual journey to continually develop, define and decide your *what, who* and *how.* When we ask these questions we commit to develop, define and decide our calling, our personal purpose. We pledge to begin knowing thyself.

To know oneself is to possess the passion to improve, to seize the opportunity for illustrating clarity, and to elect one's ongoing behavior. As we progress from the teenage years to adulthood, our likes, dislikes, interests, goals and behaviors inform how we take action on various matters. Every one of us should be constantly viewing and reviewing both work and life through acts of inspection and introspection. Such factors continue to change over time. Whether or not purpose, meaning or joy ever materializes at work is, in part, subject to personal arbitration. Of course, roles, direct manager, teams and place of work can assist or detract from the journey—as we will discover in Chapters 6 and 7—but above all, it is an individual's understanding and demonstration of *what, who* and *how* that helps determine an individual's purpose of self. This is the importance of knowing oneself.

Let me introduce Megan Smith as an example. When I was working at SAP, Megan began working with our team just after she graduated from university. She was extraordinary as an individual contributor, and over time, she began to lead projects. From there, she switched business units and began leading people. After I departed to commence employment at TELUS, she switched again, and began leading leaders as an HR business partner. Throughout her time at SAP, she has continued to develop her skills, honing her experience across multiple roles. Through new opportunities, she continues to explore roles that push her growth. The key criterion for Megan is professional growth. She is uninterested in factors such as title, team size, power or corporate fame. Megan realizes that if she is not growing, her personal sense of purpose stalls or diminishes. But she is invariably her own chaperone. She has been and continues to be in control of her purpose.

Megan does not possess a traditional ladder-climbing, career mindset either. She judges her roles as opportunities for development. They are chances to learn and expand her experience. Thus, her growth, development and passion for the work are her purpose. It is what makes her tick. As she relayed to me in an interview, "I believe that doing something I love will allow me to enjoy my work and be my best professional self." Not missing a beat, she added, "Closely linked to this, I've always aimed to be in a 'career sweet spot,' the point at which you work your hardest (because you love it) and in turn become most valuable in that area, which brings greater responsibility." The organization Megan works for continues to provide a comfortable environment—the company, for example, continues to give back to the community in philanthropic ways, something very important to her—and in return, Megan has spent a decade developing, growing, learning and generally continuing her commitment to what she does. Not only has this benefited Megan, SAP also has gained from her personal disposition.

What sets Megan apart is how she makes it a priority to continue to explore, learn and grow, not just for the sake of doing so, but for the purpose of developing passion, excitement and personal satisfaction in her roles. She is constantly defining who she is, who she is to become and how she will operate under any circumstance thrown her way. Indeed, she is constantly building her *what, who* and *how* in the context of her "why." Megan knows herself.

These qualities have become the ultimate arbiters in her life. In fact, Megan thinks people should make it their priority to love what they do, to find what they are best at and then to develop a mindset of ingenuity in order to become their best personal *and* professional self. "I see my motivators like a triangle of passion-development-reward, each in a corner and the 'sweet spot' firmly ensconced in the middle of the triangle," she concluded. Because of her commitment to continuously develop, define and decide, Megan—now married with two young children while employment at SAP continues—believes she is working *and* living a life with purpose, aided in part by her mindset, roles and the organization she works for.

By virtue of working with people like Megan, conducting interviews and poring over mounds of research—as well as launching people development programs at organizational and team levels across several large firms—I have come to the realization there are three behaviors that successful and purposeful team members seem to employ. The actions—to develop, define and decide—are perpetually in motion.

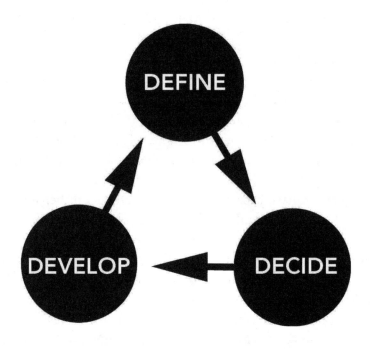

Develop

Possessing a passion for learning, growth and improvement, individuals are curious and constantly at odds with the status quo. They yearn for new experiences, knowledge and acumen whether through roles, projects or people.

> *Team members who successfully and continuously develop, answer the question:* **What** *am I doing to evolve myself?*

Define

Individuals who steadily define (and redefine) what they are in life and at work seize the opportunity for clarity. Determining and adjusting their disposition, character, identity, attributes and qualities ensure they offer themselves the chance to continually reach new levels of success.

> *Team members who successfully define, answer the question:* **Who** am I in life and at work?

Decide

Every day, we have a decision to make whether under pressure or not. How am I going to act in a given situation? We must continually choose whether to operate with truth or dishonesty, with openness or intolerance, with grit or timidity, with love or hostility.

> *Team members who successfully decide, answer the question:* **How** will I operate and be perceived by others?

The aim of this chapter is to delve into these three behaviors, highlighting examples of people (like Megan) who have successfully demonstrated the *what, who* and *how* that helps spawn their *why*. Of course, this leads to an individual's personal sense of purpose.

Develop Your What, Like Van Gogh

Studs Terkel's classic 1974 book, *Working: People Talk About What They Do All Day and How They Feel About What They Do*, provided incredible insight into the mindset of team members at work. Through hundreds of interviews, Terkel was able to investigate individuals and their quest for meaning in their work, "Over and beyond the reward of the paycheck."

Terkel found the majority of people lacked purpose in their place of work. Whether he was spending time with a miner, farmer, receptionist, press agent, publisher, truck driver, therapist or plant manager, individuals revealed with honest candor a genuine lack of meaning in the positions where they were being remunerated. One interesting response came from Nora Watson, a writer for a company that published health care literature. Watson replied to a Terkel question as follows:

> Jobs are not big enough for people. It's not just the assembly line worker whose job is too small for his spirit, you know? A job like mine, if you really put your spirit into it, you would sabotage immediately. So you absent your spirit from it. My mind has been so divorced from my job, except as a source of income, it's really absurd. You throw yourself into things because you feel that important questions—self-discipline, goals, a meaning of

your life—are carried out in your work. You want it to be a million things that it's not and you want to give it a million parts of yourself that nobody else wants there. So you end up wrecking the curve or else settling down and conforming.[3]

Did Watson possess a passion for learning and growth or a commitment to improve? Was her apathy a result of the organization, her role or perhaps a failure to evolve?

Perhaps we might seek wisdom from the painter Vincent van Gogh. When van Gogh was starting out as a painter, particularly between 1886 and 1888 while based in Paris, he would actually reuse his painting canvases. Today, van Gogh is revered as one of the world's finest painters. But things were a little different in the 19th century. He would often reuse his canvases, adding a layer of white paint on top of an original painting before starting over on a different subject entirely. This layering could happen several times in fact. To him, he was merely continuing to master his craft. To us, (well at least to me), he was painting over brilliance. Unable to pay for new canvases, he did not stop developing, and instead improvised so that he might continue building his skills and talent.

As team members contemplate what they are doing to evolve their character, no canvas should ever be thought of as complete. Each painting can build upon itself. To disregard developing is to never paint at all. To resist adding new layers to one's canvas is throwing a wet towel of apathy or timidity over the paint set, much like Nora Watson confessed to Studs Terkel. It reminds me of someone else, Céline, who continually chooses to paint over her personal canvas of purpose and overall growth in life.

Over her first 10 years of employment, Céline Schillinger worked for different companies in France, Vietnam and China, holding roles in communications, consulting and sales, as well as general management. She bounced between industries, too, including military defense, radio and media entertainment. In 2001, when she landed a position back in France at Sanofi Pasteur—the world's largest company to produce vaccines—her job-hopping continued, all the while remaining employed at Sanofi Pasteur. Céline to date has occupied positions in human resources, product development and stakeholder engagement before moving to Boston in 2015 to focus on quality innovation. "I would define myself as a person under construction," she said to me. "I'm always trying to enrich my experience by adding bits and pieces wherever I go. I experiment in my roles, push for uncomfortableness to eventually gain new knowledge out of each situation." Céline's background is another of continuous development in the pursuit of self-based purpose.

During an interview with me, Céline raised an important point about one's personal sense of purpose. Perhaps our mindset must return to the middle ages where the path to purpose was fueled by the concept of generalism. She calls herself a generalist because she believes "generalism is humanism." This depiction of humanism is how Céline sees the world, and it helps her hone her personal definition of meaning. It is what makes her grow. It is what fuels her purpose. The opportunities to learn, the diversity of people she works with, the connections she makes and the layers of gained knowledge and experience all contribute to her personal purpose. But not everyone agrees with this model—including some of the leaders at Sanofi Pasteur.

"It has been difficult at times, living and working without specialization," Céline candidly divulged. "There were lots of times I didn't feel I was good enough. People thought of my generalist background as a weakness. Generalists are frowned upon." When I asked her to provide an example of how this type of thinking affected her, she recalled a mentoring exchange. "Five years ago," she said, "I tried to explain to a top leader in the company that my purpose is to create bridges between people because I can understand what they're going through. He looked at me with a crazy look, but I insisted because this is who I am. Needless to say, our mentoring sessions ended. He didn't believe being a generalist was a good career move."

If there is one thing that is markedly poignant with Céline's insistence on a working life of continuous development—of painting over her canvases—it is her perseverance, grit and gumption. Recognizing that her organization possessed a significant gender imbalance—where the majority of senior roles were occupied by men and the majority of promotions were awarded to men—Céline wrote a letter to the CEO in January of 2011. In it, she described the problem and identified 13 ways in which to remedy the situation. The letter went viral throughout the organization, and Céline also scored a lunch with the CEO. Next she was seen launching a gender balance community to support the conversation for change. The group swelled to over 2,500 members in under two years. Later Céline, while only in her 40s, became the recipient of multiple external and international awards.

During the conversation with the CEO, Céline expressed her feelings about purpose—what could bring the company together might be introducing attributes such as openness, respect, and collaboration, which to Céline were important aspects to gender balance—and the concepts regarding humanism. He listened and agreed that gender balance was an issue and something that needed to be solved. But the community that Céline launched—which won her all of those awards—was only one facet of change, and only one element to Céline's ongoing quest for development and personal purpose.

A savvy Chief Quality Officer at Sanofi Pasteur picked up on Céline's talents (and purpose) and asked if she might be interested to relocate to Boston. Today, Céline is the Head of Quality Innovation and Engagement, working alongside a culture change consultant on the implementation of new behavioral and collaboration practices to improve various aspects of quality across the company. Then, ideally, the model will be utilized by other parts of the organization. "My passion and my purpose have turned into my dream job. I absolutely love what I do and I hope this project will bring real change across the entire organization."

Being the pragmatist of self-based purpose, Céline also laid down a personal warning shot of sorts. "I am cautious and alert and mindful that the battle is not won yet. There is still a lot of work ahead of me. I will not fall into complacency, and I need to demonstrate innovation in all of my actions. No matter what, I will continue to hone myself. My purpose will remain a development journey. You have to remain as independent as possible, not letting other people develop your path. They can help—with your role, team and organization—but you should always be in charge of your purpose."

When individuals possess a passion for learning, growth and improvement, it can help deliver on their personal sense of meaning, which can also create positive benefits for the organization in which they work. Take Henry Ford, for example. Ford was constantly learning, inquiring and investigating. Through his efforts came the invention and perfection of the assembly line needed for mass production of the automobile. He also is credited with inventing the two-day weekend, something that materialized from his learning. Or consider Steve Jobs. Aside from his notoriously bad people management skills, Jobs was famous for asking an extraordinary number of questions inside of Apple in the product development cycle, not to make himself look smarter but to learn enough such that he solidified the quest to reinvent the music, phone, television and computing markets.

Ultimately, if the team member is constantly redeveloping their skills and building up their experience—painting over their canvas—the attainment of a personal sense of purpose may become smoother and clearer. It might even become beneficial to all stakeholders, too. Céline, Sanofi Pasteur and their stakeholders clearly are reaping the benefits of her personal sense of purpose.

Define Who You Mean

Abraham Maslow once wrote, "It isn't normal to know what we want. It is a rare and difficult psychological achievement,"[4] but I contend team members ought to try to prove Maslow wrong. Aldous Huxley perhaps provided a positive antidote, when he wrote, "Knowing who in fact we are results in Good Being, and Good Being results in the most appropriate kind of good doing."[5]

Kelsy Trigg, a leader in the high-tech space, was having dinner with me one night in 2011 when she shared her personal purpose statement. She did not refer to it as such, but Kelsy highlighted something that night that made me think. Do people who exhibit purpose define themselves with some form of personal purpose statement? In the words of Huxley, does this definition aid "good being and good doing?"

Kelsy's working life purpose was and continues to be a journey. Whether as an independent contractor or analyst working for banks and insurance companies, or as a leader (director, head, vice president) in high-tech, she is highly regarded. But the path to purpose came with a few bumps along the way. Although Kelsy is someone who continuously puts purpose before profit, she had to sort through what gives her true meaning in life and at work. Her giving attitude, thoughtful character and open mind are carefully mixed with operational zest and a high degree of business stratagem. Today she is a consummate and balanced professional that sees her career as a journey of exploration.

Over that dinner, we launched into a discussion about purpose, specifically about one's personally defined sense of purpose. Kelsy pulls no punches. Her purpose is a testament to her character, and to her self-created definition of how she lives life, both at work and personally. Though it was likely years in the making, when Kelsy put pen to paper, the words came easily and she distilled it into:

- I decide to live my life filled with joy.

- I decide to be generous, open-hearted and loving.

- I decide to show up wholeheartedly and be present.

- I choose courage, integrity, peace and love.

This personal purpose statement has served Kelsy well. Her ability to define who she is and how she will operate—deciding to live and work through the behaviors and attributes outlined above—helped vault her to a level of work that continues to be grounded by her purpose. But Kelsy did not have this clarity until her late 30s. Her prior experiences, roles and organizations helped her to develop enough acumen so that she could reach a point in her life to define what truly mattered.

Indeed, over another dinner in 2015, Kelsy divulged how important the personal purpose statement had become for her. "For me, the language 'I decide' is very powerful, whether it's deciding how I show up or deciding what my next step in something is. This doesn't ensure a particular outcome or necessarily impact those around me, but it does provide a sense of grounding and choice about how I respond to my internal and external environment, no matter what my surroundings hold. When I internalized this, it brought a sense of calm for me. My happiness is my responsibility. How I show up is my choice."

Two points come to mind with respect to Kelsy:

1. Defining yourself through a personal purpose statement is an important step in the quest for workplace *and* life purpose.

2. Individuals should not be afraid to revisit the statement over time to determine if it continues to resonate.

Jill Schnarr, vice president of Community Affairs at TELUS, provides another example about the importance of these personal purpose statements. During the fall of 2013, I had the chance to moderate both virtual and face-to-face panels of TELUS vice presidents during the kickoff to the

Leadership NOW program—the high-potential leadership development program for roughly 700 TELUS team members each year. Jill kindly volunteered to be a part of a face-to-face session held in Vancouver as well as an online session. The panels were an unscripted, unrehearsed chance for senior leaders at the company to provide feedback and insight on topics such as leadership, career, work-life balance and health. I moderated the panels, and the last question at each of the sessions was for panel members to articulate three words that best described their own mantra. Not missing a beat, Jill was first to respond in the face-to-face Vancouver session with the following:

"I live by the 'be easy to' mantra. Be easy to . . . work with, do business with, talk to, connect with . . . just 'be easy to.' It is so important in our line of business, for our team members and in our communities." Jill did not know the question was coming, but had already established her purpose statement into a three-word stanza.

During Jill's 20-year career at TELUS, she continually has worked to develop her skills and experience—including roles in marketing, customer service and community investment—and throughout her tenure she has lived (and worked) by a simple yet powerful three-word professional mantra "be easy to." Later, over tea, she also noted, "I've also lived by a famous quote and have used it all the way from high school—it's published in my Grade 12 yearbook—and to this day it's hanging on a wall in my office." The quote is as follows:

> To laugh often and much; To win the respect of intelligent people and the affection of children; To earn the appreciation of honest critics and endure the betrayal of false friends; To appreciate beauty, to find the best in others; To leave the world a bit better, whether by a healthy child, a garden patch, or a redeemed social condition; To know even one life has breathed easier because you have lived. This is to have succeeded.

Despite the fact this quote has long been misattributed to Ralph Waldo Emerson by Hallmark and other misinformed companies, instead of its original 1904 writer, Bessie Anderson Stanley, you can clearly see how Jill has used this passage to help define the way in which to operate. She has developed her work self to mirror her life self, which is "be easy to" and to succeed, per the hopeful words of Stanley. For further proof, Jill continued her quest both to define and redefine herself by applying to (and being accepted into) the TELUS MBA program, commencing studies in October 2015.

In his seminal 1989 book, *The 7 Habits of Highly Effective People*, Stephen Covey encouraged people to create a personal mission statement within the second habit, "Begin with the End in Mind." While it may seem like semantics, I would prefer to call what people like Kelsy and Jill and others have defined as a "Personal Declaration of Purpose." This differs from Covey's "Personal Mission Statements," for it is purpose that one is seeking to declare and then establish, not a mission.

The question a successful team member is continuously asking and answering—who indeed is creating a personal sense of purpose—is: "Who am I in life *and* at work?" There is no one right answer, nor should it be viewed as a competitive task against peers and friends. It is an ongoing definition, not a one-time commandment. It can occur in your 20s or your 90s or at several points in between. Constantly redefining who one is in life and at work increases the likelihood that *The Purpose Effect* will be realized. Being relentless in the quest for personal purpose is key to achieving the sweet spot. An excellent starting action is to define one's self through a personal declaration of purpose. It may change over time. That can actually be healthy. The key point, however, is to take the time to define it and, ultimately, to know thyself.

Decide How To Be

Decisions. We make them every day. Whether they are big ones, little ones, important ones or novel ones, decisions are as prevalent as tourists in Paris. With respect to one's purpose of self, a decision is needed in just about every aspect of the journey. But the one ongoing decision that an individual makes to cement their personal sense of purpose is whether or not they will choose to act with integrity.

To operate with integrity is about more than making a choice between honesty and dishonesty, right and wrong. It is about wholeness, about individuation. Personal integrity, *wholeness,* is suggestive of someone who acts with a higher purpose, demonstrating their trustworthiness, reliability and authenticity. All too often, we witness the lack of such characteristics in our social, political and business leaders. An illustrative case in point was the exit of CEO Martin Winterkorn from Volkswagen in September 2015 in the wake of a scandal relating to the rigging of emission tests on diesel engines.

Integrity and the concept of being whole can help determine whether someone (or an organization) is ever going to achieve *The Purpose Effect*. How one acts is often how one will be perceived.

Eric Liddell was a British Olympian known to many through the 1981 Academy Award-winning film, *Chariots of Fire*. His decisions and demonstration of authenticity helped define his purpose. In preparation for the 1924 Paris Summer Olympics, Liddell and his coaches were informed his race specialties—100 meters, 4x100 meters and 4x400 meters—all fell on a Sunday. A devout Christian and missionary, Liddell intended to keep a promise to himself, his family and his Church; he would never run on the Sabbath.

Although the British press derided his decision—claiming he was putting God before country—Liddell remained whole, stayed true to his values and made a decision not to deviate from what mattered most to him. Instead, he requested that the British Olympic Committee allow him to train and race in the 200 and 400 meter events. Although not his preferred races, doing so would permit him to remain whole as those events were scheduled on days outside the Sabbath. Liddell went on to win a bronze medal in the 200-meter race and a gold medal in the 400-meter event. He was lauded as a hero across the United Kingdom. We might even argue Liddell and the British Olympic Committee both benefited from Liddell's decision to remain whole.

Clayton Christensen, the famous Harvard academic and author of such books as, *The Innovator's Dilemma* and *Disrupting Class*, provides another example. When he attended Oxford University, Christensen was a member of the varsity basketball team that went undefeated for a year. The only thing in the way of a perfect season was the championship game. The match fell on a Sunday. Like Liddell, Christensen was a devout Christian. What to do? Like Liddell, Christensen refused to play on the Sabbath. He decided to sit out the championship game. On the decision, Christensen remarked, "The lesson I learned from this is that it's easier to hold to your principles 100 percent of the time than it is to hold to them 98 percent of the time."[6]

The sorts of decisions that Liddell and Christensen (and arguably Winterkorn) demonstrated can ultimately impact where, with whom and how one works. It can affect one's acceptance of whether they are leading a life (or a working life) of purpose. Take for instance Michael Bungay Stanier.

"I want to infect a billion people with the possibility virus," Michael said to me. If one decides to work with authenticity, a statement like this might just do the trick. After years of toiling in roles and organizations that were not delivering much personal purpose—not making him whole—Michael made the decision to go out on his own and launch an organizational development firm he coined Box of Crayons. The company has since helped hundreds of organizations including Tesco, TD Bank, PWC, Nokia, Citibank and Nestlé. Box of Crayons wants to help people and organizations "do less good work and more great work." The person behind it all is Michael—the one who wants to infect a billion people with the possibility virus—but his decision to work in this manner was not easy.

"I've been engaged with this question, 'What the hell is the point of it all?' for quite a long time," Michael divulged during one of our discussions. "I spent a long time seeking a path that would create a more purposeful life. I've always had a slight nervousness of following the expected path. School, university, marriage, house, kids, career and so on is the commonly held preordained path, but it isn't necessarily the right path. This thesis has allowed me to stay present, and helped me figure out the right path. It helped me with my decision making."

After a few years working in various "decreasingly purpose-driven companies that led to misery all around," Michael decided that the process and the output of his working life were insufficient. The question he began asking himself—the decision he was seeking to make—was, "What sort of outcome did he want from life?" "I recognized I was simply inventing the next soup for Heinz or Campbell's," Michael indicated. He cheekily continued, "I did not want to leave a legacy of having invented stuffed-crust pizza." Michael had been developing and defining his *what* and *who* of personal purpose, but the manner in which he was operating—his *how*—was leaving him less than fulfilled. "After a significant period of self-reflection," he added, "I realized that the process of my work was insufficient. A better outcome had to become a big part of what I was doing in my life."

Michael launched Box of Crayons to complete the circle of creating his *what, who* and *how*. Michael confided that "even after creating Box of Crayons, it took some time to figure out the purpose of the company. We had to develop and decide what we wanted to be. But then this notion of the possibility virus became so much of what we wanted to do. Box of Crayons became a firm to give people the responsibility for enacting their own freedom. I can't personally touch a billion people, but I can infect people in a way that is shareable and accessible. This way of being influences me each and every day. We continually ask ourselves at Box of Crayons, 'How do we give away our content and intellectual property in a useful way—sharing with the tribe—so it helps others with their own purpose?'"

Michael may not have been prescribed to decide whether to run or play basketball on the Sabbath, but he forced himself to make a series of decisions concerning his working life. Eventually he made himself whole. Shifting himself from a mindset without purpose (floundering in an unfulfilled mindset) to one full of purpose ensured he upheld his own definition of authenticity and integrity. The decision to operate in such a manner has benefited both Michael and the thousands of people he and his organization have touched. Indeed, it seems he is well on his way to infecting billions of people with the possibility virus.

Knowing Myself

If you have ever heard the adage, "salt of the earth"—those who demonstrate great reliability and worth to others—Tim McDonald more than fits the bill. He is an example of someone who continues to develop, define and decide what his place is in this ever-changing world.

Tim started out his professional life in real estate. He was very successful. Not in the backwards Donald Trump real estate manner, but simply because he was really good at what he did. He probably could have continued in real estate until eventually retiring and would have done very well for himself and his family. In the mid-2000s when the market was crashing in his hometown of Chicago, he began observing and hanging out with some of the developers in the real estate office—college kids, as he calls them—who were exposing him to a new set of social networking tools like Facebook and Twitter. A light bulb went off. The connection time to build up potential relationships could be quickly reduced. Even more, the number of relationships one could build could increase as well.

Connections. Connecting with people. That is what brought purpose to him, not real estate. Realizing this (in fact, Tim was continuing to sort out how to *know thyself*), he set out to land a marketing job, thinking some combination of marketing, high tech and making connections was going to be the ultimate place of purpose. Although Tim eventually became the Director of Communications at the Social Media Club Chicago, it did not fill that nagging void of personal purpose. He was still empty. Tim was still analyzing his purpose of self, but the adjudication result was less than stellar. His canvas needed repainting. His definition needed reworking. He did not yet know thyself.

So he continued to hunt (more than ever) to achieve this personal sense of purpose. In the meantime, he was exposed to another term: community manager. The problem now became one of exposure. There was not a lot of information about community managers on the Internet at the time, so quite naturally, he created his own site, naming it "My Community Manager." It became a connections portal of sorts. From there, to help build up better relations with the connections (and community), he began utilizing Google Hangouts. He became "hooked" on live stream video as a means to establishing and enhancing these connections, friends and relationships. This was helping to fuel Tim's definition of himself. He was not yet done with his journey, but he was getting close to a better state of knowing thyself. Tim was inching toward a workplace scenario that began to make far more sense than any other previous role or situation.

On his trek he then took a giant leap forward to the ultimate decision of what he has become today. Based on what he was doing from the "My Community Manager" site he created on his own, *The Huffington Post* approached him to relocate to New York City and become its first community manager for their HuffPost Live service. Imagine that! From real estate to the purpose empire that Arianna Huffington built. Off he went to New York City.

But a funny thing happened during his time at *The Huffington Post*. Tim was working in a role that fueled some of his passions, but still found he was not entirely fulfilled. He finally had come to a place in his life where he could properly "define" who he was, continuing to "develop" what he was about, but he did not like *how* he was working.

He said to me during an interview, "During my time at *HuffPost*, I realized that there was so much more to life than climbing the corporate ladder or becoming the next Facebook or Twitter. It was about looking at the relationships we have in life and how we can make a lasting impact on them." It was Tim's penchant to ask the questions in his own Agora—what am I doing to evolve my character, who will I become in life and at work, and how will I operate and be perceived by others—that led him to a personal epiphany of sorts.

While taking part in a Changers of Commerce meeting in Dallas where he was speaking on stage about his role at *HuffPost*, leaders from Be The Change (BTC) Revolutions—an organization that aims to mix communities with social good—approached him. They asked Tim if he might be interested in joining their social council for the No Kid Hungry foundation. He jumped at the chance, and after a few months of his volunteer efforts—and realizing that his true purpose and focus in life was one of giving—he was asked by BTC to join them in a full-time capacity. As McDonald says, "It was like the person you have a crush on asking you if you wanted to go on a date!"

Tim knew leaving *HuffPost* would not be easy, but he also knew that "finding a place where I could live my purpose-driven life was an opportunity I couldn't pass up." He added, "Becoming more vested in working with organizations doing good has allowed for my work and life to be purposeful beyond my wildest dreams." Tim's job title at BTC Revolutions is now the Purveyor of Purpose. Not to be satisfied with the status quo, after joining the firm he also co-founded CreatingIs, a non-profit organization that brings together people (unsung heroes as Tim calls them) who are changing the world in terms of social impact.

As we will witness over the remaining chapters, one's role at work and the organization's ethos and operating practices can have a significant bearing on a team member's personal sense of purpose. But purpose always starts with the self. Without properly developing, defining and deciding one's self, the likelihood of *The Purpose Effect* coming to fruition may be minimal, if not impossible.

Megan Smith is lucky to have discovered and realized all three facets of purpose—personal, organizational and role—since she first joined SAP more than a decade ago. But her own sweet spot starts and ends with the passion-development-reward triangle she articulated. Céline Schillinger is an example of someone who has been relentless in the pursuit of personal meaning in life and at work. For her, it is a constant battle to ensure the balance of experimentation, networking and learning is front and center. Kelsy Trigg and Jill Schnarr are individuals who not only paint over their canvas to continue learning; they define themselves with authenticity and meaning. Michael Bungay Stanier was busily developing and defining himself, only to look in the mirror one day and decide the trajectory he was on was unsuitable, and unfulfilling. He decided to put purpose first. Tim McDonald suggests the personal purpose journey is never over. One ought to be constantly asking if the current situation is as good as it could be.

In the quest for and creation of personal purpose, each of these individuals continuously develop, define and decide. There is no such thing as status quo. There is no complacency. Their monocle of inspection—the emergence of meaning—hinges on the recurrent pondering of three key questions:

- *What* am I doing to evolve my self?

- *Who* am I in life *and* at work?

- *How* will I operate and be perceived by others?

William Ernest Henley ends our investigation into the establishment of one's personal sense of purpose with the following passage:

> It matters not how strait the gate,
> How charged with punishments the scroll,
> I am the master of my fate:
> I am the captain of my soul.[7]

As mentioned earlier, personal purpose is the perpetual journey to develop, define and decide your *what, who* and *how.* But unless you are independently wealthy, you must work for an organization (or start your own as was the case for Michael Bungay Stanier) in order to pay for groceries. What does the ideal organization look like? How can that organization develop, define and decide its own purpose? What exactly is organizational purpose? The next chapter explores these and other questions regarding the true purpose of the organization.

CHAPTER SIX
DEVELOPING ORGANIZATIONAL PURPOSE

If you want to succeed you should strike out on new paths,
rather than travel the worn paths of accepted success.[1]
John D. Rockefeller

One doesn't discover new lands without consenting to lose sight,
for a very long time, of the shore.[2]
André Paul Guillaume Gide

Since its inception in 1945, Johnsonville Sausage LLC has believed in delivering sound business results. It does so within a culture of fairness and organizational purpose. This company of 1,500 employees (which it has the decency to call "Members") produces all sorts of sausages, meatballs and bratwurst from various facilities, including its headquarters in Sheboygan Falls, Wisconsin. Ralph C. Stayer, who has been the visionary and owner for the past 40 years, has taken the company from a regional sausage supplier within Wisconsin to the global player it is today. The company has sales in excess of $1 billion annually.

I met Cory Bouck, a leader at Johnsonville Sausage, in 2012. I have been intrigued by the organization's purpose and operating practices ever since. Take, for example, the Johnsonville Way culture statement:

- We at Johnsonville have a moral responsibility to become the Best Company in the World.

- We will do this as each one of us becomes better than anyone else at defining, and then serving, the best interests of all those who have a stake in our success.

- We will succeed by setting near-term objectives and long-term goals that will require a personal growth and superlative performance by each of us. We will change any objectives or goals that no longer require personal growth and superlative performance to ones that do.

- As an individual, I understand the Johnsonville Way is about my performance and my accountability to the team. My commitment to stretch, grow and excel is an unending one.

- This is the JOHNSONVILLE WAY and I am committed to it.

In an interview, Cory mentioned to me that, "It's a great place to have the role that I have," indicating one of the owner's inspiring turn-of-phrase sentiments is why he and so many members have a sense of purpose in their work. As Bouck told me, Stayer often states, "Most companies use people to build their business. At Johnsonville, we use our business to build our people."

But I was not only interested in the organization's values and culture. I wanted to know how it continually delivers on its goals and objectives in what is an ultra-competitive landscape, the food industry. I wanted to know why its 1,500 members seem to perform ethically and fairly. I was curious why its members are continuously empowered by senior leadership and also thought of as family. I wondered if this sausage company was achieving the sweet spot, helping its team members do the same in the process.

"Our owner, Ralph Stayer, has incredibly high standards," said Cory. "But he also believes that it would be morally wrong to hold people to incredibly high standards without also giving them every opportunity and resource to stretch and grow themselves in order to be able to deliver against those high standards." The company has created quarterly commitments (referred to as PDCs—Personal Development Commitments), which allow its team members to report on their progress through an internal web portal. It is open and transparent, and thus anyone can see what is going on at any time with anyone's performance and objectives.

What it suggested to me was that Johnsonville possesses an internal culture that is mature, open and collaborative, but it also is one that is driven to perform. If anyone can view a PDC, you may not want to be caught napping. More importantly, the culture is so supportive, a Johnsonville member would not want to disappoint a fellow member. It is the opposite of how many organizations think of performance management today.

At the core of Johnsonville's business strategy is something they refer to as HICS: Highest Impact on Customer Success. "HICS is a tool," as Cory explained, "that is invoked in daily conversations at all levels by members from all the various teams within Johnsonville." Think of HICS as a moral and cultural responsibility at Johnsonville to ensure everything they do is with the customer in mind, at the highest quality possible, through an engaged workforce. Bouck believes its team members are continuously striving to deliver and attain purpose in their roles. The organization has created an environment for both the team member and itself to reap benefits, to operate with purpose.

The Johnsonville vision is: "To become the best company in the world that just happens to make sausage." Cory was adamant that "the difference between 'be' and 'become' is a big one." He not only believes it is aspirational, he believes the vision of Johnsonville is about the journey of the organization *and* the 1,500 team members to deliver value through a purpose. "It's a useful daily benchmark," he continued. "For example, did my actions and behaviors today reflect someone who's on a team that's trying to become the best?"[3] The types of actions and behaviors that Johnsonville has defined—and which team members carry out—are key to organizational purpose. They are an important component to the achievement of *The Purpose Effect* sweet spot.

Testing Organizational Purpose Through Cars, Pills and Sausages

In the face of adversity—when pressure mounts or calamity seems imminent—an organization's purpose is put to the ultimate test. Every organization faces one or multiple forms of stress at some point in its existence. Often an organization takes the easy route, either to uphold its profits and revenues, or to ensure power and reign continues. An organization that endures any form of financial hardship or business loss will regularly be forced to test its purpose, to test its standing in society. What did Johsonville

Sausage do when it experienced an event that could have ruined their entire culture, and perhaps their financial stability? Did the company ignore the organizational purpose it had worked hard to inculcate across its business? Did it neglect the team members who had committed to purpose, and to the organization's quest to "To become the best company in the world?" We will find out shortly, but first let us investigate two different approaches to a crisis.

When Lee Iacocca—a vice president in the late 1960s at Ford—was under pressure to combat the emergence of Japanese and European cars, he fast-tracked the design and development of a car known as the Pinto. Impervious to several design defects—including the fuel source being placed too far to the rear of the vehicle, and the omission of a small plastic insulation cap for protection—the gas tank in the Pinto was poised to rupture and leak on the force of an impact, causing a vehicle fire. Knowing this was an issue, Ford (and Iacocca) turned a blind eye. The cost-benefit analysis suggested the company could simply pay out any loss of life or injury at a lower cost versus recalling and fixing all Pinto automobiles. Several accidents resulted in catastrophic fires—including death and serious injuries—and only until the company realized it was affecting sales across the company, and lawsuits began to pile up, did it finally recall the Pinto and fix the problem. In this example, profit trumped purpose.

In 1982, seven people died in Chicago when bottles of one of Johnson & Johnson's product lines, Extra Strength Tylenol, were tampered with and cyanide was added to their contents. Johnson & Johnson's credo—written in 1943 by its CEO, Robert Wood Johnson II—includes the line, "We are responsible to the communities in which we live and work and to the world community as well." The crisis of 1982 tested both the organization's resolve and its purpose.

Without hesitation, the company pulled all 31 million bottles of the product from the shelves of its retailers across the globe. At the time, Tylenol was Johnson & Johnson's best-selling product, accounting for 17 percent of its income in the previous year.[4] However, did that stop the company? Did it deviate from its purpose statement, its credo? The organization did not buckle. In fact, Johnson & Johnson put customers, team members and the community ahead of any penchant for profit or lost revenues. It might have cost the company well over $100 million, as well as lingering consumer skepticism, but its purpose was never in question. The company asserts its credo "is more than just a moral compass."[5] That is, Johnson & Johnson does not allow its purpose statement (the credo) to merely sit on a website or company walls. It takes action as necessary.

Even in the face of adversity with the Tylenol scare, Johnson & Johnson ensured its organizational purpose did not waver, putting communities, customers and employees ahead of profits. Ironically, perhaps, its actions led to increased consumer confidence in the company. Increased revenues and profitability also continued. By the end of 2015, Johnson & Johnson had realized 32 consecutive years of adjusted earnings increases and 53 consecutive years of stock dividend increases. It earns more than $75 billion in annual revenue, but it remains steadfast to its giving mission, too. Johnson & Johnson annually donates 7 percent of its pre-tax income (cash and non-cash philanthropy) to the communities in which it serves. That percentage amounts to almost $1 billion in community giving annually, suggesting profit can indeed be paired with purpose in the face of adversity and without.[6]

Let us fast forward to the spring of 2015. Johnsonville Sausage suffered its own tragedy and was forced to test its organizational purpose. On May 11, a freak incident of physics and biology occurred at one of the company's largest facilities where it produces sausages. At this particular location in Watertown, Wisconsin, a combination of oil, pressure and heat mixed up with a pair of gloves that were inadvertently put in the wrong place, at the wrong time.

This freakish combination of the gloves and materials led to a spontaneous combustion, and the result was an explosion and resulting fire that decimated the plant. Investigators immediately ruled out any foul play. It was simply bad luck. The incident occurred in the middle of the night, so luckily there were no deaths or injuries. There were no livestock in the building either. However, the facility employed 100 Johnsonville members, and come May 12, there was nothing left to work on. After all, there was no longer a facility to make sausages. What to do?

The first order of business company executives decided was to keep all of its members "whole." They continued to pay their wages despite an obvious lack of sausage to produce. "The plant was really bad," Cory informed me in a follow-up discussion. "Everything had to be thrown away. All of the equipment was affected. Water and charred materials do not mix with stainless steel, and everything immediately became rusty. We quickly realized this was not going to be a one-week job. At the time, we felt it was likely going to be a three- to four-month job."

The Johnsonville members in Watertown helped with the facility clean-up. But after a week or so, there was nothing more for them to do at the plant. In fact, the location where the fire occurred had to be permanently closed. Executives made another decision. While arranging to purchase a new property and build a new facility, the company asked everyone to remain on staff to do two things.

First, Johnsonville arranged for each member to dedicate 20 hours per week volunteering time in the community. Landscaping, teaching and general community improvement efforts across Watertown became the objectives. Second, the members were asked to spend the other 20 hours of the work week developing, learning and educating themselves. The education happened at various Johnsonville Sausage sites as well as local education institutions.

"Treating our people with dignity," Cory said, "was our number one priority." While the fire was not the fault of any individual, the company felt compelled to treat its members as decently as it could, and no one was terminated during the months when there was no sausage to be made. After all, their team members were an important stakeholder in the Johnsonville way of doing business. Its members had always demonstrated a commitment to the Johnsonville Way, and the organization was not about to leave them out to dry. Maybe we might call this "reciprocal purpose."

The new facility did become operational again but not until early 2016. After almost a year without producing a single sausage at this location, the 100 team members affected by the fire remained on the company payroll. Their "job" through this time period? They were asked to give back to the community in which they lived, while developing themselves through various forms of education. "It was the right thing to do," said Cory. "We have a commitment and responsibility to each other. What else would we have done?"

An organization, rather obviously, is made up of people. For the organization to define and enact a more purposeful mission and strategy, it must be done by the people of the organization. For many entities, this is the work of senior leadership. The more inclusive and open organizations ask team members for their opinion. Both Johnson & Johnson and Johnsonville Sausage defined, followed and acted upon their respective purpose. Ford did not. In fact, at the time, Ford's purpose remained fixated on profit, devoid of any real additional meaning or purpose. But the company did eventually turn things around.

Like all automobile manufacturers in 2009, Ford plunged into a precarious state of financial instability due to the economic crisis, one that rivaled the 1929 depression. Alan Mulally—President and CEO of Ford at the time—worked extremely hard to avert complete ruin. One key strategy he introduced was something called ONE FORD, its new purpose.

Mulally started the initiative to restate its purpose but also to inculcate collaborative and cooperative behaviors among its team members in order to address the crisis. Introduced as a graphic, the left side contained three defining statements (ONE TEAM, ONE PLAN, ONE GOAL) that outlined "people working together" and an "exciting viable Ford for all." On the right side of the graphic, Mulally used the word Ford as an acronym further detailing how they would set a new course. The details included:

- Foster Functional and Technical Excellence

- Own Working Together

- Role Model Ford Values

- Deliver Results

The subtext included such phrases as, "Believe in skilled and motivated people working together" and "Have a can-do, find-a-way attitude and emotional resilience." Not only did Ford return to profitability under Mulally, the company was the only major American car manufacturer to avoid government intervention and bailout funds. Mulally summarized his thoughts on both leadership and purpose by stating, "Leadership is having a compelling vision, a comprehensive plan, relentless implementation, and talented people working together. People also want meaning. All of us want to know that we are doing great things, that we are touching a lot of people, and that what we are doing is something bigger than ourselves."[7]

Purpose is not an exercise in lip service. Organizational purpose—the second of three categories that help to create the sweet spot in *The Purpose Effect*—is the opportunity for a firm to define its principles, ethics, leadership and culture. It is the chance to establish who its stakeholders really are. But it is imperative for the organization to *act* on this definition, too.

Otherwise, the organization remains in jeopardy of becoming fixated on profit and/or power as its sole purpose. If it remains locked into such behavior, not only is society being defrauded, team members might never demonstrate a sense of purpose in their role at work.

A Plum Decision

Founded in 1989, Plum Creek Timber had revenues of roughly $1.4 billion in 2014, and a team member population of approximately 1,200 people worldwide. Their mission statement reads as follows:

> We are stewards of land, working forests and natural resources, dedicated to enhancing asset value while protecting the environment and promoting prosperity in the communities where we operate.[8]

Plum Creek operates the organization through eight belief statements. These belief statements, much like the Johnson & Johnson Credo or Johnsonville Sausage culture statement, help to guide the organization with business decision making. The highlights of the Plum Creek belief statements are as follows:

- Responsible environmental stewardship creates superior long-term value.

- Our people work together to achieve exceptional results.

- Intellectual capital drives innovation.

- Community engagement is an essential part of doing business.

- Our customers deserve quality goods and services.

- Partners that share common values and beliefs produce the best results.

- Superior shareholder returns come from innovation and leadership.

- Strong corporate governance and an ethical business culture drive accountability.[9]

An organization not only should define its purpose, it must actively and consistently demonstrate the behavior. If the organization is not demonstrating its purpose, it may be viewed by its stakeholders as one that is "all talk, no action," something I first surfaced in *FLAT ARMY*.

What if Johnson & Johnson did not remove the bottles of Tylenol from those shelves? What if Johnsonville Sausage decided not to keep its team members "whole" during the long months the company recovered from the fire? What happened to the reputation of Ford at the time of the Pinto crisis? It is individuals who carry out organizational purpose. It is individuals who define an organization's purpose. The organization is merely the vehicle. It is driven by individuals. In 2014, Chief Executive Officer of Plum Creek, Rick Holley, provides another example how individuals must decide how it will uphold an organization's defined purpose.

During the company's end-of-year analyst conference call in 2014, Holley was put on the spot by Chip Dillon, an analyst from Vertical Research Partners. Dillon was reviewing the company's regulatory filings and came across a particular if not unusual discrepancy. The CEO of Plum Creek had recently given back over 4,000 units of restricted stock to the Board of Directors, due to vest in just a few short years. The total personal payout to Holley would have been over $2 million.

When Dillon questioned Holley on the move, the CEO mentioned rather casually his personal level of discomfort with the stock award due in part to the sagging performance on the Plum Creek stock that year. It was as if it was no big deal to Holley. The company was not doing particularly well financially, so he decided he was not going to benefit either. An ethical culture highlights accountability. It is one of the core beliefs that Plum Creek subscribes to. Holley's decision translates belief into action.

As he went through this decision-making process in 2014, Holley was clearly demonstrating the mission and beliefs at Plum Creek. He was putting the purpose of Plum Creek well ahead of his own personal financial gains. Imagine what Plum Creek customers and employees thought once they heard about it. Part of his verbatim response on the analyst conference call provides further insight:

> As we went through the year, our stock was under-performing, per the S&P 500 and other metrics, and I went to our Board and I said I'm not comfortable taking this stock run

and I'm going to return it. So I was not pressured to do it by shareholders or by the Board. And I didn't ask the Board's permission to do it. I just said I'm not comfortable with this. The shareholders haven't had a return this year and Rick Holley is not going to get one either. I returned the 4,445 shares of restricted stock. So it's basically as simple as that.[10]

We might claim the action that Holley took was a good deed. In fact, Johnsonville Sausage, Johnson & Johnson and Rick Holley at Plum Creek Timber are all examples of firms (and people) defining *and* demonstrating organizational purpose through a number of good deeds. When an organization successfully defines its purpose to be something that consists of more than profit and/or power—while actively demonstrating said purpose at all times—it is the stakeholders that ultimately benefit. When the organization defines and demonstrates a greater purpose, it creates a scenario in which team members can feel a sense of purpose in their role, ideally complementing how they have developed, defined and decided their own personal sense of purpose. Organizational purpose is the second of three components in the quest to achieve the sweet spot of *The Purpose Effect*.

A Deed That Is Good

What is a deed? According to the Oxford Dictionary, a deed is "an action that is performed intentionally or consciously." A deed is also referred to as a legal document, something that is signed and delivered. Think of property ownership documents or an item related to legal rights. For *The Purpose Effect*, we will use the first definition and consider it alongside a well-known expression, "doing good deeds."

Good deeds can be performed for anyone. Good deeds also can be performed *by* anyone. I might shovel my neighbor's driveway after a snow blizzard, or I may donate money to my colleague Bryan Acker's worthy cause of helping to eradicate cancer. When I save 10 percent of my earnings for the future, as David Chilton taught me in his book, *The Wealthy Barber*, I am performing a good deed when it comes to my future, and *for* my family.

A stranger who opens her doors to other strangers in need of lodging, as many residents of Gander, Newfoundland, did when air travelers were stranded on September 11, 2001, is performing a good deed in the community. I once witnessed a family of four cleaning up garbage that had been collecting in the bushes adjacent to Jericho Beach in Vancouver. When I asked the father what they were doing as I was walking past, he replied rather gleefully, "It's our family's good deed of the month."

Researchers have long studied humans (in life and at work) with respect to acts of giving. Adam Grant, for example, provided us with the book, *Give and Take*. It turns out we are hard-wired to do good acts and we give (and want to do good) without the need for any kind of vainglorious recognition. Some researchers claim this is because humans are naturally pro-social. "When people are primed to see themselves as good people," claimed one study, "who do good for goodness sake, not to obtain public credit, they may be motivated to do more good."[11]

As Adam Grant writes, "The more I help out, the more successful I become. But I measure success in what it has done for the people around me. That is the real accolade."[12] In other words, a good deed helps others, and that in itself is a success. Of course, it was philosopher Epictetus who once wrote, "Know you not that a good man does nothing for appearance sake, but for the sake of having done right?"[13] Perhaps good deeds result in doing good.

This brings me to the "Good DEEDS" of the organization, the second major component to *The Purpose Effect*. As with the examples of Johnson & Johnson, Johnsonville Sausage, Ford or Plum Creek Timber, an organization's purpose defined to reflect a more harmonious society is performing a good deed. The organization can no longer fixate solely on profit or increased shareholder value, if it is a for-profit entity. It can no longer fixate on power and bureaucratic supremacy if it is a not-for-profit, public sector or even a for-profit organization. In order to help team members (and the organization) to achieve the sweet spot—in order for society to truly benefit from an organization's actions—I have discovered there are five key principles that purposeful organizations define and constantly employ. I refer to these as the Good DEEDS. They are:

- Delight your customers

- Engage your team members

- (Be) Ethical within society

- Deliver fair practices

- Serve all stakeholders

It is my intent over the remainder of this chapter to define each of the five components that make up the Good DEEDS. In Section IV of the book, I will identify tips and strategies to implement each of the five parts.

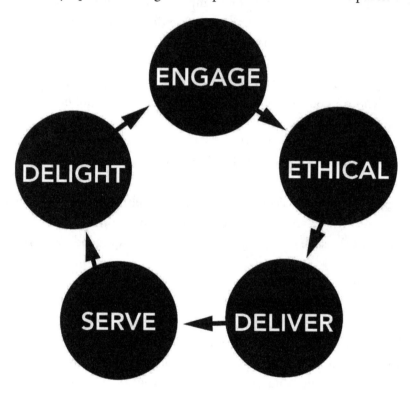

Delight Your Customers

Whether the organization is a for-profit, not-for-profit or a public sector institution, the primary stakeholder audience is the key group the organization serves. I am referring to the customer. It matters not if the organization is built to make money, to provide charitable service or to serve citizens. Organizations ought to commit to delighting its customers, remembering why the organization exists in the first place. If there are no customers, there is unlikely to be an organization. If there is no organization, somewhat obviously there are no roles. While a public sector institution will obviously remain in operation, how can it be an attractive place to recruit new team members or to innovate new services to better serve its citizens, its customers? Put simply, if the organization does not delight its customers—the people it ought to be working for—neither team members nor the organization can reach the sweet spot for there will be a damaged organization left remaining to carry out its mission.

Take for instance IKEA, the opposite of a damaged organization. This Swedish company—formed in 1943 by 17-year-old Ingvar Kamprad—continues to demonstrate the mantra of always putting customers first and subsequently impressing them. There is no other or ulterior motive at IKEA. It has continued to dedicate itself to value and service, always in appreciation for—and solely intended to delight—its customer base. We need not look any further than its simple, yet elegant vision crafted in 1943 by Kamprad himself.

> To create a better everyday life for the many people.

This is a furniture company (and maker of meatballs in the millions), but it simply wants to help its customers improve their "everyday life." Its purpose could not be any clearer for its team members, suppliers, investors or customers. It cannot be clearer for any number of stakeholders. The customer comes first. The company and its vision have certainly helped millions of families over the years. Stop for a second and try to name another global furniture brand. Furniture companies tend to be regional, not international. Why is that? How can IKEA be a global brand, committed to making everyday life better for all global citizens, yet it is a furniture company?

IKEA also created what it refers to as "The Business Plan." This is an organization intent on helping customers improve their everyday life (the IKEA purpose), but it also wants to improve the lives of "the many people" through quality, affordable, valued service and goods. IKEA's business plan—an addendum to its purpose—reads as follows:

> We shall offer a wide range of well-designed, functional home furnishing products at prices so low that as many people as possible will be able to afford them.[14]

Forbes Magazine ranks IKEA's brand as the 40th most valuable in the world (at $12.5 billion), and annual revenues are just shy of $40 billion, gained from its 345 stores in 42 different countries. Not only is there a customers-first purpose and a customers-first business plan, the company instituted the "Human Resource Idea." It reads as follows:

> To give down-to-earth, straight-forward people the possibility to grow, both as individuals and in their professional roles, so that together we are strongly committed to creating a better everyday life for ourselves and our customers.

Despite using a term like "human resource," you get the picture. From the moment the company was formed to its growth as a $40 billion company, it has consistently put its customers first, delighting them in the pursuit of value and service. This has been its overarching purpose. Its investment in its team member—who delivers value and service to its customers—is the manner in which it achieves its customers-first quest. Like Johnson & Johnson, IKEA recognized early on that without the customer (and the purpose-driven team member), there is no reason to be in business. Like Johnsonville Sausage, its belief in its team members permits its organizational purpose to be realized across the globe.

When discussing why IKEA has not ventured into a line of furniture that might be considered high-end or expensive, Kamprad responded, "All nations and societies in both the East and West spend a disproportionate amount of their resources on satisfying a minority of the population. In our line of business, for example, far too many of the fine designs and new ideas are reserved for a small circle of the affluent. That situation has influenced the formulation of our objectives."[15] As we surfaced earlier, "There is only one valid definition of a business purpose: to create a customer."[16]

The first principle of the Good DEEDS is to "Delight Your Customers." IKEA is an example of an organization that carries this trait out in its organizational mission, actions and strategies. When an organization makes delighting its customers a key component of its organizational purpose, team members are more likely to buy in and provide such value. If the customer is thought of as secondary—and profit and/or power remains the true organizational goal—it is easy to understand why team members may not be fulfilling either their personal or role-based purpose wishes.

Engage Your Team Members

The word "people" is derived from Old French "peupel," which means "mankind" and "humanity." The word also stems from the Latin "populus," which translates into "body of citizens." Mankind, humanity and a body of citizens are precisely what an organization needs if it is to successfully develop and deliver *The Purpose Effect.*

Banco Bilbao Vizcaya Argentaria (BBVA) is the second largest bank in Spain. It possesses over 112,000 team members spread across 31 countries serving 51 million customers. Total assets are approximately €600 billion. Its singular purpose is a bit like IKEA. "At BBVA we are working for a better future for people." The people it is referring to, however, is both its customers *and* its team members. The people are its body of citizens. The bank maintains that its many team members "play a key role in promoting a culture of social commitment and shared values."

BBVA believes team members are the fuel to a brighter future, both for BBVA and its customers. It insists that an engaged workforce, utilizing "new styles of behavior" is its core strength and where "increased competitive advantage" is realized. BBVA is an organization that chooses to engage its team members, knowing there is a causal relationship between an engaged workforce, customer satisfaction and business results. Consulting firm Great Place to Work placed BBVA in its top 15 best places to work global rankings in 2013. "Teamwork as the key to generating value," is one of BBVA's operating principles. Organizations that aim to establish purpose in its mission (like BBVA does) ought to be engaging its team members, instituting teamwork, collaboration and connectedness as ways in which to deliver on its (more purposeful) operating mission.

We might argue that there is an invisible reciprocal social contract between a team member and their boss, between the people of the organization and the organization itself. Any employment contract dictates a team member is remunerated for performing in a role that the organization has defined. A social contract—albeit invisible—is much more than an employment contract. It is a team member's responsibility to carry out role-based duties in a manner that is socially acceptable to the organization's strategy. A call center agent must be respectful when talking to the customer. A service technician must be polite in the home of a customer. A software engineer must not create code that harms other systems. An agency worker must not divert funds intended for the homeless. But the organization should also be responsible for upholding their end of the social contract. This comes in the form of engagement, of engaging with the team member. For organizations to deliver on the social contract, it ought to create a culture of engagement. IKEA and BBVA are but two examples of organizations that engage with their team members in order to construct organizational purpose.

When team members are authorized to innovate, contribute or to take action, their commitment to the organization increases exponentially. When this occurs, the team member has a greater chance of achieving purpose in their role. Evidence by researchers correlates a culture of autonomy and inclusion with increased engagement.[17] Peter Senge also taught us to become a "learning organization" by focusing on "the openness needed to unearth shortcomings."[18] That openness comes if the organization is engaged and engaging with its team members. If the behavior of relatedness is utilized, team members become more trustworthy of the organization, and thus the social contract might more easily materialize.

When conducting a global study of over 90,000 workers worldwide, Towers-Watson discovered that the biggest single driver of discretionary effort was senior leadership's sincere interest in team member well-being. In a follow-up report released in 2012, the firm discovered virtually no progress had been made. Only 45 percent of senior leadership admitted to a "sincere interest" in their team members' well-being.[19] If psychologists believe that the well-being of team members will lead to engagement, self-actualization at work and a sense of purpose in a team member's role, there is evidence to suggest improvements ought to be made by the organization to help team members with their well-being. This could be a helpful clue in the creation of the sweet spot.

The holy grail of engagement—and thus engaging with team members—is not a new orthodoxy, cobbled together by perquisites and happiness tricks. An organization's destiny lies in the development of an open, trusting, transparent and connected culture where team members feel safe to contribute and to consume knowledge and ideas. It is an environment of caring and of curiosity. Engaging with team members is the difference between a command-and-control operating ethos to one that is cultivating a community of collaboration.

When I asked John Helliwell, Senior Fellow and Co-Director of the

Canadian Institute for Advanced Research (CIFAR) Program on Social Interactions, Identity and Well-being, if he felt there might be a link between purpose, engagement and people, he had this to say:

> Why not treat your next elevator ride not as a short-term prison sentence but rather as a social occasion waiting to happen? Human beings are inherently social, and pro-social, beings endowed with the capacity and need to cooperate with others whom they trust, and with whom they identify. Forging new social connections broadens the scope for building trust and designing new ways to cooperate to good purpose.[20]

The social contract between team member and the firm ought to be strengthened if the Good DEEDS of organizational purpose is ever to come to fruition. In other words, the organization has a responsibility to remember the word "human" is found in the word "humanity." An organization's body of citizens—the humans—are yearning to be engaged. "Engaging with team members" is the second key principle to enacting the Good DEEDS of organizational purpose as we continue to hone *The Purpose Effect*.

(Be) Ethical Within Society

Team members are an easy and telling target to qualify an organization's ethics. After all, they work for the organization every day. They see a lot. They witness the good and the bad. When you ask team members if their organization is indeed ethical, the answer might surprise you. When Towers-Watson queried respondents concerning ethics and public believability, only 58 percent claimed their employer was "ethical and highly regarded by the public."[21] Not surprisingly, that number dropped to 29 percent for team members who considered themselves disengaged at work.

More evidence comes from the Ethics Resource Center (ERC). The ERC was established in 1922 and is "America's oldest non-profit organization devoted to independent research and the advancement of high ethical standards and practices in public and private institutions." In a research report, the ERC reported that of team members who are engaged in their organization, a shocking 61 percent had witnessed some form of ethical misconduct.[22] Being ethical within society, therefore, is the third principle to the Good DEEDS. Specifically, an organization must sort out how it can be ethical while it seeks to better society.

John Bogle was the founder and now former CEO of The Vanguard Group, an American investment management company responsible for approximately $3 trillion in assets. He is a staunch Republican. In his book, *The Battle for the Soul of Capitalism*, Bogle laments a system fixated on profit, shareholder value and what he calls "Managers' Capitalism." His entire career has been in the business of making money within the financial services sector. If a profit-minded financial investment manager worth millions is worried, I wonder if we all should be. One particular passage caught my attention in his book:

> I also see far too much greed, egoism, materialism and waste to please my critical eye. I see an economy overly focused on the "haves" and not focused enough on the "have-nots," failing to allocate our nation's resources where they are most needed—to solve the problems of poverty and to provide quality education for all. I see our shocking misuse of the world's natural resources, as if they were ours to waste rather than ours to preserve as a sacred trust for future generations.[23]

Bogle outlines ethical concerns with respect to the environment, citizens and the communities in which we live. For organizations to create a purpose, the scope of ethical interest must widen its swathe.

Is the organization concerned for society, or has its operating ethics negated a chance for higher purpose? Regarding publicly traded organizations, it is worth wondering whether existing fiduciary responsibilities to investors give them the excuse not to care about such factors as philanthropy, community investment or the environment. Are they exploiting consumers by focusing on an individual's wants versus society's needs? Are for-profit firms even permitted to look out for the interests of all stakeholders . . . and not just shareholders or profit seekers?

Forest Reinhardt, Robert Stavins and Richard Vietor, all of Harvard University, were interested in the same question. In a research paper, they wrote, "As long as managers claim some plausible connection to future profitability, the business judgment rule grants them substantial leeway to commit corporate resources to projects that benefit the public." Put differently, the researchers found it is legally acceptable for an organization to financially invest and support other causes in parallel with their quest for increased revenues and profits. There is no legal reason for a company and its corporate directors to maximize shareholder return or profits. Recall Joel Bakan's concerns from Chapter 3 and the "best interest of the corporation" principle.

While research indicates it is perfectly fine to be ethical—balancing purpose with profit—the question to ask next is whether the for-profit organization ought to do so. More importantly, would an ethical stance toward becoming a more sustainable organization impact its profitability?

On the subject of whether corporate social responsibility is an effective use of time and money for the organization, the Harvard researchers wrote, "For most firms, CSR pays for itself." On whether or not profit is surrendered, they stated, "Evidence on sacrificing profits in the social interest is lacking." It may seem ironic, but being ethical and advocating for corporate social responsibility will ultimately pay off in the end for the organization.

According to the researchers, it is perfectly fine for a publicly traded company to act ethically within their shareholder requirements. Indeed, organizations are permitted to serve interests greater than profitability.[24] Surely companies that are not publicly traded, public sector and non-profit in nature, can adopt the same philosophy. Regardless of your organization's makeup, being ethical within society is a good practice and can help the organization become more purposeful.

There are other benefits, too. In his research paper, "Authentic Purpose: The Spiritual Infrastructure of Life," Corey Keyes notes, "The ethical ethos of organizations is central, because companies in which more employees perceive their workplaces as ethical report higher retention rates, more positive work and supervisory relationships, better dispute resolution and enhanced productivity."[25]

The chair of BBVA, Francisco González, articulated the importance of ethics and its impact on BBVA's purpose:

> The BBVA team are part of a corporate culture based on the principles of integrity, prudence and transparency, which have been key in allowing us to build a strong business model that is able to grow and is very customer centric.[26]

Aristotle once wrote, "Every art or inquiry aims at some good." It is incumbent upon the organization to both define and enact a more ethical purpose. It must aim not only at being good, but *doing* good. If the for-profit firm decides that shareholder return is its modus operandi, then it becomes its sole purpose. If any type of organization decides that power or prestige is its raison d'être, then it becomes its sole purpose. If an organization cares not for the planet or the community it inhabits, should it be considered ethical? The organization has a responsibility to distinguish between what appears to be ethical, with what actually is ethical. There is no such thing as being part ethical.

Martin Luther King once said while speaking at Oberlin College, "The time is always right to do what's right."[27] Indeed, for the Good DEEDS to come to fruition within *The Purpose Effect*, organizations must make it a priority to define a new way in which it becomes ethical. If an organization wishes to aid society, being ethical ought to be a key component. When the organization does so, not only is it supporting our planet, it just may inculcate a set of purpose-driven behaviors that many team members will be drawn to, support and advocate both in their personal lives, and in their roles. If this happens, there is a greater chance for role purpose to be demonstrated by team members, too.

Deliver Fair Practices

For an organization to survive and thrive, somewhat obviously, it must deliver results. Many organizations accomplish their goals, however, saddled by a maddening display of Kafkaesque bureaucracy, antiquated procedures and disengaging personnel practices. Results are demanded from the team member, but the manner in which to improve how they come about is ignored. To accomplish its goals, the organization shifts into an obsessive demonstration of such adages as cost containment, downsizing, rightsizing, outsourcing, workforce re-balancing and the "do more with less" pitch. Many of these issues cause individuals not only to slip into workplace disengagement, but it likewise reinforces distrust between the team member and the organization.

Unsurprisingly, it can be part of the reason many of today's organizations lack purpose. It may be a clue concerning a lack of role purpose or personal purpose for team members, too. If the organization does not treat its people fairly, how will those team members feel in their roles? Conversely, if an individual's personal sense of purpose is thwarted by an organization's lack of concern to replace various workplace inanities, it is questionable whether purpose will ever be reached in *The Purpose Effect* concept.

If a team member is going to enjoy working for their organization—if they are to possess the courage to delight its customers—there is a veritable avalanche of operational practices to consider retiring or updating. If the organization aims to deliver on its goals—but doing so with purpose—there are institutional processes we must contemplate overhauling. Goodhart's Law states that any observed statistical regularity tends to collapse once pressure is placed upon it for control purposes. Perhaps the introduction of organizational purpose may trigger such a collapse. Maybe it manifests through the introduction of the fourth component to the Good DEEDS—"Deliver Fair Practices" to team members. There are three facets in particular that are in need of fine tuning: compensation, performance management and recognition.

Compensation fairness is arguably one of the toughest nuts to crack to assist organizational purpose. There are always two sides to a coin. Take for instance an example concerning McDonald's. In 2012, when the company's COO, Jim Johannesen, issued a memo to its U.S. franchise owners requiring them to stay open during key holidays (U.S. Thanksgiving and Christmas Day), the company decided that normal hourly wages would be paid on these statutory holidays. The restaurants were formerly closed on these dates. Uproar ensued among some of the McDonald's team members. Company spokesperson, Heather Oldani, said in a statement, "The staff voluntarily sign up to work. There is no regular overtime pay."[28]

Oldani is correct. The Fair Labor Standards Act (FLSA) in the United States does not require overtime pay for statutory holidays. But is what McDonald's decided *fair* for those team members who volunteered to work? Should they have been paid more? In Canada, for example, law dictates the payment of extra compensation benefits for individuals working on statutory holidays. It varies from province to province, but in British Columbia for example, any individual is entitled to 1.5 times their hourly rate for the first 12 hours. After that, it becomes double time plus an additional day off with pay. Is it fair? Is it fairer than McDonald's?

A competitor to McDonald's in some Western regions of the United States is In-N-Out Burger. With roughly 300 restaurants and $500 million in revenues, its business is a fraction of McDonald's. Interestingly, it has decided not to open on Thanksgiving or Christmas Day holidays. Furthermore, it pays its team members more than any state mandated minimum wage. In fact, the company boasts about it. "We start all our new Associates at a minimum of $10.50 an hour for one simple reason . . . you are important to us!"[29] The 2013 Quick Service Restaurant (QSR) Benchmark Study that surveyed 10,000 fast-food burger restaurant patrons ranked In-N-Out Burger first with 66 percent satisfaction and McDonald's 11th at 32 percent satisfaction.[30]

"I find it a remarkable notion that McDonald's can't afford to pay an increase in the minimum wage but In-N-Out Burger can," said United States Labor Secretary, Thomas E. Perez, in 2014, when discussing wage practices in the United States. "They [In-N-Out Burger] do it for the same reason—it's about reducing attrition and having a more effective workforce."[31] Recall the compensation story of Dan Price, CEO of Gravity Payments, from Chapter 3. Not only did he decide to raise the minimum annual wage of all team members to $70,000, he also lowered his own salary by 90 percent. Team members do not need millions in wages, but for purpose to manifest in their roles, fair compensation is something to potentially reconsider.

Current performance management practices surface another opportunity for organizations to reconsider. Companies such as Microsoft, Adobe, Juniper Networks and Expedia have all done away with the stack ranking process of performance management, where a leader pits team members against one another, ranking and placing them against an arbitrary bell curve of performance. Bob Rogers, president of DDI (a leadership development company) writes in his book, *Realizing the Promise of Performance Management* that the process of stack ranking, of segregating team members, "causes damage by filtering employees from the bottom, and causes changes in people's behavior, and not to the good."[32]

For a team member to feel and demonstrate purpose in their role—for the organization to indeed demonstrate purpose—the mechanisms by which an individual's performance is rated needs in-depth scrutinizing. If you want to demonstrate that you care about the people you work with, focus on coaching and mentoring as rankings and annual reviews rarely help.

Sir Richard Branson of the Virgin empire highlights the need for recognition. In one of his columns, Branson observes, "We give our people real autonomy, and celebrate their achievements by identifying star contributors, highlighting brand ambassadors in our internal newsletters and hosting parties for individual employees."[33] Recognition is known to help a team member feel purpose in their role, which also can benefit the organization's purpose. As Mark Twain once wrote, "I can live on a good compliment two weeks with nothing else to eat."[34]

Indeed, recognition should be practiced more widely in our organizations. A SHRM/Globoforce survey found 84 percent of leaders believe recognizing employees for their contributions and accomplishments provides a clearer understanding of the organization's objectives.[35] When team members were asked by research firm Psychometrics what leaders could do more of to improve engagement, 58 percent wished they received more recognition at work.[36] But does recognition aid an organization and its requirement for improved results?

To test the effect of recognition on performance, several academics in Europe created a work environment experiment where 363 people were hired to perform a three-hour data entry job each day over a six-month period. Workers were not aware they were taking part in the experiment, but they received a flat wage of 25 euros each day. When thank-you cards were given to all workers in one of the groups, the researchers found performance increased by 5.2 percent compared to the group that received no recognition and whose performance did not increase. What is quite interesting, however, is that the performance of those who did not receive recognition—but were aware of others in their group receiving public recognition—increased by 10 percent. This suggests individuals have a preference for both conformity (I want to be recognized like the others) and reciprocity (If I give recognition, surely my peers will give me recognition later). The result is an increase in performance.[37]

Improving compensation, performance management and recognition practices are three key aspects I recommend organizations consider as they attempt to "Deliver Fair Practices" for their team members. If an organization can indeed deliver fair practices, the likelihood of the sweet spot being created increases for all parties.

Serve All Stakeholders

John Mackey is the co-founder and co-CEO of Whole Foods. He firmly believes that stakeholders, not shareholders, should benefit from an organization's derived value. This conviction developed into his notion of *Conscious Capitalism*, which led him to co-author a book on the subject with Raj Sisodia. The authors invite the reader to, "Imagine a business that is a committed and caring citizen of every community it inhabits, elevating its civic life and contributing in multiple ways to its betterment."[38] Those benefiting from an organization's value, as Mackey suggests, ought to be all stakeholders, armed by a firm's "higher purpose, stakeholder integration, conscious leadership and conscious culture and management."

In the private firm's pursuit of profit—in some cases aided by the aggressive expansion to operate in new jurisdictions or outsource expensive costs to inexpensive markets—it seems companies serve the balance sheet rather than the customer. For *The Purpose Effect* to come to fruition, each organization must define who it really serves. The fifth and final component to the Good DEEDS, therefore, is to "Serve All Stakeholders."

The term "stakeholder" was originally coined at Stanford Research Institute in 1963 to describe "those groups without whose support the organization would cease to exist."[39] Author and futurist Don Tapscott wants organizations "to be honest and considerate of the interests of their stakeholders, and that includes society at large." In an opinion piece, Tapscott indicated we, "Need multi-stakeholder approaches" and that society will require "more complex multi-stakeholder decision-making models."[40]

Without a doubt, stakeholders ought to be made up of everyone that an organization might affect. José Ignacio Goirigolzarri, BBVA Group Chief Operating Officer, suggests his bank, "has a clear and ambitious business project in which the creation of value for all becomes our driving goal: shareholder, clients, society, and of course, our team. This is what we mean by 'passion for people.'"[41] As BBVA has done, other organizations should consider redefining their stakeholders—the groups they ultimately aim to serve and benefit. Some assistance might come in the form of work previously established by a group dedicated to such a cause, Benefits Corporation.

Benefit Corporations—more commonly referred to as B-Corps—seek to take into account the welfare and interests of all stakeholders in its operations. This position includes the communities in which the organization serves, employees, the environment, customers, partners and any relevant shareholders. In essence, the organization measures its success against each of these target audiences. A registered B-Corp (adjudicated by the Certified B-Corporation organization) must be "certified by the non-profit B-Lab to meet rigorous standards of social and environmental performance, accountability and transparency"[42] in order to achieve accreditation and good standing. As of 2015, B-Corps are legislated in 28 U.S. states, as well as in 40 other countries including Canada, France, Germany, Australia and the United Kingdom. By the end of 2015, the total number of organizations who have become B-Corp certified was over 1,400.

A B-Corp adjudicates financial, social and qualitative metrics as a basis for its success. It does not solely measure accomplishment by financial targets. A B-Corp organization does not serve shareholders or power-holders only; rather, it aims to measure its progress through all stakeholders. There may be advantages for team members when the organization redefines its stakeholders, too. Indeed, Ryan Honeyman, author of *The B Corp Handbook: How to Use Business as a Force for Good*, said to me, "Becoming a Certified B-Corporation can help unleash the passion, initiative and imagination of employees by connecting them with the larger meaning behind their work."[43]

Vermont-based King Arthur Flour is as blunt as it is deft in the kitchen when it comes to describing their purpose. "Being a good steward of our community and our environment, treating our employees and our business partners with respect and remaining steadfast in our commitment to quality has been King Arthur Flour's recipe for success for more than 220 years."[44] It is an example of an organization that purposefully redefined who it serves. The company's stakeholders are now made up of customers, owners, team members, the community and the environment. In their 2014 annual report, the company reported on each of its target audiences:

- King Arthur Flour currently pays all regular team members at least 14 percent above the state-identified livable wage.

- It invested $193,000 in team member development, exceeding the target by 49 percent.

- It spent $72,000 on employee wellness, 20 percent higher than the target.

- It donated $182,000 in dollars, goods and time to the community, up 65 percent year over year.

- It provides 40 hours of paid volunteer time per year to part-time and full-time team members, meeting their goal of donating 3,238 hours of time in the community.

- It won the "Transportation Workplace of the Year Award" in the Upper Valley region of Vermont for their commitment to sustainable transportation, saving over 80,000 miles in commuting.

- All catalogue mixes and cake flour boxes are now made with 100 percent recycled fiber.

- The company gives back 1 percent of its sales to non-profits dedicated to protecting the environment.

- It achieved over $100 million in revenues, and remains 100 percent team member-owned, utilizing profit sharing and allocations of stock through an Employee Stock Ownership Plan (ESOP).[45]

King Arthur Flour successfully redefined who it serves, but was not shy to report it had not met certain targets either. Its attempt to implement a more significant solar installation failed and attempts to evaluate the social and environmental impact of its suppliers did not occur.

In Summary

Collectively, the Good DEEDS can, in fact, "do good." When an organization's senior leaders purposefully decide to delight its customers, engage with its team members, become ethical within society, deliver fair practices across teams and serve all stakeholders as it operates, organizational purpose can become well within reach.

On the subject of stakeholders, work and humanity, American inventor and author, Buckminster Fuller, introduced something he referred to as "The World Deal." He, too, believed in good deeds. To conclude our investigation into the Good DEEDS of organizational purpose, Fuller's statement captures what any organization might consider:

> Make the world work, for 100 percent of humanity, in the shortest possible time, through spontaneous cooperation, without ecological offense or the disadvantage of anyone.[46]

Next, we will investigate the third and final component of *The Purpose Effect*—role purpose. This is informed by a team member's personal purpose, the organization's purpose, and various factors within the position itself. When in a role, team members will elect to work in either a job, career or a purpose mindset. The sweet spot shines brightly for both the individual *and* the organization if the purpose mindset is demonstrated a majority of the time. Let us find out next *why* and *how*.

CHAPTER SEVEN
ESTABLISHING ROLE-BASED PURPOSE

"The true way to render ourselves happy is to love our work and find in it our pleasure."[1]
Françoise Bertaut de Motteville

"Work and purpose are so closely connected that your work comes to an end, once your purpose is achieved."[2]
David Steindl-Rast

In his book, *The Pleasures and Sorrows of Work*, Alain de Botton offers his own atypical perspective on working life:

> Our work will at least have distracted us, it will have provided a perfect bubble in which to invest our hopes for perfection, it will have focused our immeasurable anxieties on a few relatively small-scale and achievable goals, it will have given us a sense of mastery, it will have made us respectably tired, it will have put food on the table. It will have kept us out of greater trouble.

It struck me as an odd way to end what I thought to be an otherwise splendid book. I could not disagree with his particular assessment more. Work is not to be a distraction for people but an important component to creating the sweet spot of *The Purpose Effect*. The roles we hold ought to be part of a greater purpose both for the organization *and* the individual. Individuals work to earn a wage, but also to provide additional meaning in their lives. The roles we fulfill every day at work are an important part of our identity. Is the work that we perform and the roles that we hold, therefore, merely a perfect bubble?

In his book, *Drive*, Daniel Pink clarified for us that mastery, autonomy and purpose were the key facets of personal motivation, not the quest to put food on the table.[3] Of course, there will be many instances and times when work feels less than desirable, almost like walking barefoot on shards of broken glass. But our roles and the work we perform should not be a distraction. Contrary to what de Botton portends, the roles people hold in an organization should not be thought of as vehicles simply to keep us out of trouble.

One specific goal we should contemplate is how to seek out a role in an organization that helps fulfill our personal sense of purpose. Maybe the position is full-time, part-time or even on contract. Whatever the case, there is a responsibility on the individual's part to seek it out, and (ideally) to achieve it. Just before his death—in an interview with Bill Moyers on PBS—Joseph Campbell encapsulated the end result of those who find such purpose in their lives:

> If you follow your bliss, you put yourself on a kind of track that has been there all the while, waiting for you, and the life that you ought to be living is the one you are living. Wherever you are—if you are following your bliss, you are enjoying that refreshment, that life within you, all the time.[4]

By continuously developing, defining and deciding our "why," team members are in a better position to adjudicate which organizations and roles are an appropriate match with their interests, values, beliefs. Their bliss, in other words.

Organizations have a part to play, too. As we discovered in the previous chapter, an organization can provide a purposeful experience (and mission) for team members by implementing the Good DEEDS concept. It is in the best interests of the organization, however, to enact the Good DEEDS if it wants to retain and attract team members now and into the future. It is quickly becoming a "team member's market." An organization without purpose is running the risk of missing out on keeping or hiring high-performing individuals.

But the organization *and* team members possess a rather unique relationship in this third component to *The Purpose Effect*. In its simplest form, role purpose occurs when personal and organizational purpose aligns. Role purpose answers the question "why" a role exists in the organization, but it also will result in a team member demonstrating one of three workplace mindsets. In *The Purpose Effect*, those three role-based mindsets are: job, career and purpose.

The ideal scenario is for team members to possess a purpose mindset as often or for as long as possible, spending as little time as is feasible in the job or career mindsets. (We will revisit those definitions shortly.) If this purpose mindset materializes, the chances of the sweet spot being achieved by both the team member *and* the organization greatly increases. One exciting benefit of working more often in the purpose mindset than the job or career mindsets is that the benefits begin to multiply for all stakeholders.

Calling Purpose

Yale professor Amy Wrzesniewski and her colleagues were some of the first researchers to define an individual's mindset at work. In a seminal paper published in 1997, they pointed out that regardless of the type of profession, team members end up classifying themselves into either a job, a career or what was termed a "calling." The breakdown was as follows:

- Job—work is not a major positive part of life

- Career—focus on advancement and growth

- Calling—focused on the enjoyment of fulfilling, socially useful work.[5]

As it pertains to a team member within *The Purpose Effect*, I propose slightly tweaked definitions of the three categories that Wrzesniewski and her colleagues identified. In fact, depending on the individual, I have discovered over my working life and through my research that some people might employ all three types of mindsets at various stages of a role or when performing specific duties.

Someone who possesses or demonstrates a job mindset is performing transactional duties in their role in return for compensation. These individuals who demonstrate the job mindset normally do so for one of three reasons:

- *It is a choice.* The only outcome an individual seeks from a role is to be remunerated.

- *It is a result.* The job mindset is the outcome of misalignment between personal and organizational purpose.

- *It is temporary.* From time to time, functions of the role will simply feel "like a job," but it is ephemeral.

If an individual portrays a career mindset, they are generally trying to increase what I refer to as "workplace girth." That is, the intrinsic motivation of an individual is selfish (versus selfless) and their role revolves around a personal crusade to advance one's salary, title, power, team size and/or span of control. Individuals who exhibit the career mindset (determinedly or periodically) normally do so for one of two reasons:

- *It is a quest.* The sole purpose of one's role is to climb the "career ladder," caring little about the collateral damage.

- *It is a pre-requisite.* Whether to develop, learn or grow, an individual chooses to advance their role or position.

When an individual's personal purpose (develop, define and decide) is aligned with an organization's purpose (demonstrated by the Good DEEDS) the team member is likely to demonstrate purpose in their role more often than not. It may not be 100 percent of the time—based on episodic moments of job or career mindset situations—but it can be a predominant portion of the time. Someone who manifests a purpose mindset is passionate, innovative and persistently committed to working in meaningful and engaging ways to serve all stakeholders. Perhaps it results in an ethos that puts "Society First."

As previously mentioned, *The Purpose Effect* is a companion book to *FLAT ARMY*. It is the interdependency between the three mindsets (job, career, purpose) and team member engagement and culture—the thesis of *FLAT ARMY*—that explains why there is such a difference between those who demonstrate purpose in their roles and those who do not.

Craig Dowden was thinking along these same lines. Research he spear-headed while working in Ottawa looked at the link between team member engagement and whether they were occupying a job, career or calling mind-set. Craig discovered that those who possessed a job mindset were rarely if ever engaged in their work. On the contrary, for those who believed their role fell into the calling category (what we are referring to as the purpose mindset in *The Purpose Effect*), roughly 76 percent were "always engaged" at work.

Furthermore, 83 percent of individuals in the calling category were highly committed to their organization while only 16 percent of those with a job mindset considered themselves committed to their place of work. Previous points I have raised in this book articulated the incredible impact a disengaged or uncommitted employee can have on customer relations, interactions, innovation, productivity and bottom-line results.

I interviewed Dowden, asking about the importance of role-based pur-pose. "Meaning is becoming increasingly important in today's workplace," he said. "Employees and leaders are spending more time figuring out their 'why.' Research continually shows that employees and organizations that are clear on their purpose benefit from higher levels of engagement, which positively impacts their bottom line." Additionally, on the topic of benefits, Dowden explained, "Most people have lots of choices in terms of where to work. Most of us want to contribute to something beyond ourselves. Those companies who can tap into that need will really benefit."

Wrzesniewski and Dowden, however, are not the only professionals to come to the realization there is a job, career and purpose mindset demar-cation with respect to workplace roles. Author Chip Conley, for example, suggested in his book *Peak: How Great Companies Get their Mojo from Maslow*, "When someone finds meaning in their work (they like what they do each day) without meaning at work (they aren't enthused by the com-pany's mission), it is much less likely that there is a 'halo effect' or indirect payoff in helping to improve their commitment with the organization."[6] Again, there is a lot riding on role-based purpose for both the organization *and* the team member.

It should not be a surprise, but it is the organization that defines all roles needed to carry out its strategy and mission. An individual applies for a role—full-time, part-time or contingent—and performs any of the duties required in order to be remunerated. Those roles could end up being highly engaging or excruciatingly transactional for a team member. The organization creates the role, but it is the individual, of course, who must perform in it. What seems like workplace bliss for one team member may be painful for another.

The more alignment there is—the more a team member believes in the organization's purpose and its relationship to their personal purpose alongside the role they occupy—the greater likelihood there is for an individual to reach the purpose mindset and thus the sweet spot. If this happens on a continuous basis, both the organization *and* the team member will have created *The Purpose Effect*.

What happens to the team member, however, if they detest the role? What of those who are fixated on bullying their way to larger teams, fancier titles and greater power? What if the organization permits the operating culture to collapse, falling hard into a world devoid of collaboration or openness? Enron, Nortel and Volkswagen are examples of organizations that fell from grace, dismantling any sense of organizational purpose in the process. Johnsonville Sausage, Box of Crayons and TELUS are organizations that have defined their purpose in order that customers, team members and society get equal billing with profitability. Do those team members find it easier to demonstrate purpose in their role than those working in organizations without a strong purpose?

The rest of this chapter is devoted to the job, career and purpose mindsets that make up the third and final component of *The Purpose Effect*: role purpose. Team members tend to occupy one, two or all three of these mindsets as a result of the make-up of their role, their personal purpose and, of course, the organization's purpose.

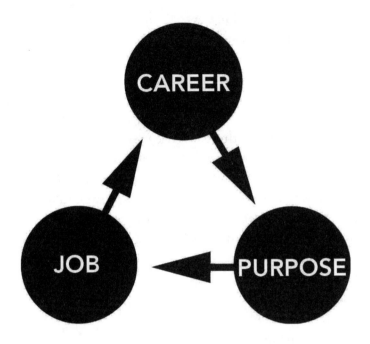

Making Mary Merry

Mary Hewitt was not the first team member I had ever dismissed. But she was—and continues to be—my most memorable.

When I started working at Crystal Decisions in 2002 as an Education Director, Mary held the title of Trainer. She had been performing the role for three years prior to my arrival. As a trainer, she would traverse the North American continent, delivering different types of instructor-led classes to customers, partners and employees alike. When Mary was back in the office, away from airplanes and training rooms, it provided a chance for the two of us to catch up on her well-being, the team and so on. It is fair to say we did not exactly get along at first. Those early conversations through my initial year as leader were at best perfunctory and at worst labored.

After a year or so, I invited Mary into one of the breakout rooms and asked how she was doing. I wondered if she was truly feeling good, full of meaning. By immediately shifting the focus of our conversation, Mary indicated she would be extremely grateful if I could eliminate some of the travel in her role. In fact, she hated being a trainer, particularly because of the travel. After some personnel shuffling, Mary switched roles and became a courseware developer, parking herself each day in an office chair rather than an economy class airplane seat.

After another year or so, Mary and I began having more conversations, this time focusing on her career and her life. Over a period of time and plenty of discussions, Mary shifted into a project management role. She remained grounded, working only in Vancouver. One day, after roughly a year in the new role, and getting the sense that things still were not right, I pulled Mary aside again and asked, "Do you think it is time you embarked on something that really is of interest? Do you know your true calling?"

Perhaps it was tough love. Maybe it was my attempt to help her to find her why, her bliss, her purpose. Whatever the case, it turns out Mary was feeling the same way. She wanted out. We then figured out a way to terminate her contract—together with a severance package—and she went out the front door of the office ready to begin seeking her personal purpose. She was escaping the job mindset that had characterized her roles as trainer, courseware developer and project manager. Her focus now was on developing, defining and deciding her new "*why.*" She took no issue with the organization—in fact she loved volunteering, being part of the team's community involvement and to this day remains dear friends with several ex-colleagues—but she simply had been occupying time in various roles that were not fulfilling her personal purpose. The alignment between personal, organizational and role purpose was missing. Mary needed to seek out and establish the sweet spot.

For the next several years, she continued to develop, define and decide who she was going to be in life and at work. We continued to meet from time to time as well. Eventually, she meandered back into social work—achieving another Master's degree—and it all came together. Today, her working life is now dedicated to the betterment of those in need. Mary works with personal and role purpose as a Clinical Therapist in Halifax at the Nova Scotia Health Authority, an organization that bills itself as "a community of caring, compassionate people who care deeply about health, healing and learning."

One aspect of Mary's story relates to her perseverance. She did not let the trappings of a job or paycheck mentality become a lifetime crutch. It took a while, but she eventually figured out her ideal path. She also refused to climb the career ladder for more pay or power. Mary was steadfast and determined to find an organization that matched her redefined personal purpose. Put differently, she had to first rediscover her goals and her interests and then she had to seek out an organization and a role that matched.

"I realized and then decided," Mary informed me, "that what I get paid to do needs to fit with what I know and feel to be my personal purpose." She knows some jobs and even some tasks in a job will not always be rewarding. But along her journey, she discovered a key difference. "Where it became soul-destroying was when I realized I had done the 'work for a paycheck job mindset' for so long that I was out of alignment with my principles, values and beliefs. They were still at my core, but my core had gotten very small and personally, harder and harder for me to connect with."

But there was another lesson Mary shared with me. "Certainly not everything I do, even now, fits exactly with my personal purpose. I have had to realize that some of the uncomfortable steps are still in the overall picture, contradictory to my overall purpose." Mary had recognized that any role, in any organization, is going to be made of elements from the job, career and purpose mindsets. "But by recognizing," she continued, "that personal purpose is not always consistent with what I get paid to do, I get to make a conscious, informed choice. The paycheck job mindset may in fact be enabling the steps toward role purpose."

Role purpose is tricky. Mary's story demonstrates it can take a while to achieve, too. As we explore the rest of this chapter, keep in mind Mary's last point. More often than not, a role will be made up of aspects of the job and career mindsets. How one defines their personal purpose—and how the organization demonstrates its purpose—will be factors in achieving role purpose. But, there will always be elements of a role that are uncomfortable. Perhaps it is the alignment between personal and organizational purpose that predicts whether the majority of time spent in a role can be accomplished with purpose. Let's next delve specifically into the job mindset and understand its makeup.

The Job Mindset

Authors John Hagel, John Seely Brown, Alok Ranjan and Daniel Byler discovered a "passion gap" in America's workforce. The researchers found close to 90 percent of workers were "not able to contribute to their full potential" due to a lack of "passion for their work." Not surprisingly, they also found that only 12 percent of the workforce possesses the attributes that define a passionate worker. The authors suggest this so-called "passion gap" is important to pay attention to because "passionate workers are committed to continually achieving higher levels of performance."[7]

If one occupies a job mindset—working in a role to carry out transactional duties solely in return for a paycheck—can an increased level of passion lead to meaning in an individual's role? Or, can the job mindset invoke any level of passion? Mary was arguably devoid of passion in various roles when she worked with me—leading to the job mindset—but once she developed, defined and decided her personal purpose, she quickly established her new passions and the sweet spot materialized, aided by the role and the organization that created the alignment.

Passion is one element related to a meaningful role (and potentially mitigating the job mindset) but so, too, is enthusiasm. Oxford Strategic Consulting (OSC) backs up this claim. OSC is a human capital consultancy business, doing work in Europe and countries that make up the Gulf Cooperation Council (GCC). It suggests that engagement is mainly impacted by three factors:

- One's immediate leader or line manager (40 percent)

- An individual's own propensity for enthusiasm and positivism (40 percent)

- The current work environment (20 percent)[8]

Perhaps passion *and* enthusiasm are underserved attributes in the makeup of today's team member, which may be causing the job mindset to materialize more easily.

When someone possesses a job mindset, purpose is not the goal for the individual. They are content with the paycheck and possess no aspiration for a higher level of meaning at work. Further, the job mindset can become the result when poor team dynamics, negative leadership practices and an organization's misaligned purpose and culture are paramount. (Many of these patterns and symptoms were surfaced in Chapters 3 and 4.) Furthermore, if the team member has developed far too many extrinsic motivators as a basis for role happiness, they will undoubtedly remain in a job mindset.

Indeed, Ratan Tata, former chairman of the Tata Group in India, believes far too many organizations have been constructed around extrinsic motivators such as individual perquisites, financial rewards as well as the fear of reprimand or the potential loss of one's role. This potentially negates any possibility of a team member demonstrating behavior linked to intrinsic motivation. "Doing good" for the sake of "feeling good" becomes far less possible. Tata noted in *MIT Sloan Magazine*, "There is mounting evidence that employees throughout the world are hungering to find and bring their values to work," but unfortunately for the individual, "they have not felt comfortable in doing so."[9]

Place yourself for a moment in a medical clinic, hospice or hospital. No doubt you have been in one of those environments at one time or another, either as a patient or as a trusty supporter of some sort. When you interact with one of the professionals—be it the desk administrator, nurse, anesthesiologist, technician or doctor, among others—you immediately can recognize if the person you are conversing with is either there for the money or they are effortlessly working on cloud nine in their role. You recognize the signs like the Big Dipper might shine brightly on a starry summer night.

Is the nurse devoid of a smile, audibly exasperated as you begin listing your symptoms? When you approach the front desk to admit your family member, does the administrator even look up from the computer screen they are mesmerized by, possibly enthralled by a game of solitaire? Then there is the x-ray technician who does not seem to care about how hard he placed the lead apron vest on your chest.

Compare these overtly job-mindset individuals with medical professionals who seem to effortlessly float on the floors they patrol. Recall the attendant who not only smiles, but jokes around as you describe an ailment that has become bothersome. How about the doctor who does not simply rush in and out of the windowless room you have been waiting in, but sits down with zeal and curiosity truly wanting to get to know what discomforts you? What of the pinstripe-clothed volunteer who easily smiles, handing out lollipops to those passing by? My favorite is the retirement home caregiver who treats anyone in their vicinity—the deaf, incoherent, able-bodied, visitors or colleagues—as though they have been a lifelong best friend. Regardless of salary or title, these individuals seem as though they are truly purpose-filled professionals—intrinsically motivated—in their roles and likely in their life overall.

Previously I suggested that a job mindset refers to someone who believes they are employed to perform transactional duties in return for compensation and not much else. For a portion of the population, the job mindset is perfectly fine. They want nothing from work other than the paycheck. These types of individuals fully understand the social contract between team member and employer. They do not seek to rock the boat nor do they expect anything more than the wage (and possibly any healthcare and related benefits) that accompany such an employment situation. Some organizations refer to this as "peace and pay."[10] For those within this particular job mindset, their entire sense of identity (and personal purpose) might be found elsewhere in life.

The individual possessing a job mindset that accepts and acknowledges the job is in fact a remuneration transaction will demonstrate a job mindset—perhaps peace and pay—that is otherwise harmless to the organization. It may not be great for innovation, levels of increased productivity or decreased instances of absenteeism, but it does not cause any major or detrimental issue either. There will always be a percentage of team members in the organization who have this type of job mindset. Indeed, peace and pay is a rather appropriate term.

The far greater concern, however, rests with team members who are not aligned with the organization or cannot figure out why they are even in the role that actually provides them with a paycheck. It could be as a result of not properly establishing their personal purpose, being significantly misaligned with the organization's purpose or perhaps the duties laid out in the role they hold are causing ruinous or questionable behavior. When a team member spends far too much time within the job mindset—and who does not demonstrate peace and pay—it creates issues for both the team members *and* the organization. The job mindset can result in any number of disengagement issues identified earlier, as well as in my first book, *FLAT ARMY*.

Of course everyone must recognize there will be aspects of their role where they will have to perform boring, tactical if not repetitive tasks. There is no role in any organization where all job description requirements will match one's personal purpose. A call center agent may not like solving a particular problem with a customer who is abrasive or loud. A project manager may not like having to chase after colleagues for overdue actions. A CEO may not like discussing particulars of the past year at the annual general meeting with the public. I do not know of anyone who actually enjoys submitting expense reports. But they are all facets of particular roles—disliked actions everyone must come to terms with.

In summary, all team members will have to come to grips with the job mindset. It is inevitable. It is unavoidable. What is the larger question to answer? Will team members temporarily find themselves in the job mindset? Is this mindset permanent and the result of misalignment between personal and organizational purpose? Or is it a choice to simply be remunerated for tasks accomplished?

The job mindset can be detrimental to *The Purpose Effect*, to the sweet spot ever being created. The job mindset wreaks havoc with the alignment between the team member and the organization. What will you do to avoid it, temper it, if not eliminate it? I posit some strategies in Chapters 8 and 9. For now, let us investigate the next type of mindset: the career mindset.

The Career Mindset

Marcia has a managerial role at a highly successful creative marketing agency. She has been at the company for just over a year. Marcia does not have any direct reports, but is part of a team of 12. There are approximately 300 people who work at the company. Since joining, Marcia has been developing her role-based competencies, learning her way around the organization, building internal and external networks and getting various tasks and objectives accomplished. She reports into a director, James, who has been working at the organization for four years.

Marcia has become disillusioned—James is the reason why. He is renowned for taking credit for ideas that surface from the team, including Marcia. He uses those ideas to gain positive reviews from leaders at the vice-president level. James also occasionally uses his power as director to force his team to stay late—claiming senior leaders are watching—but refuses to thank any of the team members for doing so. From time to time, he remarks there is a long list of individuals wanting to join the company.

Adding insult to injury, James has issued vague threats to Marcia and her colleagues, citing potential termination if they do not complete their tasks on time. What has also become very clear is that the director is doing everything in his power to become a vice president. There are two roles opening up due to retirement in just over a year's time. James has also been known to hoard key pieces of client information and refuses to collaborate effectively with others in the organization lower than the director level.

Ironically, he is seen as a far more positive person when in the company of other senior leaders. It is as though he is being an irrational professional.

Marcia came into the organization having already achieved a sense of role purpose in her previous company and role. She knows what it means (and what it takes) to be passionate, innovative and dedicated to a meaningful and engaging workplace, committed to serving all stakeholders. The organization where she previously worked had achieved a Good DEEDS ethos. Marcia knows what the sweet spot means. This sort of mindset is not new to her. Her former leader was open, transparent, collaborative and, most importantly, a listener. While working in San Francisco, Marcia and the company she worked for were both demonstrating purpose: personal, organizational and role.

However, James has become the blocked artery of Marcia's current journey. Although she joined the New York-based organization thinking she would be able to recreate the sweet spot (and thus role purpose) from her previous company on the west coast, so far in the new organization it is beginning to look like she will regress into the job mindset. Marcia seems a likely candidate to be employed to perform transactional duties in return for compensation and not much else.

This anonymized story outlines the damaging effect a career mindset can have on others. But the damage affects many parties. Clearly Marcia is caught in the middle, possibly set to veer into a job mindset. But what of the other team members James has come into contact with? What of the customers? Finally, what about James? How does this fixation on power, title and promotion help him ever achieve a sense of purpose at work, or in his own life?

I interviewed Dr. Linda Duxbury, noted trailblazer in the field of organizational health. Not only is she interested in researching the changing workforce and organizational dynamics, she has become a provocateur of sorts. "Look after yourself," she said to me when I asked what team members should be doing in today's work environments, particularly as it relates to the career mindset types. "Employees need to take control," she continued, "otherwise someone else is going to take control of their well-being at work." Linda was referring to the "develop, define and decide" categories of personal purpose from Chapter 5, and the importance of being in control of one's own purpose.

But my conversation with Linda reminded me of the situation between Marcia and James. James—with his career mindset firmly intact—has begun to control Marcia and her attempts to re-establish the purpose mindset she once held. Marcia is inching her way downward toward the job mindset, encroaching a percentage greater than 50 percent of the time. I asked Linda about it. She continued, "If you hate your boss, your boss probably hates you, too. Don't keep yourself in your role if it's hurting your health, family and life." Indeed, Marcia is beginning to hate her boss. Is it reciprocal?

Linda published a research paper, "The Implications of Subjective Career Success," where she stated, "An employee's achievement of fulfilling work is the strongest predictor of their attitudes toward the job and organization."[11] If James continues to be the blocked artery in Marcia's quest for role purpose, the bottom line is that everyone is going to end up a loser, and a spiral into the job mindset will become inevitable for Marcia and potentially others. But make no mistake, it is James' career mindset that is causing Marcia's suffering and damage at work.

James is determined to increase three key facets of his role: salary, title and power. For some individuals drawn to the career mindset for the wrong reasons, money (or more of it) becomes the quest rather an outcome of good work. This frame of mind impacts others. It is certainly impacting Marcia. Indeed, as Swarthmore psychology professor Barry Schwartz wrote in his book, *Why We Work*, "When we say of someone that 'he's in it for the money,' we are not merely being descriptive; we're passing judgment."[12]

For individuals locked into a career mindset, there is a very low level of selflessness in their demeanor and actions. I liken it to a soap box derby, motorless wooden vehicles children build and then race against one another in a public competition.

While people may have helped you to build your vessel on wheels, even pushing you up the hill to the start line, when the race commences, it is you against everyone and your entire quest is to win. You do not care who might be in your way. The career mindset is a form of tunnel vision, analogous to the rider in the soap box derby. While the soap box derby is good fun for kids, if this competitive, solo-driven mindset were how children acted all the time, trouble would be brewing in many a household. Perhaps it is comparable to the way James is treating his role, his organization and Marcia.

The career mindset individual is seeking to advance personal and professional status, not stakeholder well-being. They want to win, and at all costs. The career mindset individual is one who abuses their role in order to gain an upper hand on their colleagues, customers and society. It often manifests in the form of power and control, including much of what we covered in Chapters 3 and 4.

Earlier I indicated the career mindset can become either a *quest* or a *pre-requisite*. James is demonstrating how the myopic and often bully-like pursuit of these sorts of attributes can denigrate a team's culture, if not besmirch a team member's personal sense of purpose. James is hell-bent in his quest and does not care about those he is negatively impacting. He has his helmet and goggles on and is racing his soap box derby car down the hill. In contrast, though, there also will be times a team member employs the career mindset as a pre-requisite, a more harmonious attempt to revisit one's personal purpose. Let us consider a few different examples.

A school teacher of seven years may seek out a Master's degree to prepare herself for a potential pay grade increase or vice-principal opportunity. A government analyst may secure the services of a coach and/or mentor to help him shift from one ministry to another. A director of sales may apply to take part in a non-profit governance program aiming to become part of a not-for-profit board. When a team member looks to continue honing their personal purpose—developing, defining and deciding—to grow their career and experience, make no mistake, this should be encouraged. This is not a bad thing. But when the action becomes a quest at the expense of others—versus a pre-requisite necessary to continue building out one's personal purpose—the differences become stark and dismal.

In the end, what happened to Marcia? She put up with James for another two months, not only hoping things would change, but going above his head and speaking with the unit's vice president about the situation. Although noble and arguably the right thing to do, nothing changed. Even though the organization was demonstrating most components of the Good DEEDS, James remained locked into a workplace attitude that was power-, money- and title-driven.

In this particular example, the career mindset of James pushed Marcia to the brink of frustration—to the cusp of the job mindset—but instead of collapsing, Marcia took it upon herself to quit the company and start again. In line with Linda Duxbury's counsel, Marcia left the role in an attempt to re-establish her sweet spot, and the achievement of fulfilling work. She returned to the "develop, define and decide" stages of personal purpose, trying again to land in an organization that was exemplifying the Good DEEDS and finding a role that would be purposeful.

It took three more months of searching and "purpose testing," but Marcia did in fact re-establish the sweet spot again. Four years later, Marcia is still in New York, still in the same organization she moved to and is still in complete alignment between the personal, organizational and role categories of *The Purpose Effect.*

The Purpose Mindset

Dr. Jennifer L. Aaker, social psychologist and professor at Stanford University's Graduate School of Business, published results proving "serious involvement with things beyond oneself and one's pleasures promotes meaningfulness." She goes on to state that purpose and meaning are "linked to doing things that express and reflect the self and in particular to doing positive things for others."[13] Indeed, on the subject of giving to others when at work, author Adam Grant opined, "You may be pleasantly surprised by the wealth of opportunities to express your values and find meaning in helping others without compromising your own success."[14]

There is more research that proves organizations and leaders who put purpose first will reap benefits. For example, several academics analyzed the interviews of 18,673 people located in various countries (including the Czech and Slovak republics, Hungary, Bulgaria and China) regarding an individual's definition of work. The majority of team members believed work should be defined "in terms of a social contribution" so that "everybody contributes according to his/her abilities to the benefit of the whole community."[15]

Backing up this research is another example where academics analyzed work design theory of "motivational, social and work context characteristics" from nearly 220,000 participants. Researchers analyzed 260 different academic studies and hundreds of mainstream media articles. They concluded, "Perhaps it should not be surprising that experienced meaningfulness is the best mediator of the relationships between motivational characteristics and work outcomes." Quite simply, if there is to be purpose in the work for team members, their output must benefit and have a positive impact on all stakeholders, including themselves. To underline the point, the researchers wrote, "The ultimate goal of human beings is to pursue meaning in our work and non-work lives."[16]

I mentioned Dr. A. R. Elangovan of the University of Victoria earlier in this book. During one of our lunches, I asked Elango why purpose is so important to one's role at work. "When someone's role offers direction and criteria for making important decisions," he said, "when it exposes us to the joys of continuous growth, sparks creativity, builds resilience toward setbacks, inspires a quest for excellence and leaves us with a sense of profound satisfaction, it makes the work-life balance issue moot and allows us to be fully and truly present at work." He later added, "And when one can feel 'so alive' just being in a role with purpose, what more can one ask for?" Elango believes the authenticity that is rooted in such clarity of purpose motivates team members in their roles to greater effort and contributions.

Apple co-founder Steve Jobs delivered a commencement speech at Stanford University in 2005 that has been viewed several million times on YouTube. He closed his speech reminding us what was displayed on the back cover of the *The Whole Earth Catalog's* final issue. It was a photograph of "an early morning country road" and the caption beneath read, "Stay Hungry. Stay Foolish." Jobs urged the graduates of Stanford to do the same, as he had done in his life. Stay Hungry. Stay Foolish.

Tim Cook succeeded Jobs as CEO of Apple. He too delivered a commencement speech. In 2015—10 years after Jobs' speech at Stanford—Cook spoke on the National Mall in Washington to graduates of George Washington University. Cook pleaded with the graduates to seek out a role and an organization "that's infused with moral purpose" and to "find work that pays the rent, puts food on the table and lets you do what is right and good and just." He suggested individuals did not have to choose "between doing good and doing well," that work ought to be "about improving the lives of others." He encouraged attendees to be impatient with progress, but perhaps more importantly he wanted graduates to be in a role full of purpose, passion and meaning. "Otherwise," as he concluded, "it's just a job, and life is too short for that."[17]

Meaningful, positive and motivating work that improves the lives of others is indeed the purpose mindset of a role. I argue that Cook's commencement speech has far greater gravitas than what Jobs urged us to consider. Elangovan, Grant, Pink, Aaker and other researchers do not recommend team members stay hungry and foolish. On the contrary, they have proven that individuals who establish their purpose in work and elsewhere in their lives, have discovered an alignment between their role, their organization and themselves; one that provides a flourishing sense of meaning and worth in all of their actions. But it does not magically happen. The purpose mindset takes action. It takes leadership.

In 1990, at the age of 19, Brian Scudamore started a junk-removal business called The Rubbish Boys. "It was to pay for university," Brian divulged to me over an interview. With 11 employees and $500,000 in revenues that year, Brian more than paid off his tuition fees with the start-up venture.

A few years later, The Rubbish Boys became 1-800-Got-Junk. His original partners did not understand the true purpose of being in business, so Brian dissolved The Rubbish Boys partnership and started anew. By 2015, Brian had successfully launched three more brands (O2E, Wow 1Day Paint, You Move Me) alongside 1-800-Got-Junk, employing more than 300 people at his headquarters while indirectly employing thousands of people across the globe working for franchise partners of Scudamore's empire. But the goal—after university tuition was paid for, of course—was not profit or revenues or success per se. The quest was purpose; it was about a meaningful life and place of work. Brian wanted his role to be a giving role, and equally important he wanted his team to feel the same way.

"I definitely have an entrepreneurial spirit," said Brian, "but I quickly realized my gift—my purpose—became the impact I could have on others and in the community. I always say, 'Make meaning not money' because when you have meaning in your life and you create a greater purpose for your company and society, you don't have to worry about a thing."

Brian does not believe money or power makes people happy, nor does he think it delivers any sense of purpose in one's role. "You need money for freedom and to make choices," he continued, "but look at Wall Street. There are a lot of people there living quarter-to-quarter, a lot of unhappy people who are not paying attention to the moments in life, making connections with people or showing that they care. These types of people don't get that it's about making meaning not money."

Brian's organization is one that empowers its team members to "make the right decisions." Whether it is removing junk, painting houses or moving furniture, Brian believes the role of each team member is a manifestation of "doing good" in life, and in society. But interestingly, role purpose for the firm's team members (and Brian) actually comes not solely because everyone is empowered; it comes as a result of being able to contribute to a community.

"If you look at the definition of a company," he explained, "it's simply a gathering of great men and women working together. The term 'company' is more synonymous with the machine. I think of our organization and our team members more as a community, doing great things for people through roles that have been created to deliver a purpose."

The ultimate arbiter of alignment between an individual's personal purpose and an organization's purpose is for that team member to achieve a purpose mindset in their role. Leaders like Brian Scudamore and Tim Cook have come to the realization that when an individual performs in a role so that meaning and fulfillment is demonstrated, good things can happen for all stakeholders. After taking the reins from Jobs, Cook began investing in community outreach, volunteer programs and other forms of philanthropy as part of Apple's restated purpose. To reiterate Joseph Campbell, perhaps the purpose mindset *is* about the possibility of bliss at work. "If we treat people right in our organizations—in the community—who are then able to inspire others, the alignment is unmistakable and purpose in their role is easily attainable," Brian concluded.

When the purpose mindset in a role has been achieved, a distinct alignment between an individual's personal purpose and the organization's greater purpose is paramount. Without it, team members will end up in a job or career mindset greater than 50 percent of their time at work, pushing the sweet spot further out of reach. If these two mindsets materialize more often than not, then yes, Alain de Botton's point that work inculcates a bubble-like protection will ring true.

But when the purpose mindset is being demonstrated by large swathes of team members for a predominant portion of time in their roles, this is truly when the sweet spot forms and when community grows.

And when community grows, communitas is forged, the focus of our next chapter.

SECTION IV

CHAPTER EIGHT
COMMUNITAS–
A COMMUNITY OF PURPOSE

To forget one's purpose is the commonest form of stupidity.[1]
Friedrich Nietzsche

Two roads diverged in a wood, and I—
I took the one less traveled by,
And that has made all the difference.[2]
Robert Frost

Mana Ionescu is the head and founder of Lightspan Digital, a digital marketing company based in Chicago that specializes in social media, email and content marketing. Before moving to the United States, Ionescu was raised in Romania and later lived in Bulgaria.

On pace for a $150,000-a-year job and in line for the Director role at the U.S.-based company she was working for, Ionescu took a deep breath one day, and asked herself, "What am I really doing?" Life, her career and the company she was working for had become too transactional. The creativity was minimal. The inspiration was nominal. The evidence of a job and career mindset was everywhere. Mana knew who she was, but her personal sense of purpose was going unfulfilled in her role and through the organization that employed her. She mused to herself, "There must be more to my working life than just sitting here making money, fixating on profit and not actually making an impact."

Mana was frustrated. The company she was working for was devoid of any meaningful outward purpose. Her own role clutched like a job or, worse, a career-laddering exercise. The alignment between personal, organizational and role purpose was missing. What to do?

She set out to fix things. In her eyes, too many businesses only see themselves through the lens of profit, whereas in reality she believes there are always two other points of impact. When we discussed what was the true purpose of an organization, Mana admitted to me far too many are solely "win" organizations, preoccupied with profits and revenues. She believes organizations should strive to become "win-win-win." Firstly, Mana indicated to me that "one should never lose site of the planet, the community or society." Further, she felt there were groups directly related to the business that it ought to keep whole. The three "wins" Mana wanted to align included:

- The necessity to make a profit and deliver value to customers.

- The individuals that make the business successful (team members, suppliers, buyers).

- Society, including the environment and members of the external community.

To curb her state of discontent, Mana decided to start her own business. When she created Lightspan Digital, as expected, the value proposition of the firm was not solely on profit. It was balanced between her "win-win-win" stakeholders theory. The purpose statement for Lightspan Digital, developed in partnership with her team, portrays these beliefs:

> To deliver clear, simple and direct digital marketing solutions. We believe in social media marketing done with purpose, not just for the heck of it.

Purpose is two-fold for Mana and Lightspan Digital. First, there must be purpose in the work that affects their clients, suppliers and their business. Second, there must be purpose in the actions the Lightspan Digital team members take to serve their customers, partners, community and society. The core values at Lightspan Digital solidify this point:

- Love our clients.

- Drive marketing with purpose.

- Be brave, adventurous, creative and accepting.

- Learn all the time.

- Teach at every occasion.

- Build strong relationships with communication.

- Do more with less.

- Be determined and passionate.

- Think, do, keep moving forward.

- Be kind, humble and honest.

"If you establish a lighthouse," Ionescu said to me, "you're creating a social contract with your employees, suppliers and customers, and it will help you sail the big waves." The lighthouse she was referring to was a purpose-filled mission, corresponding core values and a strong sense of community. Ionescu continued, "We've had situations where we had to go through our mission and core values to see if a client or employee was matching up." Purpose is so important to Mana and the Lightspan Digital team that they have parted ways with clients and team members, because the lighthouse was shining a light on troubled waters. "It takes a lot of guts when you need the money," she added, "but leaders and organizations need to set and stick to their values if they want to stay true to being purpose-driven."

Being purposeful takes courage, determination and a high degree of gumption. Difficult decisions are often required to continually enact purpose. Whether on an individual or organizational basis, team members must determine whether purpose is valued at the same level as or above profit, power, performance management and prestige. This is akin to Mana's lighthouse metaphor. When the community acts as one and is able to shine a light against issues that run counter to purpose, team members and the organization benefit. Of course, society can benefit as well.

On the other hand, purpose is not a moment in time. The lighthouse must be constantly scanning for impediments or infractions to purpose. The establishment of community, of communitas, occurs through a perpetual state of transition, of liminality. It ought to be done as a team as well. When an organization and its team members are indeed on the same page—when the sweet spot is being demonstrated by all parties—a collective sense of community can be felt. The state when team members and the organization are on the same page, jointly using the lighthouse, and building its community to serve personal, organizational and role purpose is aided by the concept of communitas. It is this concept of transitioning to communitas and the corresponding "sweet spot" that will be explored throughout the remainder of this chapter through various stories and examples, including companies off the multi-national beaten track such as Market Basket, Waggle, ViRTUS, LSTN and Earls.

Togetherness in Transition

The term *liminality* comes from Arnold van Gennep, the Belgian anthropologist who first outlined the common patterns in cultures and how they mark transitions from one human state to another (for example, from adolescence to adulthood). In his 1909 book *The Rites of Passage*, van Gennep described three stages of separation from one world and entry into another with the liminal (or threshold) stage being key to such a transition. Another anthropologist, Victor Turner, explained later on that liminality was "a moment when those being moved in accordance with a cultural script were liberated from normative demands, when they were, indeed, betwixt and between successive lodgments in jural political systems. In this gap between ordered worlds almost anything may happen."[3]

It was Turner, a professor at the University of Chicago, who took the research and findings of van Gennep much deeper to bring us a term he coined as communitas. Turner spent time testing his anthropological theories with the Ndembu tribe in Zambia, where he discovered that the liminal stage was a separation from "normal social roles" to contemplate, reinterpret and embrace alternatives to the current status quo. This is important to denote as we introduce the concept of communitas within *The Purpose Effect*.

At its core, Turner argued that liminality represented the opportunity for a group to strip down existing structural status and customs to create new ones through both intellect and spirit. He developed the notion of "anthropological communitas" as a way to define what happens to groups of people when they enter the stage of liminality. He believed a sense of solidarity emerges at the liminality stage (when people shift from one state to another) that is then backed by feelings of equality, spirit, joy, belonging and overall well-being. These feelings—ideally shared by all—lead to a better future state as an outcome. These feelings actually help to shift the status quo. They dissolve any prior rigid obligations of the old world in favor of a new and authentic manner of behavior in the new world. Turner found these feelings to be social and cooperative.

In its simplest form, communitas is both the feeling and spirit of togetherness. It is a term used to distinguish community, the point at which members feel as though they are on an equal level with one another, achieving its purpose in unison. Communitas is the ultimate definition of a purpose-driven solidarity between the organization and team members. As it relates to *The Purpose Effect*, I liken communitas to achieving the sweet spot for both team members and the organization. Communitas instills humility and humanity, inculcating a high degree of compassion and understanding among its members. In essence, communitas is the shared journey of putting "Society First." Communitas *is* the sweet spot.

Elango Elangovan informed us of his belief that those individuals wishing to achieve a purpose mindset can be seen "living life and earning a livelihood" equally and in harmony. He continued this thread during one of our interviews. "The notion of a 'fit' is not new—we have all heard of person-job fit, for example. But think about what happens when there is person-organization fit for most, if not all, employees in the organization. This is where the employees of an organization are able to understand the purpose of the organization, realize the convergence with their own values and purpose in life and enact a fluency of functioning that offers mutual benefits." Elango was honing in on the need of establishing true community in the organization.

Elango insisted that there are no inherent tensions between what the team members aspire to and what the organization's mission is. He said, "What's good for the company is good for the employee and vice versa." When competition is intense and the environment dynamics are volatile, this is an extremely unsettled position to be in. "In such a context," he said, "the leaders of the organization can rest assured that employees will doggedly pursue the best interests of the organization since they would just be doing it for themselves anyway. So an organization that can instill a sense of purpose through its mission, reinforce it in its values and culture, and live it via its strategy would be like a beacon to employees—they need to see it first and those who find it resonates with them will be drawn to it, and flourish as true corporate citizens."

This is my point with communitas, with community. When team members are committed, driven and feel as though they are an integral part to the success of the organization, in the words of Mana, everyone is able to win-win-win. The liminal stage—transitioning from what was to what should be through a continuously scanning lighthouse—is the act of creating a community so that all team members not only demonstrate purpose in life and in their role, but they "doggedly pursue the best interests of the organization." This state of being can become a dynamic and influential community that is indeed emboldened with purpose, for a purpose.

A (Market) Basket Full of Purpose

Market Basket is a supermarket chain of over 70 stores throughout Massachusetts and New Hampshire that employs over 25,000 people. In 2013, when its CEO, Arthur T. Demoulas, decided to offer customers an additional 4 percent discount—suggesting customers could probably use the money more than the company's shareholders—a coup d'état was put in motion. Led by factions of the board, which included direct relatives of Demoulas, he was removed from his senior role. Even after volumes of sales increased, and the company's already low turnover dropped further still, Demoulas was sent to the sidelines, wondering what had gone wrong. The sweet spot for him—and the organization—had been eviscerated.

Market Basket team members receive better pay than those working for the competition, customers enjoy lower prices than its rivals, a focus on community and the environment is a fixture with its operating culture and all of this is accomplished by paying shareholders smaller dividends than other supermarket chains. Indeed, Market Basket aims to serve all stakeholders, an element of the Good DEEDS we discussed in Chapter 6. The community spirit that Demoulas had created with Market Basket team members, customers and suppliers was about to be put to the ultimate test. Would Elango's theory that team members willingly pursue the best interests of the organization ring true? Were team members using Mana's lighthouse metaphor, scanning for potential issues and threats, trying to ensure the state of communitas (the sweet spot) would be top of mind?

Shortly after Demoulas was ousted, team members indeed demonstrated their purpose mettle. They walked out. Over a six-week period, the Market Basket team members stuck up for their leader (and the sweet spot that they had previously enjoyed in their roles) by refusing to work. Customers started boycotting the company's stores as well. Consequently, those members of the Demoulas family and board who favored higher profit margins versus price drops were forced to negotiate with the purpose-based Demoulas. Both parties eventually came to a negotiated settlement. Demoulas bought the company back for $1.6 billion. He assumed operations and leadership of the chain again in the summer of 2014. Once news reached the team members, they immediately went back to work and customers again started shopping at Market Basket, ending their six-week-long boycott, too.

When he returned to work, Demoulas spoke to employees from the back of a pickup truck during a rally at their company headquarters. "Words cannot express how much I appreciate each and every one of you," he said. "You are simply the best. As I stand here, there is very little that I could ever add to your brilliant work, your extraordinary display of loyalty and the power of your enduring spirit over the past several weeks."[4]

Market Basket provides us with a lesson. As Elango indicated, most team members do want to be part of something special at work. They do want to contribute to the greater good of society, too. They do want to pursue the best interests of the organization, but they expect the firm to do the same for them in return. They do want to feel a part of a team, of a community; they want to be in that sweet spot.

Michael Papay, co-founder and CEO of Waggle—an online feedback and engagement platform—told me in an interview that feeling heard as part of the greater team is a huge part of purpose for team members. "If you're in an organization that you are aligned to and inspired by its purpose as an individual," he said, "you want to feel as though you are contributing every day to the organization, your role and your personal purpose. You have great ideas and insight, so the question is how do you play that back with the organization in mind to make a difference."[5]

Michael's observation is similar to the manner in which team members at Market Basket acted when Demoulas was ousted as its most senior leader. Perhaps their notion of "doing good" in society was what defined Demoulas. When he was forced out, as a united community of Market Basket individuals, the team members took action. Michael works with hundreds of organizations through his company, assisting various leaders with culture, engagement and leadership improvements. He often has seen a fixation on profit and a lack of community overthrow common sense, like with the example of Market Basket. "Any entrepreneur has to make a choice," Michael added. "What is the goal of the organization? Profit or purpose or both? Organizations are inherently made to die. There are many ways to re-frame an organization, but leaders ought to be building something that is more enduring, generating a lot more value for the community, humanity, employees and social causes for the long term."

The sense of community and of purpose that Market Basket had created between team members, its customers and each other led to the team member revolt, the customer boycott and then the eventual return of Demoulas. This demonstration of the sweet spot cemented the company as both an employer of choice, and an organization set to increase its already loyal customers. On the basis of its purpose, profitability was set to surge. Michael concluded our interview by saying, "Creating a more authentic and inclusive way for employees to have a voice and express themselves—through wisdom and knowledge—in alignment with the organization's more altruistic purpose is where the magic starts to happen." Indeed, there was some magic happening at Market Basket.

Mike Desjardins, CEO of ViRTUS—a leadership development firm working with clients throughout North America—sees things the same way as Michael of Waggle. "Profit and purpose are not in conflict," Mike confirmed. "The closer and tighter we focus on purpose, the more profit grows. The more we focus on profit, the less we make."

Mike believes an organization and its team members are differentiated by its purpose. "It's not easily repeated," he said, "because if a competitor is unable to match an organization's purpose, they are never going to win." When I asked Mike specifically about the organization that he runs, he said, "The better we get at demonstrating our purpose up front at ViRTUS is how we end up making more profit in the end. It's not about pricing for us, per se. How we do a better job in being explicit with our purpose is what makes us successful. Further, if a client does not care about purpose, then we don't want to be involved with them."[6]

Market Basket team members, customers and its leader somewhat quickly returned to the sweet spot following the return of Demoulas to the CEO chair. Despite losing $405 million during the turmoil of 2014, company executives were happy to report purpose was indeed creating financial benefits for its stakeholders in 2015. Market Basket products continued to be priced significantly lower than its competitors, so customers were winning, and coming back in droves. During the first six months of 2015, products were priced 15.9 percent cheaper than its nearest competitor, yet sales were up 4 percent over the previous year. Demoulas predicted sales would surpass $4.8 billion, a $700 million increase over the previous year by the end of 2015. Team members were being taken care of, too. More than $129 million in various bonuses and profit-sharing contributions were also being distributed, on par with previous years.[7]

Hearing Aid for Good

LSTN is a company based in Los Angeles that produces and sells high-quality wooden headphones. It is an example of how the three categories of purpose (personal, organizational and role) can eventually align through a continual state of transition. Its mission suggests it not only wants to produce headphones, it wants to better society. It reads as follows:

> We believe that what's good for business should be good for the world. When we started LSTN, our mission was to create a company that could create global change by providing high-quality products that help fund hearing restoration and spread awareness for the global problem of hearing loss and hearing impairment. We didn't just want to create another headphone company. We wanted to create something that could change the world.

Indeed, LSTN has partnered with the Starkey Hearing Foundation, and for every pair of headphones it sells, the company commits to helping restore hearing loss for someone in need. Founded by Joe Huff and Bridget Hilton, LSTN calls itself a for-purpose company that "connects individuals, families and communities through sound." Its founders have created the sweet spot that balances purpose with profit. Furthermore, it has inculcated a culture with its team members that ensures society is constantly being bettered through improved hearing.

"Whether it's sales meetings, production, development, distribution or marketing," Joe informed me, "every single decision has to be able to first answer to: 'Will this help give more people the gift of hearing?' We want to make sure that even if people are talking about selling more product or making better products or marketing better, it's all really about the bigger end result and the real bottom line of helping people. That's enabled everyone in the company to realize that every single person is a part of the change we create, and we all can celebrate our collective achievement together because each role is crucial to the success of the mission."[8] I wondered if this type of thinking about a greater purpose came as a result of happenstance, or was it learned. Did Joe and Bridget have an innate sense of *The Purpose Effect*, or did it come from a place of past experience?

Both Joe and Bridget learned what their true sense of personal purpose was over a period of time. It was roughly a 10-year period of transition for both of them. Through their learning, they then wove their "true purpose" into LSTN and into the organization's roles.

For more than a decade, Bridget worked in the music industry. She started out in the mail room at Universal Music Group (UMG) and eventually wound up helping market and launch some of the biggest names in the music business. Her journey was a constant exploration of developing, defining and deciding who she wanted to become in life. Along the way, she worked in various roles and became inspired by brands like Warby Parker and Toms Shoes. It was during the personal purpose phase where she developed a strong desire to start a venture that could help change the world for the better. One day, Bridget watched a video of a woman who was given a contraption that permitted her to hear for the first time in her life. It was that moment when everything clicked for Bridget. Although still related to audio, she felt compelled to help others by figuring out how to give the gift of hearing.

Joe had spent a similar 10-year period building out his personal purpose, sorting out his why. But many of us hit speed bumps or potholes along the road of life. It is inevitable. Joe began to experience a few rough patches in his life. He lost his father to cancer and his dog suddenly died. Then, he and his wife divorced. "These events made me realize with total clarity," Joe confirmed, "that what matters most is what we do to make the world a better place. So I decided then and there that I wanted to create a business that could do just that."

Shortly after Joe's rough patch, he met Bridget. She showed him the video of the woman hearing for the first time. From that point forward both of them committed to spending all of their time building out the LSTN idea. "When I decided to spend all of my time working on a business that could really affect change and inspire others to do the same, is when I met my purpose," said Joe.

But why not simply create a headphones company? Why not focus on profit, and not purpose? Why not create an organization that simply ignored creating the sweet spot for both the firm and its team members? "I believe that balancing profit and purpose is always the hardest part of any social enterprise because the 'giving' mentality that most social entrepreneurs possess naturally makes them want to give more than they actually can and should." Joe was admitting that organizations that might put purpose before profit—even with the sweet spot in place—might end up shooting themselves in the foot, faltering to the graveyard of bankruptcy.

Joe continued on this thread. "Since the reason we started the company was to fund hearing restoration, we built in the giving component right off the bat. It's a part of the core business plan and financials, so we knew what we could afford to give while still growing the business." While everyone at LSTN is crystal clear with its purpose in terms of societal good, team members are also acutely aware that the business plan must balance purpose with profit, not the other way around, and not one in place of the other. He introduced an interesting analogy to further explain his point.

"We always use the airplane safety instructions as the perfect example," he said. "When the oxygen mask comes down, you have to put yours on first before you help anyone else because if you don't make sure you're healthy, you can't help anyone at all." Joe was not suggesting purpose should overtake profit, or that profit overtakes purpose. On the contrary, he and Bridget have built LSTN balancing purpose with profit and ensuring this is the key principle to its business plan, its culture, its operating processes. The oxygen mask is both purpose and profit. This is how the sweet spot has been achieved at LSTN, for its team members, and for Bridget and Joe individually. This is how communitas is being demonstrated across all LSTN stakeholders.

The Delicate Act of Balancing Purpose with Profit— Part I

In Viktor Frankl's book, *The Doctor and the Soul*, the famous Holocaust survivor and psychiatrist suggested that people can use their work to help establish their personal sense of purpose, so long as their role allows them to use their skills to benefit others. In part, this is the alignment we have been discussing between personal, organizational and role purpose throughout *The Purpose Effect*. Frankl pointed out that when an individual's role allows them to learn, permits them to give back and encourages them to deliver value, both society and the individual come out a winner. He wrote:

> Work usually represents the area in which the individual's uniqueness stands in relation to society and thus acquires meaning and value. This meaning and value, however, is attached to the person's work as a contribution to society, not to the actual occupation as such.[9]

Frankl's research and writing echo points discussed in Chapters 3 and 4 about power, role and performance. If the individual (and the organization) is unwilling to transition—where there is alignment between the three categories of purpose—it may continue to result in what has plagued much of the working world: disengaged workforces and myopic profit or power-focused organizational missions.

Led by their most senior leader, there are two firms who decided to buck that trend, transitioning their organizations to make better contributions to society. Unilever and Etsy made mindful decisions to define both meaning and value in their organizational missions in order that potential benefits to society could be on par with the need to grow revenues and profitability. Like LSTN, these organizations believed that by "doing good" and making it a part of their company ethos, communitas could come to fruition by aligning a holistic purpose with profit mission.

In the late 2000s, although Unilever was doing reasonably well financially, its directors determined something was lacking. Employee engagement sat at 57 percent. That was not a horrific measure, but certainly not best in class either. Its environmental record was being questioned and targeted by organizations like Greenpeace. There were other issues percolating as well. The company needed to transition, to review and revise its mission. The Board agreed to bring in a new CEO, Paul Polman, effective January 1, 2009.

Polman, a 27-year veteran of Proctor & Gamble and the reigning CFO at Nestlé before joining Unilever, was as daring as he was caring in his quest to redefine Unilever. On day one of his CEO tenure, Polman informed various analysts and financial markets that the company would no longer be providing short- or long-term guidance, a blasphemous action if there ever was one in the financial community. In an interview with *Harvard Business Review*, Polman was asked by the editor-in-chief, Adi Ignatius, if other companies should follow suit. He answered, "Oh, definitely. I did it the day I started this job because I figured I couldn't be fired on my first day." He later added in all seriousness, "It has allowed us to focus instead on a mature discussion with the market about our long-term strategy."

When interviewed by *Management Today*, the Unilever CEO crystalized the point about the company's newly redefined long-term strategy:

> To drag the world back to sanity, we need to know why we are here. The answer is: for consumers, not shareholders. If we are in synch with consumer needs and the environment in which we operate, and take responsibility for society as well as for our employees, then the shareholder will also be rewarded.[11]

It was not long after Polman took over as CEO at Unilever when he and his team introduced a manifesto known as the Sustainable Living Plan.[12] The company promised to cut its environmental footprint in half by 2020, dramatically improve the sourcing and supply chain of the goods it turns into food or products and to double its total revenues. The plan aims to improve the health and well-being of one billion people by ameliorating nutrition, health and hygiene factors. "The essence of the plan," said Polman, "is to put society and the challenges facing society smack in the middle of the business."

When asked why Unilever made the corporate shift in philosophy, Thomas Lingard, Global Advocacy Director of the company, said not everyone on Earth will "necessarily aspire to a Western lifestyle, but they will aspire to an improved quality of life."[14]

For Unilever, purpose has turned into a driver of both growth and profitability. Put differently, increased financial results have become an outcome of a purpose-driven ethos. For example, in their 2014 full-year performance announcement, Polman wrote, "The Unilever Sustainable Living Plan continues to underpin all aspects of our business model from the way we source materials through to our product innovations. Our activities enhance our reputation and corporate brand. They are well recognized and an important way of reducing cost and risk in increasingly well-informed and challenging societies."[15]

Despite Unilever's bold move to put purpose on par with profit—ignoring calls from financial analysts to reinstate financial guidance—the company continued to grow its business results. Over a five-year period, profits have risen from €5 billion in 2009 to €8 billion in 2014. The organization's combined market capitalization increased from €63 billion to €94 billion. Unilever's diluted earnings per share have also risen, shifting from 1.16 in 2009 to 1.79 in 2014. Not to be forgotten, Unilever has also dramatically reduced its use of CO2, water usage, waste sent for disposal and accident rates, all components of their Sustainable Living Plan.[16]

When Paul Polman became CEO of Unilever in 2009, it was an organization operating much like many other for-profit companies. Today, employee engagement at Unilever sits at 87 percent—a 53 percent jump—and almost all financial metrics are up. The company has firmly set its sights on creating a more sustainable, harmonious and purpose-driven society as its overarching mission. It made a decision to transition—to balance purpose with profit—and as Frankl suggested, this purpose-driven focus is now delivering contributions to society through the workers.

The Delicate Act of Balancing Purpose with Profit—Part II

Unilever is an example of a long-standing organization that shifted its purpose on the fly. As we introduced earlier in the chapter, they entered a liminal state to create the sweet spot. What if you were a start-up, high-tech firm and decided to go public? Could purpose be balanced with the various requirements of becoming a publicly traded company? Founded in 2005 by Robert Kalin, Chris Maguire and Haim Schoppik, Etsy is an online marketplace for artisans and others to sell unique goods to citizens of the world. Etsy was about to test its purpose.

Since its foundation, Etsy has witnessed remarkable growth. Subsequent to its opening in 2005, Etsy's revenue has grown at an incredible 72 percent annual rate, while their advertising and payment processing revenues have increased by close to 80 percent. The Etsy business model consists of charging artists a listing fee for items to be sold, and a transaction fee on the total cost of the sale price of the good if it is sold. Over time the company has witnessed a 31 percent annual increase in new items listed. With well over 43 million Etsy members and more than one million active Etsy shops in over 200 countries, it is not surprising to discover that Etsy sellers have grossed more than $1.5 billion in annual sales over its tenure.

The company's mission begins to tell a bit about where its purpose lies:

> Etsy's mission is to reimagine commerce in ways that build a more fulfilling and lasting world. We are building a human, authentic and community-centric global and local marketplace. We are committed to using the power of business to create a better world through our platform, our members, our employees and the communities we serve. As we grow, commitment to our mission remains at the core of our identity. It is woven into the decisions we make for the long-term health of our ecosystem, from the sourcing of our office supplies to our employee benefits to the items sold in our marketplace.[17]

Notice how they commit to bettering the world, inclusive of customers, team members and the community. From its inception, Etsy wanted to build an organization that would take into account all stakeholders, not simply profit seekers. It sought to build an ethical business, delivering results through a dedication to value and service, by an engaged workforce. They were not an organization (or a founding leadership team) that put profit *before* purpose. On the contrary, profit became balanced with purpose. As a result, thousands of stakeholders have benefited, including its customers, artists, team members and investors. Let's examine their values as another indicator:

- We are a mindful, transparent and humane business.

- We plan and build for the long term.

- We value craftsmanship in all we make.

- We believe fun should be part of everything we do.

- We keep it real, always.

Etsy Chief Executive Officer, Chad Dickerson, had this to say about purpose: "Etsy is proud to be a part of what I see as the defining trend of 2015 and beyond, an expectation that companies must articulate the social purpose of their businesses to retain customers."[18] Etsy's business model reminded me of a passage from Jeremy Rifkin's book, *The Zero Marginal Cost Society*, which juxtaposes profit versus purpose:

> While the capitalist market is based on self-interest and driven by material gain, the social commons is motivated by collaborative interests and driven by a deep desire to connect with others and share. If the former promotes property rights, caveat emptor, and the search for autonomy, the latter advances open-source innovation, transparency and the search for community.[19]

The technology and investment worlds were abuzz in 2015 as Etsy finally went public and launched an initial public offering (IPO). It was an unusual public offering in that the company allocated 5 percent of its IPO shares to its Etsy vendors before the stock went live on NASDAQ. What it demonstrated, however, was the company's commitment to serving all stakeholders. That is the good news.

In terms of its first day of trading, by all accounts it had a fantastic one with shares gaining 88 percent to $30 on an IPO benchmark of $16. The bad news, however, is that by June of that same year, the stock was trading at $15, almost 7 percent below its IPO price. By December 31st, it had dropped to under $8.26. Despite the fact its 2015 third-quarter financial results witnessed $65.7 million in revenues—a growth of 23 percent year over year— things were not going well with "The Street." Although Etsy announced it had grown its active buyers and sellers list to 1.5 million and 22.6 million, respectively, trouble was brewing and the investment community was growing increasingly impatient. One might look at this as really bad news.

As the company plots a course for its future, the question it will have to ask is if its previously established mission and core values will continue so that it remains committed to balancing purpose with profit. Will it remain in its sweet spot? Will all stakeholders continue to be served, delivering value across the board? Or will the organization succumb to maximizing shareholder value, an affliction that so many publicly traded companies alarmingly succumb to, ultimately failing to shine the lighthouse light on such a plight.

John Mackey, the co-CEO of Whole Foods, believes that in the long run, being purpose-driven produces business benefits. He once wrote, "Although it may seem counterintuitive, the best way to maximize profits over the long term is not to make them the primary goal of the business."[20] Indeed, this is similar feedback to what Mike Desjardins of ViRTUS shared. Only time will tell if Rifkin's point about self-interest and a drive for material gain is lurking inside of Etsy, a company that arguably was already demonstrating *The Purpose Effect*.

Cooking Up Purpose

"We weren't really putting purpose first. We were almost lying to ourselves, faking it."

Those were not the words I was expecting to hear from Brenda Rigney, vice president of People Operations at Earls, but she expressed them nonetheless. "We used to make promises about our purpose and culture, and then we wouldn't do it," she continued. "We didn't know how to make purpose intentional, so we consciously decided to change things. We decided to focus on purpose—on our purpose—so that our employees could understand it, and bring it forward to our customers."

Earls commenced operations in 1982, opening its doors and first location in Edmonton, Alberta, as a family-style restaurant. These days, Earls Restaurants can be found in over 60 different cities including Chicago, Toronto, Miami, Vancouver, Denver and Calgary. It employs over 7,000 people across North America who cook and serve food to over 10 million customers each year.

"We didn't know what we stood for," continued Brenda. "What were we proud of? How does that fit in with the employee life cycle? None of it was clear or intentional, so we had to re-establish our brand, operationalize our culture and define our purpose."

The story of Earls Restaurants Limited is one of transition to eventually create the sweet spot. When Mo Jessa was promoted to president, 25 years after starting at the company as a prep cook, he and Brenda began discussing what was needed to make Earls the career destination place of choice for young people in North America. It was a tall order, you might say.

Earls refers to its team members as partners, and in order to attract new ones (and to retain those already working there), Mo and Brenda felt they had to sort out its purpose. "Until partners see a correlation with what they want in life, with what Earls wants," said Brenda, "in order to get partners to buy in, we wanted the experience of working at Earls to be real, attainable and something the partners wanted themselves. We wanted employees to feel as though Earls was an integral part of their life."

One of the first actions the company took was to redefine its purpose through the development of a new purpose statement. It reads:

> We believe in people living large purposeful lives, filled with fun.

Another transitional action it took was to define new "Leadership Commitments":

- Integrity: The assurance of an ethical environment for all partners. You can expect this.

- Authenticity: What we say we're going to do, is what we do. Authenticity is continuous.

- Something bigger than yourself: Don't talk behind the backs of people. Do everything possible to be present in the moment.

- Cause in the matter: Be the center of change, the epicenter of doing. Everyone can be a leader.

From there, the company began working with legions of chefs, cooks, servers and managers to discuss, teach and learn about purpose and the organization's wishes to improve its operating practices. One particular story Brenda shared with me outlined the benefit of restating its organizational purpose, and how it affected the company's bottom line.

There was one Earls location in particular that was really suffering. Sales were declining, the morale and engagement of its partners were low, and there were some customer service issues that began to percolate. The store was on the verge of collapsing. Tough decisions had to be made. A general manager (GM) who had been in the location for the previous 10 years was moved to another restaurant. A new GM was brought into the struggling restaurant—one who had recently been educated about the new purpose mission of Earls, who adopted the practices right away—and her work began to pay immediate dividends.

After only three months, sales began to increase sharply. Three months after that, profits began to increase, too. Not surprisingly, team member engagement scores went from the low 30s to 75 percent, and customer satisfaction was repaired as well. "This new GM simply believed in a purpose-driven and fun environment, caring about the partners, the guests, the community and herself," said Brenda. "She just began knocking it out of the park for us." Ever the pragmatist, Brenda concluded, "We're always trying to help leaders and partners 'see the purpose light,' but ROI and better numbers do not come overnight. Everyone has to be patient. It's about people . . . not robots and it's these people who have to choose, learn and make mistakes. Purpose is not going to happen instantaneously."

Continuing her pragmatism, in late 2015, Brenda took on another personal purpose challenge, accepting the position of vice president of people operations at Nurse Next Door, a local home care provider. With 100 locations in Canada and the United States and growing, the company provides quality home care assistance that is "about caring, not just health care." As Brenda remarked, "This role fits perfectly within my plan to gain global opportunities and to diversify my industry experience. I loved my time with Earls, with their leaders and transforming the way we think about development, culture and our soul. Earls will redefine careers for young people in the hospitality industry for years to come."

Indispensable Purpose through Disposable Diapers

The story of Earls reminds us that continual effort is required on behalf of the organization (specifically its senior leaders who own the organization's strategy and purpose) and of team members (who own their personal purpose) if the sweet spot is to be achieved for both parties. But so, too, it exposes another fundamental discovery. As with Unilever, any organization currently devoid of a balanced mission will have to enter into a period of transition in order to reach the sweet spot. For-profit organizations may have to solve the imbalance between the need for profit and defining a higher purpose. Some not-for-profit or public sector organizations may have to sort out how to balance power, bureaucracy and the shift to a higher purpose. In any event, it is a transition to such a state.

Authors Teresa Amabile and Steven Kramer state in their book, *The Progress Principle*, "Of all the events that engage people at work, the single most important—by far—is simply making progress at meaningful work."[21] While this point is undoubtedly helpful, as I have argued throughout *The Purpose Effect*, meaningful work comes when there is an alignment between personal, organizational and role purpose. Earls recognized this potential and set about a transition path in which to put it into motion. Unilever did the same by focusing on community and societal improvements only to see team member engagement and various financial metrics correspondingly improve. But what happens if you are an individual seeking to transition?

Meet Kim Graham-Nye. "When I arrived in Australia, I needed money, so I ended up in telecommunications selling airtime." Kim said the money was great, extremely profitable in fact, but the job quickly became meaningless. "I would also lie to people. I wouldn't even tell them I was in telecommunications or what my job was. From there, it got worse. I became solely focused on money. My soul became empty and I got sick. I started asking myself, 'How did I go from being about meaning to being about money?'"

Kim was a 25-year-old recent immigrant to Sydney, trying to figure out her personal purpose. Growing up in Canada, she was supported by two loving parents who provided many lessons in the balance between meaning and a living. When Kim was 12 years old, for example, she witnessed her dad quit his high-paying but somewhat less meaningful job. He did so in order to marry his passions and personal purpose by taking an elite athlete coaching position. It was a pay cut for the family, but it was an early example for Kim to learn from. It was an example of someone who was not in it for the money, but for the pursuit and accomplishment of all facets of *The Purpose Effect*.

During her early days in Sydney, Kim met Jason. They eventually married. Between them for several years, they held various positions, hunting for their personal purpose to materialize. It was an arduous time, but they never lost hope. They continued to develop, define and decide who they wanted to be on this planet. In the early days, Jason was a stock broker, and although very good at it, he recognized something was missing, too. Together, they decided to make some changes. Kim sold the telecommunications business she had started, and Jason left stock broking. As Kim suggested, "Jason observed our lives were a mess, and that we had to make a change."

They began writing a book about "great dates in Sydney." Jason also became a Japanese language teacher. Kim launched an events management company. They began cleaning houses in order to make a mortgage payment. It continued to be a trying time. "There was loads of stress, of wasting time, and not knowing where we were going," she said. Very deliberately, they next decided to have children.

"Our grandparents thought we were absolutely crazy when we announced we were pregnant," said Kim. "I recall a few of those conversations, most ending with 'What the hell are you two doing with your lives, you can't bring children into this world?'" But what both Kim and Jason were adamant about was not caring about how people would see them in the world, rather, what types of contributions they could make in order to improve the world. As it turns out, the first child was a catalyst to finally unleashing their personal purpose and improving the world.

Shortly after giving birth, the couple were shocked by the waste caused by baby diapers. Kim said, "We found out that millions of disposable diapers were being thrown away each year into landfills, and these same diapers utilized 20 times more raw materials than cloth diapers. It also took 500 years for one diaper to biodegrade. We had to do something. It got personal real quick. This was our calling."

In 2005, the couple moved from Sydney to Portland, Oregon, and launched gDiapers, a disposable and home-compostable diaper inserts company. Licensing technology from an inventor and biochemist in Tasmania, the family set into motion the plan to start up a business that was ideally about to fulfill their personal purpose alongside a new type of organizational purpose. From there, they wanted to ensure that their role purpose would be in alignment with the other two categories. The ultimate question was whether they could finally achieve the sweet spot that they had been seeking.

Equally important, Kim and Jason began building the company, ensuring family, society and business could go together. Yes, they had to make a profit, but they wanted to ensure there was balance among all stakeholders. They employed Fair Dinkum, an Australian term that calls on people to be genuine with everyone that they work with. "Fair Dinkum is our bottom line, our values," said Kim. "It affects how we conduct our business, how we interact with people and how we care for the planet. We believe being genuine, real and honest, while demonstrating integrity in everything we do, is everything we ought to be doing."

Some 10 years later, gDiapers is continuing its mission, and its founders remain steadfast in living their lives with purpose. They remain grounded yet committed to organizational and role purpose as well. Their gDiapers team is also thriving with role purpose. They even moved back to Australia, with the business operating globally. "It's this unwavering belief in the pursuit of the greater good, doing business differently," Kim described, "that makes us believe our customers will continue to connect with those values wherever they are, perhaps wherever we are."

She added, "And if for whatever reason gDiapers isn't meant to be, we can take these learnings of the past decade and go do something else. It's our life; we own it. We own our purpose now."

The story of gDiapers and of Kim and Jason is one of transition, from liminality to communitas—the sweet spot. As individuals, they spent years developing, defining and deciding *who* they were, *what* they were about and *how* they were going to approach their lives. They transitioned, eventually coming to a point in which they could state what their personal purpose was all about. When the idea of gDiapers presented itself, they purposely created an organization through the notion of Fair Dinkum, their variant of the Good DEEDS, as a basis for how they wanted to operate.

When their personal purpose and the organizational purpose were aligned, their own roles and those of team members consistently resulted in the purpose mindset. Yes, there were times when the roles became tedious or even difficult (components of the job and career mindsets), but Kim and Jason have never allowed an overarching misalignment between personal, organizational and role purpose to come to fruition. Certainly not to the level that they experienced during those days of cleaning houses and teaching Japanese a decade prior.

The example of gDiapers, of Kim and Jason's background, illustrates *The*

Purpose Effect in full. The alignment of personal, organizational and role purpose is not easy, but nor is it completely out of reach, as Kim and Jason demonstrate.

While this story provides some illustrations of what to do, and what not to do, the final chapter of this book will summarize and highlight additional guidance for team members *and* organizations aiming to create the sweet spot, otherwise known in this chapter as communitas.

CHAPTER NINE
SWEET SPOT GUIDANCE

*It is in the character of growth that we should learn
from both pleasant and unpleasant experiences.[1]*
Nelson Mandela

*What man actually needs is not a tensionless state but rather the striving
and struggling for some goal worthy of him. What he needs is not the
discharge of tension at any cost, but the call of a potential meaning
waiting to be fulfilled by him.[2]*
Viktor Frankl

Marshall McLuhan, the Canadian scholar and media theorist, was famous for coining terms such as "the global village" and "the medium is the message." His prescient thinking is often taken for granted, but, in fact, it was his work and research during the 1960s and 1970s that paved the way for the forms of collaboration and communication we are witnessing in today's constantly connected and Internet-fueled society.

One aspect of McLuhan's research that is less well known is his "tetrad of media effects," which are featured in his posthumous 1988 book, *Laws of Media*. A tetrad simply means a group of four. McLuhan's tetrad was written to help explain the effects technology can have on society. McLuhan proposed four questions (i.e., the tetrad) that helped to explain how technology was changing life itself. Co-authoring the book with his son Eric, they wrote, "We propose no underlying theory to attack or defend but rather a heuristic device, a set of four questions, which we call a tetrad. They can be asked by anyone, anywhere, at anytime, about any human artifact." The questions they posed were:

- What does it enhance or intensify?

- What does it render obsolete or displace?

- What does it retrieve that was previously obsolesced?

- What does it produce or become when pressed to an extreme?[3]

It was not until I put the concept of *The Purpose Effect* through those four questions that the final working thesis for the book clicked into place, allowing me to both sharpen and broaden my thinking. This related to how I thought about purpose in general terms, as well as about personal, organizational and role purpose specifically. The tetrad's questions enabled me to treat the concept of purpose as an artifact—any object made by a human being—but also to lead me to a key lesson: Purpose is all about people.

The results of *The Purpose Effect* tetrad are as follows:

What does *The Purpose Effect* enhance or intensify?

- To develop, define and decide one's personal self becomes core to the purpose journey.

- All stakeholders benefit when organizational purpose is revised to include the Good DEEDS.

- Society prospers when personal, organizational and role purpose are in alignment for a majority of team members in the organization they serve.

- The purpose mindset becomes a continuous transition; always in motion, disentangled from the status quo.

What does *The Purpose Effect* render obsolete or displace?

- Wider disillusionment regarding the true purpose of the organization.

- Disengagement and potentially life dissatisfaction for the team member.

- Increasing levels of societal issues (mental, physical, emotional, financial).

- Widening gaps in pay and power and decreasing levels of productivity and innovation.

THE PURPOSE EFFECT TETRAD

What does *The Purpose Effect* retrieve that was previously obsolesced?

- "There is only one valid definition of business purpose: to create a customer."[4]
—Peter Drucker

- "Communityship: Effective organizations are communities of human beings, not collections of human resources."[5]
—Henry Mintzberg

- "The capacity to hold two opposing ideas at once, then generating a new one that contains elements of the others but is superior to both."[6]
—Roger L. Martin

- "The purpose of a business, in other words, is not to make a profit, full stop."[7]
—Charles Handy

What does *The Purpose Effect* produce or become when pressed to an extreme?
(i.e., the negative consequences due to a lack of purpose)

- Job (paycheck, apathy, disregard) or career (laddering, bullying, greed, power) mindsets.

- Increased levels of team member disengagement and/or disillusionment.

- Harm to society by insistence on shareholder or bureaucratic supremacy.

- Dearth of personal purpose; continued confusion with self-identity leading to angst, health issues and lack of fulfillment.

The stories in this book are about continuous journeys, perpetual transitions from one state to another. People like Bas van Abel, Mary Hewitt, Mana Ionescu, Joe Huff, Bridget Hilton, Kim and Jason Graham-Nye and Tim McDonald, to name a few, have taught me that if one's personal purpose is not evident, defined or being fulfilled, it is time to redefine and rethink what it should be. These people and their stories taught me that the sweet spot is only possible if one is open to change and willing to be fully committed to the journey of transition. That journey is what we call life.

The establishment of an individual's personal purpose is, above all, the only way in which *The Purpose Effect* and the sweet spot can truly come to fruition. The interviews, conversations with friends, tetrad and extensive research led to *The Purpose Effect* model found in its entirety below:

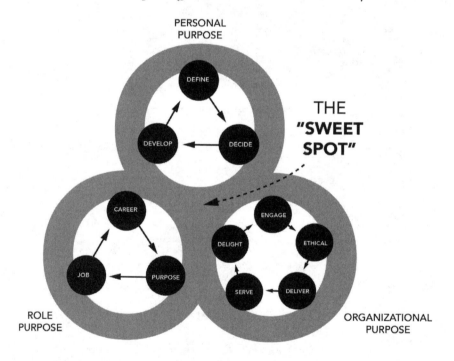

But the sweet spot is elusive. It can suddenly or unexpectedly disappear, too. What was the sweet spot for a team member one day in their role can vanish the next when, for example, an unexpected workforce reduction plan is put into motion. Even after an organization reaches the sweet spot and is fully demonstrating the Good DEEDS, market forces may cause it to deviate from its previously established purpose mindset. Panic ensues, senior management begins making myopic decisions for short-term gains and scores of team members are left wondering what happened. In such scenarios, there can be debilitating effects on a team member's personal purpose. Clearly, the collective also regresses in terms of organizational purpose.

Although this book has focused mainly on the organization and its team members in full-time roles, we must not forget that there is an ever-growing number of people working for multiple organizations at the same time. These contingent or independent workers—not the focal point of this book, but possibly the main attraction in another—are not only on the rise, they, too, pursue a personal purpose in what they do. Despite the fact these types of individuals may be working in multiple roles for more than one organization at a time, it does not absolve an organization from incorporating them in the path toward assisting role-based purpose. Likewise, there are no reasons contingent workers should not reach the sweet spot.

Notwithstanding, all of us must recognize that personal purpose should always be thought of as in perennial motion, something that must be constantly tended to. Throughout the journey—by way of gaining new experiences, insights and knowledge—our personal purpose can shift, too. But an individual must not rely solely on the organization for the sweet spot to materialize. Any alteration in our understanding (and redefinition) of personal purpose requires realignment with the organizations we work for, the roles we fulfill, and our responsibility to society. Anything less than being 100 percent attentive to personal purpose may result in the sweet spot being lost, or never being achieved in the first place.

One key point to surface is that the sweet spot is not the final destination. Rather, it is an outcome of the alignment between personal, organizational and role purpose. If a sense of personal purpose has been lost, the likelihood of organizational or role purpose greatly diminishes. It may even be impossible. After putting *The Purpose Effect* through the tetrad, this was a lesson I learned. My original thesis contested that if a balance between the organization's purpose and purpose in someone's role existed, that life would be better off for the individual, and that personal purpose would either materialize or solidify. I was wrong.

What I discovered is that an individual's sweet spot will manifest if personal purpose becomes the top priority and it is constantly tended to. People must also allow their personal purpose to evolve. Personal purpose can grow and mature so long as team members continue developing, defining and deciding their *what, who* and *how*. While it may start with *why*, as Simon Sinek claims, for the sweet spot to be realized, personal purpose must be in perpetual motion. It must be at the forefront of one's self.

Janice Williams had this to say regarding the need for continuous development and perseverance: "It is entirely possible to be in the sweet spot, happily going about your career, excelling in every way imaginable and then to find that the purpose of the organization has shifted, your role has shifted, or you have shifted in some way, for it all to grind to a heart-crushing halt. The key is to recognize when you are no longer in that sweet spot, to understand yourself, your role, your organization and your environment. Fix it if you can, but if you cannot, you owe it to yourself to believe that another sweet spot is out there. Do whatever you can to get there. Understand yourself, understand the roles you can play well, and find or create an organization that shares your purpose. Persevere—pause if you must, but do not stop."

The focus of this final chapter is to provide guidance to help create and maintain the sweet spot. This is informed both by my research and personal experience, as well as by the individual stories of people we have encountered during the course of this book. Advice is offered for both an individual and organizational perspective.

Guiding Tip—
Write a Personal Declaration of Purpose

In a 2014 *Harvard Business Review* article entitled "From Purpose to Impact," authors Scott Snook and Nick Craig indicated, "Fewer than 20 percent of leaders have a strong sense of their own individual purpose. Even fewer can distill their purpose into a concrete statement."[8]

The consulting group Imperative and New York University corroborated this point. The authors discovered that only 28 percent of the workforce "defines the role of work in their lives primarily as a source of personal fulfillment and a way to help others."[9] If team members do not possess an understanding of their personal purpose, the first step is to create a personal purpose statement. But something stronger is required. It should not be a simple statement, rather a declaration. A necessary action, therefore, is to define a personal "declaration of purpose."

Elango Elangovan believes that for the sweet spot to materialize, deciphering one's personal purpose should become priority number one. "We spend an extraordinary amount of time establishing organizational purpose and role purpose, but we hardly pay attention to personal purpose," said Elango. Through his research and teaching, he has witnessed far too many team members putting extraordinary effort into organizational purpose (mission, vision and values) as well as role purpose (job descriptions, objectives and evaluation criteria) that dwarfs the effort individuals *should* be investing with respect to the definition of one's personal purpose.

"We can't get to the sweet spot without making sense of our personal purpose," he added. Elango believes there is a large deficit between the three types of purpose. Individuals possess the ability to define their personal purpose, but an alarming amount of time is spent on organizational and role purpose instead. "Especially in contrast to organizational and role purpose, where multiple stakeholders shape the outcomes," Elango warned, "my advice would be to invest as much effort, if not more, in figuring out our personal purpose as we would in establishing the other two."[10]

Examples of various personal declarations of purpose were mentioned earlier from the likes of Kelsy Trigg, Jill Schnarr and Michael Bungay Stanier. Perhaps my favorite came from Brian Scudamore of the 1-800-Got-Junk firm. His was simple and to the point: "Make meaning not money."[11]

To create a personal declaration of purpose, individuals can utilize the following techniques:

- Incorporate how you decide to operate your life—how you will show up—each and every day.

- Be succinct, specific and jargon-free, but ensure the declaration is equally expressive.

- Make it personal, make it yours and incorporate strengths, interests and/or core attributes.

Once an individual's personal purpose has been declared, the next step is to ensure they take ownership of what has been crafted. If the declaration is the commitment to "define" one's purpose, acting upon it is to "decide" how someone is going to carry out their purpose each and every day. Each of these actions come from the work we discussed in Chapter 5 regarding personal purpose.

When I created my own personal declaration in the late 1990s, I realized it had to be something that defined me, allowed me to continue developing and forced me to decide how I would behave in any situation. How was I going to show up each and every day? My personal purpose declaration statement has been the following ever since:

> We're not here to see through each other;
> we're here to see each other through.

This declaration has guided me through life-altering decisions, often acting as my personal compass, my North Star. Of any action you plan to take to achieve the sweet spot, based on my research, interviews and personal experience, I cannot stress how important the personal declaration purpose statement can be to your long-term prosperity.

Guiding Tip— Don't Stop Believing (and Developing)

Variety is one of the keys to establishing and maintaining one's personal purpose. For individuals truly to achieve personal purpose, they need to come into contact with a multitude of situations and participate in a variety of projects in order to grow. This also helps individuals learn what is pleasing to them in life. If one stops growing, experiencing and developing, personal purpose may be inhibited. It took Bridget and Joe of LSTN 12 years to sort out their personal purpose. It took Kim and Jason of gDiapers a similar amount of time. Mary Hewitt took even longer. Yes, some people discovered it very early on in their lives—the likes of Mark Zuckerberg, John Lennon and Oprah Winfrey are famous examples—but for most of us, developing, defining and deciding our personal purpose is a long and continuous journey.

Johnsonville Sausage's Cory Bouck is a fan of author Stephen Covey's "best self," concept from the book, *The 8th Habit: From Effectiveness to Greatness.* He sees a connection between one's best self, developing personal purpose and the sweet spot. "Highly skilled, constantly developing, mobile people will always be able to find a role," said Cory, "but when they are living Covey's 'best self' they are more likely to be a high achiever—doing something they love, are good at, that fills a need and feels noble—and that generates the confidence to set out and achieve their own sweet spot."[12] The "best self" Covey outlined in his book refers to what someone is good at—what they love to do—pitted against what needs there are in the world. This is mapped alongside what one's soul and conscience drive them toward. If one is constantly developing themselves toward a "best self," it can help them reach personal purpose.

There are certain tactics I recommend for individuals to help create and continue developing their personal purpose.

If it is available, team members could participate in programs such as a short-term rotation, job shadowing, as well as being part of cross-departmental project teams. Exposing oneself to a variety of experiences and opportunities at work is critical to increased knowledge and learning. Outside of work, there are innumerable ways in which one can help develop their personal purpose. Joining a club, volunteering at the community center, registering for a local program, being part of your city's various initiatives or meeting new people at local events are ways to learn from others in the attempt to develop and hone personal purpose. Of course, any type of formal, informal or social learning opportunity is going to assist as well.

The concept of networking and building relationships is also important. Team members who have warm relations with people across various stake-holders—internally and externally—will feel more connected to their life, role and organization. When someone is connected to other human beings, they end up feeling a greater sense of self-worth. The Grant Study from Harvard University, for example, famously proved that people who were more connected with others were three times as likely to have achieved success compared to those without such relationships.[13]

Phil Noelting is the founder and CEO of Qwalify, an organization committed to creating intuitive technology to power the future of hiring. He, too, believes networking and relationship building are key to personal purpose. "To me, it all comes down to relationships—from professors and advisers, to colleagues and customers, people are what bring real purpose and meaning. Not only did I find my purpose and current opportunities through these relationships, but they are also the glue that keeps everything that we do together, on track and constantly pushing forward. With alignment in vision and ambition, the purpose becomes much more than a job that brings a paycheck; it's a mission powered and empowered by people and relationships. Every day is a new opportunity to further that purpose, and we are all more confident and able knowing we are living that purpose together."[14]

In addition to relationships, when a team member seeks to improve a cause or situation, research also suggests it can lead to personal purpose. We might say there is "joy in giving," which in turn creates a "helper's high." Through the act of giving, individuals end up stimulating areas in the brain associated with trust, social connection and pleasure, creating a "warm glow" feeling for their contributions. It is these types of activities that can also prompt the development of one's purpose.[15]

Jeffrey Puritt of TELUS chimed in on this point about giving. "An example of the sweet spot for many of our team members is around 'We give where we live,' a core pillar and essential element of our culture to give back to the communities where we live, work and serve. Corporate social responsibility drives the engagement of our team members and also acts as a draw for recruiting. Our team members, particularly this next generation of millennials, are proud to work for a company that shares their values and supports causes that are important to them. Ultimately, if employees are aligned with and truly engaged in a company, they develop that deep sense of trust and respect that drives them to do remarkable things for their peers, their organization, their customers and the community where they live, work and serve."[16]

Building upon one's networking skills (and boosting relationships), getting involved inside *and* outside of work, being exposed to variety, adapting to be a constant learner and becoming a contributory or giving person are likely to assist in the development of personal purpose. The ultimate point to remember is that people continually need to be developing if they are to remain in the purpose mindset and within the sweet spot itself. The "best self" *is* out there, but as Tim McDonald suggested with a contrarian opinion, "Stop trying to establish the sweet spot and start discovering where it already exists."[17] To *discover* the sweet spot, however, requires the individual to be constantly *developing* themselves, *defining* and *deciding* how they want to be each and every day.

Guiding Tip— Write an Organizational Declaration of Purpose

John Cage, famous essayist and artist, once wrote, "Look at everything. Don't close your eyes to the world around you. Look and become curious and interested in what there is to see."[18] A team member's role-based purpose mindset is aided by an organization that commits to a purposeful way of operating. Thus it is the organization that must be opening its eyes to the world around it.

As we have discovered, those organizations fixated solely on profit or power often do not enable an individual's personal or role-based purpose. For many it does the opposite. When team members are empowered to help, innovate and collaborate—be it with one another, customers, the community or society—both the organization and the team members benefit. Most individuals are on a quest for recognized self-worth in their work in order to provide benefits to others.

To help achieve this state, an organization's senior leadership team could start by redefining its organizational purpose. It is a tall order, but one that can pay huge dividends. By establishing a purpose-first strategic intent that serves the interests of all stakeholders, an organization likely will have far greater buy-in from its team member population to achieve its mission and objectives. When team members are bought in and able to demonstrate purpose in their role, the organizational benefits begin to quickly accrue. Thus, the creation of an organizational "declaration of purpose"—as we discussed for personal purpose—helps deliver *The Purpose Effect*.

Rick Wartzman is the executive director of the Drucker Institute at Claremont Graduate University. He believes that leaders have to be much clearer about their organization's larger purpose in order for both individuals and the collective to enjoy success in the future. He said, "It begins with a clear understanding of who their customer is, what the customer values and needs and how the organization is fulfilling that need."[19]

Rick has been studying purpose for years. In *Fortune Magazine,* he once wrote, "In an era in which cultivating talent is increasingly essential, building a deep and authentic sense of purpose could be a company's ultimate competitive advantage."[20] This was in response to his discovery that Unilever was in the number three spot on LinkedIn's "most sought-after employers in the world" list. Unilever's quest to ensure both the declaration of organizational purpose as well as profits is somewhat unique, but so, too, is its insistence that team members be treated fairly and that talent development programs align to its "purpose first" mission. Unilever's declaration of purpose is "to make sustainable living commonplace. We work to create a better future every day, with brands and services that help people feel good, look good and get more out of life."[21]

Another example is Quicken Loans, a financial lending company. The United States' largest online retail mortgage lender and second largest overall retail lender firmly believes purpose balanced with profit is the key component to both team member and organizational health. The firm encourages its team members to "chase the skills that will make you great at what you are doing or what you are building" and not to chase money because "then, and only then, do the better numbers or the good money follow you." Not only does the firm believe customers are their primary focus, its purpose includes the development of its people in a way that reinforces a "money doesn't come first" distinction. Quicken Loans' declaration is "Every client, every time, no exceptions, no excuses."[22]

To create an organizational declaration of purpose, the following techniques may be helpful:

- Embed stakeholders into the declaration, ensuring all applicable interest groups are addressed.

- Be succinct, specific and jargonless, but ensure it is equally expressive.

- Make it relatable to both customers and team members.

There are examples from organizations in machinery, grocery and clothing we can learn from too, including:

- John Deere: We are committed to serving those linked to the land, thereby helping to improve living standards for people everywhere.[23]

- Whole Foods: Helping support the health, well-being and healing of both people—customers, team members and business organizations in general—and the planet.[24]

- Patagonia: Build the best product, cause no unnecessary harm, use business to inspire and implement solutions to the environmental crisis.[25]

Guiding Tip—
Serve All Stakeholders

Of course, if an organization is going to create a declaration of purpose, it should also be prepared to serve all of its stakeholders. The importance of such a change is arguably best summarized by Frank Abrams, chairman of Standard Oil of New Jersey in the late 1940s and early 1950s. In a 1951 public address, Abrams remarked, "The job of management is to maintain an equitable and working balance among the claims of the various directly affected interest groups . . . stockholders, employees, customers and the public at large. Business managers are gaining professional status partly because they see in their work the basic responsibilities to the public that other professional men have long recognized as theirs."[26] Imagine that. The chairman of an oil company urging us to balance an organization's purpose against the needs of all stakeholders.

There is a fairly easy way to summarize all of the stakeholders the organization ought to be serving. If it is putting its customers first, it does so through its team members (who are ideally engaged, demonstrating personal and role-based purpose) who then aim to assist the community in which they live, and the society they are a part of. Additionally, the organization will provide a return to owners and/or shareholders where applicable. Of course, this is an outcome of a properly aligned strategy that addresses the needs of other stakeholder groups *before* shareholders:

- Customers

- Team Members

- Community

- Society

- Owners/Shareholders (if applicable)

To actually serve all stakeholders, a few more steps and considerations might be contemplated for each of these groups.

Customers:
Outline the importance of your customers by redesigning all organizational

practices to prioritize and serve the customer first. Regardless of business unit, objective or geography, all team members must be aligned with the reason the organization exists in the first place. This ought to be the common DNA for all team members, everywhere. Then, if you are not doing so already, survey your customer base regularly for insights and feedback. This sort of customer intelligence ensures the organization is meeting or exceeding customer service levels, but it also aligns the entire organization to its organizational purpose.

Mark Colgate, Associate Dean of the University of Victoria, suggests three key attributes be continually demonstrated and assessed: reliability, responsiveness and relationship. An organization must be looked upon as reliable (does what it commits to), responsive (proactive versus reactive) and then relatable to the customer. As Mark said, "It's about the warmth and wonder of the human conversation, even remembering the customer's name, giving them special attention and asking questions so you can get to know them even more."[27] These "three Rs" could become factors that help the organization determine whether it is indeed putting its customers first. Additional customer actions are detailed later.

Team Members:

Whether directly or indirectly, any customer deserves to be served by an engaged team member. To offer an interaction between a team member and a customer that is unreliable, unresponsive or failing to be relatable can often be pinpointed to a disengaged individual. But a team member equally deserves to work in an engaging, connected, collaborative and open environment in their place of work. Anything less is a failure on behalf of an organization's senior leadership team to recognize the importance of team members and their contributions to its overarching mission. To create an organizational culture in which a majority of the team members are engaged, may I recommend putting into action the ideas contained within my first book, *FLAT ARMY*.

This book aims to cultivate an environment that results in "an unobstructed flow of corporate commonality." *FLAT ARMY* in its simplest form refers to the point at which all team members act as a unified corporate organism using clear and succinct goals. When an organization is united such that duplication is negated and a selfless amount of collaboration is the norm—when it no longer operates a culture of "command and control," but rather one of "engage and empower"—it has become an open, engaged and connected *FLAT ARMY*. With a view specific to *The Purpose Effect*, some distinct organizational engagement actions are outlined below in another guiding tip example.

Community:

Jill Schnarr is a staunch proponent of doing good in the community. Jill argues that, "Organizations need to think beyond profit and product and have a social mission or vision that makes their employees feel as if they are contributing to a greater good." She claims, "A team member's objectives must be tied back to the overall company mission, and they must have a clear understanding of how their activities impact the overall corporate performance and social mandate."[28]

The importance of Jill's observation is subtle, but important. As we have been detailing, the mission and mandate of the organization (its purpose) must be redefined and declared to involve all stakeholders. As we have discussed, it must then also include the community. What does that mean? Somewhat obviously, any organization operates and is located in a community. Perhaps it operates in several. Multi-nationals can conduct business in hundreds of communities. Whatever the scenario, the organization must consider giving back to the community in which it operates, for the community is a part of the organization's purpose.

The easiest manner in which to serve the community is through organizational sponsorship of volunteering. It can manifest through labor (e.g., cleaning up garbage), compassion (e.g. donating time at a hospice) or intellect (e.g. teaching at a local school or retirement center). But, of course, any organization should also be earmarking a portion of its budget or revenues for the community, donating money on top of volunteer time. Most for-profit companies do give, but the question quickly becomes "how much?" The average giving since the early 1980s has amounted to 2 percent of pre-tax profits. Between direct financial giving and in-kind gifts, I argue that the percentage amount should be far greater. For public sector organizations, there really is nothing stopping them from attributing a small portion of their budget to further community causes. After all, public sector team members live in the community, too.

Society:

Take a moment to observe what you are currently wearing. Now picture the contents of your closet. What do you see? You may not know it, but the social impact on the production of clothes is often harming our society, our planet. In Tiruppur, India, researchers found dyeing and bleaching units from local garment factories were generating 87 million liters of untreated wastewater per day, most of it dumped into the Noyyal River. Not surprisingly, locals have reported large increases in health defects and other immune issues. In Bangladesh, four million garment workers across the country make less than $100 a month each in wages. Cotton farmers in Africa and Central America use pesticides with faulty or dated equipment, while pickers, including children, are exposed to toxins, ingest the poison and suffer some form of malady thereafter.[29]

The garment industry is but one example of how we are detrimentally affecting society in our quest for profit and/or power among other organizational inanities. Emissions, pollutants, water utilization, electricity consumption and other environmental factors cannot continue to be treated as greenwashed promises. As it considers all of its stakeholders, the organization likewise must prioritize improvements in the way it treats our physical society. Fairphone and gDiapers are excellent examples of organizations getting it right. Next, an organization must ensure its labor practices are fair and ethical. Whether onshore or abroad, how an organization treats its team members, contractors, suppliers or partners must become better than today's practices. Safe and healthy work environments are a must. Fair living wages are another absolute. These types of factors ought to be targeted, tracked and made publicly available. I discuss this tactic in *The Purpose Effect* scorecard below.

Owners/Shareholders:

Lynn Stout argues in her book, *The Shareholder Value Myth*, "Many people are 'pro-social,' meaning they are willing to sacrifice at least some profits to allow the company to act in an ethical and socially responsible fashion." She adds, "Others care only about their own material returns."[30] To achieve this, it is going to take serious courage and gumption on the part of senior leaders to eliminate the latter and improve the former.

A profit is obviously required for a for-profit organization to stay in business. But how much is enough? Of course, as history has demonstrated and as I have shown here, increased profits and revenues—upheld at all costs, including team member layoffs amid other unethical acts—are tied to stock market price gaming and stock option rewards. William Lazonick pointed this out in a Roosevelt Institute white paper when he wrote, "This toxic combination [stock market manipulation and stock-based pay as incentives] is at the core of the failure of the U.S. economy to achieve stable and equitable economic growth."[31]

There have been many opponents to the adage, "maximizing shareholder value," backing up Roger L. Martin's thesis in his book, *Fixing the Game*. What to do? The problem, sadly, is far too complex to unravel in this book. But more guidance comes from Charles G. Koch, chairman and CEO of Koch Industries, Inc. He has gone on record as never having been guided by the maximization of profit, rather the creation of value. Koch wrote in his book, *Good Profit*, "Our vision is based on what we believe is the role of business in society: providing products and services that customers value more than their alternatives while more efficiently using resources. Consequently, we strive to profit only from benefiting both our customers and society as a whole."[32] The pursuit of profit must be balanced by the benefits derived by customers and broader society, too. Maximizing shareholder value is not a goal, rather an outcome of a purpose-driven organization. As Roger L. Martin previously outlined, perhaps stock options and restricted stock units should simply be eliminated as features of the compensation portfolio in favor of actual cash awards.

For each of the five stakeholders an organization now aims to serve, I recommend setting targets and to then publicly publish the results to a new dashboard website. This is not a Corporate Social Responsibility document or report. It is a thoroughly defined and proactive set of targets and measures that are established, which the organization holds itself accountable to on a quarterly and annual basis. CSR documents tend to be reactive and, too often, toothless. A cumulative score or target can be created from all targets measured against all stakeholders, one we will coin *The Purpose Effect* scorecard. This is applicable for public sector, not-for-profit and for-profit entities as well.

An inability to meet the overall targets does not result in lip service either but genuine penalties. How? The easiest penalty might be adjusting remuneration. If an organization is publicly traded, part of the punitive measure ought to be related to a decreased level of RSUs (restricted stock units) and/or stock options awards. Various governance protocols could be put in place to ensure this occurs. The penalties might be applicable to only senior leaders. The resulting effect would not result in previously issued RSUs or stock options being rescinded, rather a lower allotment being made available in the pool for that year. That seems both fair and ethical. Taking it a step further would be to—as mentioned earlier—eliminate any type of RSU or stock option award in favor of a cash bonus pool. This may stop executives and boards from "gaming" the stock market system and the fabrication of stock price volatility. (Read the book, *Fixing the Game*, for more information.)

If an organization has either a profit-sharing pool, annual-bonus pool or annual-salary increase pool—with the latter occurring in any type of organization—those, too, could be earmarked for penalties or, even better, in rewards. For example, if targets are set that are met or exceeded, accordingly the organization can reward team members at all levels for a job well done with increased outcomes that financially benefit all team members. The program does not have to be thought of as only punitive in nature. Perhaps the organization could take things even farther with additional benefits being applied to the community if results were positive. Imagine how motivated the team members would become if the organization commits to donating more of its profit to the community if targets were met. Imagine how the reputation of the organization could increase in the eyes of its customers and community citizens. Imagine how that may positively impact customer satisfaction and in some cases revenues or profits.

The targets that are set annually and then tracked quarterly (and publicly published) ought to include the following:

- **Customers:** customer satisfaction scores through various factors including reliability, responsiveness and relationship. Other metrics could be devised by the organization.

- **Team Members:** engagement scores and sub-drivers, diversity breakdown, acts of internal recognition, positional changes/promotions and learning and development expenditure.

- **Community:** team member volunteer hours, organizational philanthropic investment, in-kind donations, number of community members impacted, etc.

- **Society:** CO_2 and greenhouse gas (GHG) reductions, water utilization/reuse, energy consumption/redesign, material consumption/lessening. Other examples from the Dow Jones Sustainability Indices (DJSI) could also be utilized.

- **Owners/Shareholders** (applicable to for-profit firms): Profitability, revenue and shareholder return (if publicly traded), but all metrics set to levels that are appropriately fair.

Each stakeholder holds a 20 percent share of the overall scorecard. (In the case of public sector or not-for-profit organizations, the first four stakeholder groups are utilized, each accounting for a 20 percent share, but the final stakeholder might be renamed "budget," ensuring the organization does not overspend. Each of the measurement categories found within each stakeholder also can be broken down by a percentage weight. For example, under Community, the organization determines how many hours it should be volunteering, its community investment level and amount of in-kind donations. These are raw values. But the three categories (and others if it chooses) are then broken down by a weighting. Perhaps volunteering holds a 50 percent weight, whereas community investment and in-kind donations hold 25 percent each. Whatever gets reported then feeds the 20 percent category of Community, which then feeds the overall score of *The Purpose Effect*.

When the organization achieves its overall target for the year, that is the point when other incentives kick in. An example of *The Purpose Effect* scorecard for a for-profit organization is outlined below:

THE PURPOSE EFFECT SCORECARD
(EXAMPLE FOR ILLUSTRATION PURPOSES ONLY)

CUSTOMERS

	WEIGHTING		RESULT	
	· 20%		18.2%	
	Target	FY Result	Weight	Result
Reliability	75%	70%	33%	31%
Relationship	90%	95%	33%	35%
Relatedness	80%	60%	33%	25%

TEAM MEMBERS

	WEIGHTING		RESULT	
	20%		19.4%	
	Target	FY Result	Weight	Result
Engagement	77%	73%	50%	48%
Diversity	50%	35%	20%	14%
Positional	150	170	20%	23%
L&D Spend	$1m	$1.2m	10%	12%

COMMUNITY

	WEIGHTING		RESULT	
	20%		24.2%	
	Target	FY Result	Weight	Result
Volunteer Hours	600	900	40%	60%
Investment	$500K	$550K	30%	33%
In-kind Donations	$1.5m	$1.4m	30%	28%

SOCIETY

	WEIGHTING		RESULT	
	20%		21%	
	Target	FY Result	Weight	Result
GHG CO_2 (tons)	25T	24T	40%	38%
H_2O (liters)	500L	450L	20%	22%
Energy (kWh)	200k	180k	40%	44%

OWNERS/SHAREHOLDERS

	WEIGHTING		RESULT	
	20%		20.8%	
	Target	FY Result	Weight	Result
Revenues ($)	$5m	$5.2m	50%	52%
EBITDA ($)	$500k	$520k	50%	52%

SUMMARY

	WEIGHTING	RESULT
Customers	20%	18.2%
Team Members	20%	19.4%
Community	20%	24.2%
Society	20%	21.0%
Owners/Sharesholders	20%	20.8%

Organizational Target:	100%
Organizational Result:	103.6%

Guiding Tip—
Delight and Deliver Value to Your Customers

Regardless of its makeup, an organization exists for its customers. As we have discussed, an organization's purpose is not to drive shareholder value, for that is an outcome of delivering sound customer value. An organization's purpose is not to uphold power or to "command and control" team members either. The organization ought to be initiating and committing to a strategy that ensures it is putting its "customers first." Whether the organization is for-profit, not-for-profit or public sector, securing and serving a customer—delivering value throughout the entirety of the relationship—is the only reason an organization exists. Customers *are* the primary stakeholders.

An organization ought to embed all facets of its customers-first paradigm into as many outlets as possible, including learning and development, community investment, recognition practices, recruitment, succession planning, performance development, as well as all communication channels and methods. It is highly advantageous to embed the customers-first strategy into all go-to-market processes as well (e.g., marketing, supply chain, partnering). It takes time, but once the organization makes the decision to put the customer first, all practices are in need of being rewired, redeveloped and reconciled due to pre-existing norms and processes.

In addition to the organizational declaration of purpose, a corresponding set of customers-first values and behavioral attributes should also be developed. These new and updated values and attributes become the basis on which the team members and the organization operate with one another, delighting and serving the customer. When the customer is put first, the organization more easily can rally around the common cause.

While organizations like Qwalify, Lightspan Digital and Etsy have the benefit of being relatively young firms that established their customers-first, service-oriented culture from inception, that does not mean older organizations cannot alter their operating practices and put its customers first, too.

By way of example, TELUS, which dates from 1880, developed 11 values attributes in 2010. These focused on its customers-first strategy launched the same year. In 2012, it then developed "Customers First Commitments" that further aligned behavior to customer interaction expectations. Both were created through hundreds of team member focus groups, online discussions and contributions. It might have taken longer to achieve the end result, but it created an earlier level of team member engagement and buy-in. The customer-first commitments that TELUS eventually introduced included:

- We take ownership of every customer experience.

- We work as a team to deliver on our promises.

- We learn from customer feedback and take action to get better, every day.

- We are friendly, helpful and thoughtful.

While it is true the commitments support the organization's values and attributes, they are also the basis for its various customer service feedback practices. Each quarter, TELUS surveys customers in the consumer, enterprise and health segments, asking key questions that map back to its declaration, strategic intent, values, attributes and commitments. An overall score is assigned—called likelihood to recommend—and documented on the company's corporate scorecard. It is an example of alignment between putting customers first and measuring progress and satisfaction.

Any organization intent on bringing added worth to its customers should align team members' objectives to its customers-first mission. The hardwiring of accountabilities—be it individually or team-based—for putting customers first should be embedded in each team member's way of operating going forward. It is this sort of alignment that ensures the customer will, in fact, be delighted and delivered value. A failure to align can lead to many of the issues we surfaced in Chapters 3 and 4.

Guiding Tip— Create an Engaging Workplace and Be Ethical

Regardless of your role at work, ask yourself this question:

Am I *a part* of the organization I work for, or am I *apart* from it?

When I am working with team members on various aspects of culture, engagement or collaboration practices, I invariably ask this question. More often than not, the answer is quick. "I am *a part* of it," they respond. Various data points suggest a large swath of individuals are actually *apart* from the organization they work for. There are a few guiding tips to surface— between engagement practices and instituting an ethical workplace—that can help shift this predicament and support team members to achieve a purpose mindset in their role.

Direct face time with your manager is another tip to help create an engaged workplace. A study from management consulting firm, Leadership IQ, suggested team members who spend approximately six hours per week with their direct supervisor are far more likely to deliver results and become engaged than those who do not. The research indicates individuals are 29 percent more inspired, 16 percent more innovative, 15 percent more intrinsically motivated and 30 percent more engaged at work when spending at least six hours per week with their manager. Unfortunately, the data also suggests that leaders are currently spending three hours or less per week interacting with their team members. In fact, 20 percent spend only one hour per week working alongside their direct leader.[33]

In a column Sir Richard Branson wrote on his company's website, he stated, "We give our people real autonomy, and celebrate their achievements by identifying star contributors, highlighting brand ambassadors in our internal newsletters and hosting parties for individual employees."[34] Recognition is another critical lever to improve the delivery of results and engagement. Implementing sound recognitions practice will also help team members reach the purpose mindset in their roles. As Josh Bersin, Principal at Bersin by Deloitte, pointed out, "We found that 'high-recognition companies' have 31 percent lower voluntary turnover than companies with poor recognition cultures."[35] It literally pays to introduce and inculcate a culture of recognition. For the giver of recognition, as Paul Zak, neuroscientist at Claremont University, informed us, the hormone oxytocin is released, which creates joy and happiness in ourselves.

Another piece of guidance deals with flexible work. If a team member is expected to contribute, the question to ask is whether the work can be performed from anywhere. If it can, let the work *be* performed from anywhere. There are many roles where a team member is required to be on-site: hair stylists, painters, construction workers, restaurant cooks, etc. But there are many more where the work can be performed from home or in other mobile situations. By recognizing that team members can work from anywhere, an organization is far more likely to become purposeful. This has been proven to lead to increased engagement. Not only that, the organization is building up trust with the team member to do what is right (from wherever) as it continues with the mission to put its customers first.

The second half of this section pertains to an organization's ethics. The Ethics Resource Center discovered, "In stronger ethical cultures, employees feel engaged and committed to the company."[36] Ethics ought to rest at the core of your organization, as opposed to sitting on the periphery. When it comes to ethics, it must be established at the top, and it has to be demonstrated each and every day. Prioritizing an ethical culture is a critical step to gaining the respect of customers, team members and the community in the pursuit of becoming a purpose-based organization.

While the world has certainly witnessed enough ethical question marks from the likes of Enron, Worldcom, Volkswagen and Tyco, financially motivated misgivings are only half the problem. If the organization were to devise a standard of ethics regarding its financials—and holds itself accountable to those standards—questions regarding what to do and what not to do become rather moot. Organizations could include standards that address our place in society inclusive of "doing good" in the community. The standards of ethics that the organization creates is a publicly available document outlining what the organization stands for and how it operates ethically at all times.

Once the standards have been developed, the next step is to set targets, which are incorporated into *The Purpose Effect* scorecard. The targets are not frivolous nor are they marketing attempts to "greenwash" any social or sustainability responsibility either. The dashboard is a proactive action to outline how the organization will act ethically over its next fiscal year, regardless of it being for-profit or not. The problem with the current state of CSR publications is that they merely summarize what the organization accomplished in the previous year. It does not go far enough.

Many organizations use this document to justify its attempts at becoming ethical within the community and society itself. Although a summary document is fine, to truly become ethical across all stakeholders, it behooves the organization to be proactive and to publicly set its targets. It should then be held accountable by society, community citizens and shareholders alike, if applicable. In other words, there ought to be a day where organizations stop producing the CSR document and start establishing targets that are publicly available on its website and updated quarterly with results. As previously discussed, the outcomes can materialize in various rewards or penalties for senior team members.

Final Words of Advice

While *The Purpose Effect* is unambiguous, it does take hard work, perseverance and an ability between the individuals *and* the organization to achieve the sweet spot. It is not impossible, but it can and will be difficult. Choices must be made. Decisions may even be painful. But remember, your effort stands in close proximity to your will. After all, it was Pythagoras, Greek philosopher and mathematician, who once observed, "Ability and necessity dwell near each other."[37]

This book was written for both individuals *and* organizational leaders. Regardless of your role or position within or in relation to the organization, you can put into action the ideas written, or you can let things lie dormant and hope for the best. I sincerely wish you choose the former.

During my interviews, many individuals provided thoughts and advice regarding the achievement of the sweet spot. It was not called "the sweet spot" when I started writing this book, but after three years of researching, interviewing and thinking, I went back to a few of them to see what they thought about the intersection between personal, organizational and role purpose. The feedback ranged between the expectations of team members, leaders and the organization.

Michael Papay advised that the quality of a relationship between a team member and the organization is at its best when each party cares as much about the success and well-being of the other as it does themselves. Perhaps it is a form of mutual altruism. Michael remarked:

Under this symbiotic relationship bound by mutual trust and respect, each party will support one another as they respectively shape and evolve their purpose. That's the sweet spot; that's when the magic happens.

Mana Ionescu of Lightspan Digital suggested a 360-degree view of purpose is required to be successful:

> To create alignment, you first have to fully understand the three purposes. I've worked with large and small businesses, and one thing is pervasive: Individuals may know their purpose but not that of the organization and vice versa. All three have to be very clear, and we have to be open to put in the work to fully understand. That understanding will not be magically given to us. We have to become "good listeners" of purpose if we want to find the sweet spot.

Kelsy Trigg believed that the collective good of all team members was forever omnipresent, but that it is the leaders' responsibility to help build a purposeful culture which leads to the sweet spot:

> Create an inclusive environment where team members can show up with their "whole selves" because it's the unique strengths we each have that tap into "purpose."

Brenda Rigny, now of Nurse Next Door, wanted us to remember personal purpose comes first in the quest toward the sweet spot:

> Teach your people to create a vision for their life and create authentic goals to mobilize their vision. Once your people create their own purpose, they will see how their personal goals link to your company's goals.

Harvard Business Review editor and author, Julia Kirby, provided pragmatic advice for individuals to achieve the sweet spot:

> Set goals for mastery of new skills and achieve them. Generously help others achieve their goals. Make friends with colleagues. Always take the high road and don't engage in office politics or intrigue. Learn to suffer fools.

Herminia Ibarra, Professor of Organizational Behavior at INSEAD cautioned that not everyone will be able to achieve a sense of purpose in their role unless they continue developing:

I advise people to always take the time for extracurricular activities and side projects that allow them to explore new avenues and different facets of themselves, and then let their experience with these be a guide to finding the sweet spot.

Along the same lines, Megan Smith encouraged us to "know thyself":

Know your strengths, talents, passions and, almost as importantly, your challenges, weaknesses and dislikes. If you are in tune with these, you're bound to find a role that brings you a sense of purpose because you likely do it well, and you will likely love doing it.

Box of Crayons' Michael Bungay Stanier advised us to be comfortable with discomfort:

The sweet spot is less a gentle overlap between three categories of purpose, and more the result of dynamic tension between three often contradictory demands. So the first is to understand there will be tension. Which means, the more you're willing to "sit with" the discomfort of it, the better. There will be awkward conversations and moments of doubt, and that's just part of the deal of pursuing this.

Tim Kastelle, Associate Professor at the UQ Business School within the University of Queensland, wants both team members and the organization to define its purpose, but to ensure both groups are solving important problems for society:

This might sound trivial, but you have to really think through what your purpose is—both as an individual and as an organization. Too many take this for granted. The point that then follows is: Focus on solving important problems. I was recently talking with a colleague about a start-up. They're building an app that you use when you make a bet with a friend. You register the bet, and then it forces your mate (or you) to pay up once it's settled. They've got investors lining up for miles to give them money. And it's for the most trivial problem imaginable, with an incredibly impoverished view of friendship (and humanity). That's anti-purpose. Who wants to devote their careers to forcing friends to pay off bets? People and firms really need to think this through—why do we exist? What is the problem that we're obsessed with? How will we make the world a better place?

At the close of Chapter 2, I promised to refrain from any further autobiographical examples. As the book comes to a close, I will deviate ever so slightly and end things with one final, personal anecdote.

I have had the good fortune of leading people and teams since 1998. I never sought out leadership roles; rather, I sought out positions that would fuel my personal purpose, as long as the organization was in alignment with my values and wishes. Not surprisingly, I have learned that people come and go during your work life. Whether you are leading them directly or working with them indirectly, people changes are constant in an organization. Some people exit through painful layoff procedures. Others continue to seek out their personal purpose taking on new roles elsewhere. Some decide to have a family and never come back to work. Some go back to school, perhaps heeding the advice to be constantly developing. There are others who retire. There are those who are contingent workers, only there for a short period of time.

One act that is relatively constant among anyone who leaves the organization is the good-bye email.

I must be approaching 500 such emails. The pattern is eerily similar. It does not matter if they were working with me, employed on another team or working for another firm outside of my own organization; the cadence and tone are relatively consistent. A fictitious example follows:

> Today is my last day, and I'm moving on from <insert organization name> to do <whatever is next>. For the past <insert number of years> I have enjoyed my time at <insert organization name>. We did some great things together such as <insert long line of accomplishments>.

> But it is the people that I will miss. How lucky am I to have worked with you for these years? I am going on to be <insert role name or life adventure> but rest assured I will look back with fond memories on my time with you. Saying good-bye is the hardest thing to do, because I won't be able to work with you at <insert organization name> on a daily basis going forward. Please stay in touch. Here is my personal email address.

Pasted below is an actual excerpt from one of those 500 emails I have received. So as to ensure anonymity, I have removed the date, name and anything identifiable:

> Retirement—I'm ready! Work—I don't think I'll miss it. Co-workers—yes, I'm going to miss each and every one of you.
>
> With tears of sadness, I say thank you to all of you for being such a wonderful group of people to work with. It truly has been a pleasure.
>
> I wish for all of you a retirement (or better yet, a winning lottery ticket!) that comes sooner rather than later so that you, too, can be a part of that magical world where you get paid not to work.

My point?

I would like to see the "lottery ticket" this individual wrote about become the harmony that is found between one's life, their organization and their role. The lottery ticket ought to become the sweet spot. We should not be gambling on a life without work. We must not be wagering on a role that delivers no meaning. We need not parlay an organization's quest for profit and/or power as accepted practice.

Ultimately, we cannot be living a life *without purpose*. We cannot be working for an organization *devoid of purpose*.

Each of us deserves a life where we get paid to fulfill our purpose, in an organization that consciously chooses to do good.

An individual without personal purpose is rudderless against any body of water. Organizations lacking a higher purpose must not calcify into common wisdom. A team member bereft of role purpose is a needless calamity.

Let us now deliver the sweet spot and commit to not souring it. We must not demur.

Let us—both team members and the organization—espouse a more purposeful, hopeful society.

Let us live and work a life of purpose.

Let us now affect *The Purpose Effect.*

Faber est suae quisque fortunae.

ABOUT THE AUTHOR
DAN PONTEFRACT
Author, Speaker, Chief Envisioner

Besides *The Purpose Effect*, Dan is the author of the bestselling leadership book, *FLAT ARMY: Creating a Connected and Engaged Organization* (May 2013). He is Chief Envisioner of TELUS Transformation Office, a future-of-work consulting group that helps organizations enhance corporate culture, leadership, learning, work styles and collaboration practices. He is a passionate leader in the leadership and social collaboration technology spaces and is uniquely skilled to ensure an organization can move from traditional cultures to healthier ways of working.

His career is interwoven with both corporate and academic experience, coupled with an MBA, B.Ed. and multiple industry certifications and accreditations. Dan is also a renowned speaker, including three different TED talks, and has appeared on the front cover of *T+D Magazine* and *Chief Learning Officer Magazine*.

In 2010, Dan was acknowledged by CLO as a "Vanguard Award" winner and is a two-time winner by the Corporate University Best in Class Awards of the "Leader of the Year" in both 2010 and 2011. In 2012, SkillSoft awarded Dan the "Learning Leader of the Year" for his work at TELUS, and CLO Magazine bestowed the "Learning in Practice Innovation Award" as well. He is also the recipient of the 2012 Brandon-Hall "Gold Award in Strategy & Governance." In 2014, his team became a nine-time winner of the prestigious "ATD BEST" award.

He and his wife, Denise, have three young children (Claire, Cole and Cate) and live in Victoria, Canada.

You can reach Dan on Twitter (@dpontefract) or via his personal site at www.danpontefract.com. Dan also writes on *Forbes, Harvard Business Review* and *The Huffington Post*.

INDEX

1-800-Got-Junk, 10, 147, 181

1950 Performance Rating Act in
America, 75

*7 Habits of Highly Effective People,
The,* 94

*8th Habit: From Effectiveness to
Greatness, The,* 182

A

Aaker, Jennifer L., 145, 146

Abrams, Frank, 187

absenteeism, 28, 44, 55, 140

Accenture, 78

Acker, Bryan, 110

Adobe, 78, 122

adversity, 53, 103, 105

Aesop, 83

Agora, 83, 98

AIG, 28

Amabile, Teresa, 170

anthropological communitas, 155

Aon Hewitt, 23

Apple, 90, 146, 148

Apply.co, 71

Aristotle, 26, 120

"Authentic Purpose: The Spiritual
Infrastucture of Life," 119

average revenue per user (ARPU), 44

B

*B Corp Handbook: How to Use Business
as a Force for Good, The,* 125

Bakan, Joel, 62, 63, 119

Banco Bilbao Vizcaya Argentaria
(BBVA), 115, 116, 119, 124

Battle for the Soul of Capitalism, The,
118

BC Ferries, 58

Be The Change (BTC) Revolutions, 99

Beck, Martha, xv

bell curve, 77, 78, 122

Benefits Corporation (B-Corps),
124, 125

Bersin, Josh, 197

best self, 182, 183, 184

Bleier, Paul, 16, 18, 54

Bock, Laszlo, 45

Bogle, John, 118

Bouck, Cory, 101, 102, 103, 105, 106, 182

Box of Crayons, 96, 97, 134, 201

Branson, Sir Richard, 9, 122, 197

Bravo, 43

British Columbia Institute of Technology (BCIT), 37, 38, 40

British Olympic Committee, 95

Brown, John Seely, 137

Business Objects, 38, 39, 40, 41

Byler, Daniel, 137

C

Cage, John, 184

Calof, Jonathan, 73

Campbell, Joseph, 24, 130, 148

Career Mindset, (author definition), 22

causal relationship, 23, 54, 69, 115

causality, 54

Chariots of Fire, 95

Chilton, David, 110

Christensen, Clayton, 95

Churchill, Winston, 35

Citibank, 96

cognitive dissonance, 69, 71

Colgate, Mark, 188

collaboration, (author definition), 59

communitas, 11, 148, 151, 153, 154, 155, 156, 157, 159, 161, 162, 163, 165, 167, 169, 171, 172, 173

Conference Board, The, 56

Conley, Chip, 133

Conscious Capitalism, 124

continual fluid process, 19

Cook, Tim, 146, 148

Cordes, Liane, 67

Corporate Social Responsibility (CSR), 9, 46, 119, 184, 191, 198, 199

Covey, Stephen, 94, 182

Craig, Nick, 180

CreatingIs, 99

Credo, 104, 105, 108

Criveau, Debra, 29

Crystal Decisions, 38, 40, 135

Culbert, Samuel, 76

Customer First Commitments, 195, 196

customers-first strategy, 195, 196

D

Daft, Richard, 75

de Botton, Alain, 129, 130, 148

de Motteville, Françoise Bertaut, 129

De Tocqueville, Alexis, 30

Deaton, Angus, 57

decide, (author definition), 20, 87

deed, (definition), 110

Deere, John, 186

define, (author definition), 20, 86

Deloitte LLP, 5, 27, 28, 55, 197

Demoulas, Arthur, 156, 157, 158, 159

Department of Motion Graphics,
    The, 67

Desjardins, Mike, 158, 167

develop, (author definition), 20, 86

Dickerson, Chad, 165

Dillon, Chip, 109

disengagement, 23, 29, 55, 69, 70, 71,
    74, 120, 140

Disrupting Class, 95

Do Purpose, 8

Doctor and the Soul, The, 162

Douglass, Frederick, 35

Dowden, Craig, 133

Drive, 130

Drucker, Peter, xv, 29, 31, 32, 33, 52, 58

Duxbury, Linda, 142, 143, 144

E

Earls Restaurants Limited, 10, 154, 167,
    168, 169, 170

Easterlin Paradox, The, 57

Easterlin, Richard, 57

Economic Policy Institute, 58

Economist Intelligence Unit (EIU), 28

ecosystem, 2, 6, 21, 165

Elangovan, Dr. A. R., 26, 27, 145, 146,
    155, 156, 157, 180, 181

Ellsworth, Richard, 32

employee, (author definition), 18

"Employee-Customer-Profit Chain
    at Sears, The" (*Harvard Business
    Review*), 54

engaged workforce, 23, 27, 28, 38, 54,
    55, 56, 103, 115, 165

engagement, (as defined by Gallup), 56

Enron, 134, 198

Entwistle, Darren, 18, 42, 45, 47

Epictetus, 83, 111

Ethics Resource Center, 117, 198

ethics, 7, 21, 107, 117, 118, 119, 198

ethos, 7, 16, 41, 42, 44, 74, 78, 99, 116,
    119, 132, 142, 162, 164

Etsy, 10, 162, 164, 165, 166, 167, 195

eudaemonia, 26

Expedia, 122

F

Facebook, 97, 98

Fair Dinkum, 172

Fair Labor Standards Act (FLSA), 121

Fairphone, 1, 2, 3, 4, 6, 7, 18, 30, 54,
    190

Fayol, Henri, 75

Federal Employee Viewpoint Survey
    (FEVS), 30

Festinger, Leon, 69

Finding Your Own North Star, xv

Fixing the Game, 20, 191, 192

FLAT ARMY: Creating a Connected and Engaged Organization, 23, 24, 36, 59, 109, 132, 140, 188, 189, 205

flexible work, 43, 197

Forbes Magazine, 114, 205

Ford, 104, 106, 107, 109, 111

Ford, Henry, 90

Fortune Magazine, 185

Frankl, Viktor, 162, 164, 175

Friedman, Milton, 63, 64

"From Purpose to Impact" (*Harvard Business Review*), 180

Frost, Robert, 151

Fuller, Buckminster, 126

G

Gallup, 23, 56

gDiapers, 171, 172, 182, 190

gender balance, 89, 90

generalist, 89

George Washington University, 146

Get Rid of the Performance Review!: How Companies Can Stop Intimidating, Start Managing and Focus on What Really Matters, 76

Gide, André Paul Guillaume, 101

Give and Take, 15, 111, 145

global employee engagement surveys, 31

Globoforce, 77

Goirigolzarri, José Ignacio, 124

Goldman Sachs Focus List, 28

Goldman Sachs, 28

González, Francisco, 119

Good DEEDS, 20, 21, 110, 111, 112, 114, 117, 118, 120, 121, 124, 126, 130, 132, 142, 144, 156, 172, 178

   Delight Your Customers, 112

   Engage Your Team Members, 115

   (Be) Ethical Within Society, 117

   Deliver Fair Practices, 120

   Serve All Stakeholders, 123

Good Life, The, 8

Good Profit, 191

Goodhart's Law, 121

Google Hangouts, 98

Graham-Nye, Jason, 10, 170, 171, 172, 173, 178, 182

Graham-Nye, Kim, 10, 170, 171, 172, 173, 178, 182

Grant Study, The, 183

Grant, Adam, 15, 111, 145, 146

Gravity Payments, 57, 58, 122

Great Place to Work, 115

Great Recession, 60

Greenpeace, 162

Gulf Cooperation Council (GCC)

H

Hagel, John, 137

halo effect, 133

Handy, Charles, 33, 60, 61

Harvard Business Review, 33, 54, 65, 74, 75, 163, 180, 200, 205

Harvard University, 75, 95, 118, 119, 183

"Has Financial Development Made the World Riskier?," 64

Helliwell, John, 116

Henley, William Ernest, 100

Heraclitus, 47, 83

Hewitt, Mary, 10, 23, 135, 178, 182

Hieatt, David, 8

Hierarchy of Needs, 31

Highest Impact on Customer Success (HICS), 103

Hilton, Bridget, 159, 160, 161, 178, 182

hoarding, 25, 75

Hoffman, Reid, 41

Holley, Rick, 109, 110

Honeyman, Ryan, 125

Huff, Joe, 159, 160, 161, 178, 182

Huffington Post, The, 10, 98, 99, 205

Huffington, Arianna, 10, 98

Human Resource Idea, 114

humanism, 89, 90

Hurst, Aaron, 31, 32

Huxley, Aldous, 91

I

i4cp, 78

Iacocca, Lee, 104

Ibarra, Herminia, 201

IBM, 39

Ignatius, Adi, 163

IKEA, 113, 114, 115, 116

IMF, 60, 64

Imperative, 180

"Implications of Subjective Career Success, The," 143

In Search of Excellence, 15

In-N-Out Burger, 121, 122

Individualism, 30

Innovator's Dilemma, 95

INSEAD, 201

integrity, 21, 92, 94, 95, 97, 119, 168, 172

Ionescu, Mana, 10, 151, 152, 153, 156, 157, 178, 200

J

Jessa, Mo, 168

Job Mindset, (author definition), 22

Jobs, Steve, 90, 146, 148

Johannesen, Jim, 121

Johnson & Johnson, 104, 105, 106, 108, 109, 110, 114

Johnson, Robert Wood, 104

Johnsonville Sausage, 10, 101, 102, 103, 105, 106, 108, 109, 110, 111, 114, 134, 182

Johnsonville Way, 101, 102, 106

Juniper Networks, 122

just-world-phenomenon myth, 72

K

Kahneman, Daniel, 57

Kalin, Robert, 164

Kalixa Pro, 69

Kamprad, Ingvar, 113, 114

Kanter, Rosabeth Moss, 74

Kastelle, Tim, 201

Kaufer, Katrin, 26

Kelly Services, 78

Keyes, Corey, 119

Keynes, John Maynard, 59

Keys to Performance Management, 78

Kierkegaard, Søren, 19

King Arthur Flour, 10, 125, 126

King, Martin Luther, 120

Kirby, Julia, 200

Klein, Dan, 40, 41

know thyself, 83, 94, 97, 98, 201

Koch Industries, 191

Koch, Charles G., 191

Kramer, Steven, 170

L

Laws of Media, 175

Layard, Richard, 59

Lazonick, William, 65, 191

Leadership IQ, 197

Leadership NOW, 93

Leading From the Emerging Future: From Ego-System to Eco-System Economics, 26

Leading with Purpose, 32

Lennon, John, 182

Liddell, Eric, 95

Lightspan Digital, 151, 152, 153, 195, 200

liminal stage, 154, 155, 156

liminality, 154, 155, 172

Lincoln, Abraham, 33

LinkedIn, 41, 185

Lois, George, 28

long-term incentives (LTIs), 76, 77

LSTN, 10, 154, 159, 160, 161, 162, 182

Lufthansa Technical Training (LTT), 37

M

Mackay, Hugh, 9

Mackey, John, 123, 124, 167

Maguire, Chris, 164

Management by Objectives (MBOs), 76

Management Today, 163

Mandela, Nelson, 175

Market Basket, 10, 154, 156, 157, 158, 159

Marks, Andrew, 29

Martin, Richard, 29

Martin, Roger L., 20, 191

Maslow, Abraham, 31, 91, 133

Mayo, Elton, 75

McDonald, Tim, 10, 97, 99, 100, 178, 184

McDonald's, 121, 122

McKinsey & Company, 28

McLuhan, Eric, 175

McLuhan, Marshall, 175

McNaughton, John, 29

Meaning of Life, The, 9

Microsoft, 39, 78, 122

Mintzberg, Henry, 71

MIT Sloan Magazine, 139

Monty Python, 9

Moral Molecule, The, 69

Motorola, 78

Moyers, Bill, 130

MSCI All Country World Index, 28

Mulally, Alan, 107

My Community Manager, 98

N

Nanterme, Pierre, 78

National Mall, 146

Ndembu tribe, 154

Nestlé, 96, 163

New York University, 180

Nietzsche, Friedrich, 151

Nin, Anaïs, 15

No Kid Hungry, 99

Noelting, Phil, 183

Nokia, 96

Nortel, 72, 73, 74, 134

Nova Scotia Health Authority, 136

Nurse Next Door, 169, 200

O

O2E, 147

Ofactor, 69

Oldani, Heather, 121

ONE FORD, 107

Opener Institute for People and Performance, 55

Oracle, 39

Overnight Test, The, 67, 68

Oxford Dictionary, 110

Oxford Strategic Consulting (OSC), 138

P

Papay, Michael, 157, 158, 199

passion gap, 137, 138

Patagonia, 186

Pathways to Bliss, 24

Peak: How Great Companies Get their Mojo from Maslow, 133

people, (definition), 115

Perez, Thomas E., 122

performance management, 75, 76, 78, 103, 121, 122, 123, 153

reviews, 75, 76, 77, 78

Personal Declaration of Purpose, 94, 180

Personal Development Commitments (PDC), 102, 103

personal purpose, (author definition), 83

Peters, Tom, 15

Pfeffer, Jeffrey, 71, 72, 74

Pink, Daniel, 130, 146

Pinto, 104, 109

Plato, 83

Pleasures and Sorrows of Work, The, 129

Plum Creek Timber, 108, 109, 111

Polman, Paul, 9, 163, 164

possibility virus, 10, 96, 97

Power: Why Some People Have It—and Others Don't, 71

pre-requisite, 144

Presencing Institute, 26

Price, Dan, 57, 58, 122

Princeton University, 57

Progress Principle, The, 170

pro-social, 190

Psychometrics, 123

Puritt, Jeffrey, 45, 46, 184

Purpose Driven Life, The, xv

Purpose Effect Scorecard, The, 194

Purpose Effect tetrad, *The*, 177

Purpose Mindset, (author definition), 22

purpose, (etymology), 31

PWC, 96

Pythagoras, 83, 199

Q

Queen's University, 55

Quick Service Restaurant (QSR) Benchmark Study, 122

Quicken Loans, 186

Quillen, Robert, 30

Qwalify, 183, 195

R

Rajan, Raghuram G., 64

Ranjan, Alok, 137

Realizing the Promise of Performance Management, 122

Redding, Linds, 67, 68, 69

Reinhardt, Forest, 118

remuneration, 11, 30, 57, 59, 79, 140, 191

Renjen, Punit, 27

restricted stock units (RSUs), 192

Rifkin, Jeremy, 166, 167

Rigney, Brenda, 167, 168, 169, 200

Rites of Passage, The, 154

Rockefeller, John, 51, 101

Rogers, Bob, 122

Rogers, Carl, 19

role-based mindsets, 131

    job, 132, 137

    career, 132, 141

    calling (purpose), 132, 145

Roosevelt Institute, 190

Roosevelt, Theodore, 61, 62

Rout, Lawrence, 76

Rubbish Boys, The, 147

S

Salary Reform Act, 75

Sanofi Pasteur, 88, 89, 91

SAP, 29, 39, 40, 41, 46, 84, 85, 99

satisfaction,

    customer, 28, 41, 42, 44, 54, 55, 115, 122, 192

    employee, 54

    job, 30, 56

Scharmer, Otto, 26

Schillinger, Céline, 10, 88, 89, 90, 91, 99

Schnarr, Jill, 92, 93, 94, 99, 181, 189

Schoppik, Haim, 164

Schultz, Howard, 9

Schwartz, Barry, 143

Scudamore, Brian, 147, 148, 181

Sears, 54, 55

self-understanding, 83

Seneca, Lucius Annaeus, 15

Senge, Peter, 116

serial creative, 70

Shapiro, Lorna, 57

Shareholder Value Myth, The, 190

Shaughnessy, Haydn, 2

Shift: A User's Guide to the New Economy, 2

"Short Lesson In Perspective, A," 67

Sibson Consulting, 76

silos, 73, 75

Sinek, Simon, xv, 6, 180

Singh, Praveen, 29

Singla, Sanjee, 70, 71

Sisodia, Raj, 124

Smith, Adam, 60

Smith, Megan, 84, 85, 87, 99, 201

Snook, Scott, 180

social contract, 115, 116, 117, 140, 153

"Social Responsibility of Business Is to Increase Its Profits, The" (*The New York Times Magazine*), 63

Society for Human Resource Management (SHRM), 76, 123

Socrates, 83

stakeholder, (definition), 124

Stanford Research Institute, 124

Stanford University, 69, 70, 146

Stanier, Michael Bungay, 10, 96, 99, 100, 181, 201

Stanley, Bessie Anderson, 93, 94

Starbucks, 9

Starkey Hearing Foundation, 159

Start With Why, 6

Stavins, Robert, 118

Stayer, Ralph C., 101, 102

Steindl-Rast, David, 129

Stout, Lynn, 190

Sustainable Living Plan, 163, 164

sweet spot, xvi, 6, 7, 8, 10, 11, 12, 15, 17, 18, 19, 20, 22, 29, 31, 33, 34, 35, 37, 38, 39, 40, 41, 42, 47, 53, 65, 69, 79, 84, 85, 94, 99, 102, 103, 107, 110, 111, 113, 116, 123, 127, 129, 131, 134, 136, 138, 141, 142, 144, 145, 148, 154, 155, 156, 157, 158, 159, 161, 164, 167, 168, 169, 170, 171, 172, 173, 175, 177, 178, 179, 180, 181, 182, 183, 184, 185, 187, 189, 191, 193, 195, 197, 199, 200, 201, 203

T

Tapscott, Don, 124

Tata, Ratan, 138, 139

Taylor, Frederick, 75

TD Bank, 96

team member, (author definition), 18

TELUS Leadership Philosophy (TLP), 42

TELUS Transformation Office (TTO), 47, 205

TELUS, 10, 16, 18, 41, 42, 43, 44, 45, 46, 47, 54, 55, 84, 92, 93, 94, 134, 184, 195, 196, 205

Tempest, The, 12

Terkel, Studs, 87, 88

Tesco, 96

tetrad of media effects, 175

tetrad, 175, 176, 178, 179

Thatcher, Margaret, 75

The Corporation: The Pathological Pursuit of Profit and Power, 62

The Purpose Economy, 31, 32

The Wealth of Nations, 60

three Rs, (reliable, responsive, relatable), 188

Toms Shoes, 160

Towers-Watson, 116, 117

Trigg, Kelsy, 91, 92, 94, 99, 181, 200

Turner, Victor, 154, 155

Twain, Mark, 123

Twitter, 51, 97, 98, 205

Tyco, 198

Tylenol, 104, 105, 109

U

Unilever Sustainable Living Plan, The, 164

Unilever, 9, 162, 163, 164, 169, 170, 185

United States Government, 30

Universal Music Group (UMG), 160

University of Business Intelligence (UBI), 38, 39, 41

University of Ottawa, 73

University of Oxford, 55, 95

University of Pennsylvania, 54

University of Warwick, 54

V

van Abel, Bas, 1, 6, 18, 54, 178

van Gennep, Arnold, 154

van Gogh, Vincent, 88

Vanguard Group, The, 118

Venn diagram, 7, 9

Verizon, 44

Vertical Research Partners, 109

Vietor, Richard, 118

Virgin, 9, 122

ViRTUS, 154, 158, 167

Volkswagen, 95, 134, 198

W

Waggle, 154, 157, 158

Wall Street Journal, 55, 58

Wall Street, 65, 147, 166

Warby Parker, 160

Warren, Rick, xv

Wartzman, Rick, 185

Waterman, Robert, 15

Watson, Nora, 87, 88

Wealthy Barber, The, 110

Whole Earth Catalog, The, 146

Whole Foods, 123, 167, 186

wholeness, 94

Why We Work, 143

Wikipedia, 11

Williams, Janice, 51, 55, 64, 180

Wilson, Woodrow, 67

win-win-win, 152

Winfrey, Oprah, 182

Winterkorn, Martin, 95

Work Foundation, The, 26

Work Rules! Why Google's Rules Will Work for You, 45

Work Styles program, The, 43

Working: People Talk About What They Do All Day and How They Feel About What They Do, 87

workplace girth, 132

World Bank, The, 65

Worldcom, 198

Wow 1Day Paint, 147

Wrzesniewski, Amy, 131, 133

Y

You Move Me, 147

Zak, Paul J., 69, 197

Z

zeitgeist, 8

Zero Marginal Cost Society, The, 166

Zuckerberg, Mark, 182

REFERENCES

Dedication

1. Ehrmann, M. (1995). *The desiderata of happiness: A collection of philosophical poems.* Crown.

Introduction

1. Deloitte, (2014). *Culture of purpose—Building business confidence; driving growth: 2014 core beliefs & culture survey.* [Survey]

2. Sinek, S. (2011). *Start with why: How great leaders inspire everyone to take action.* Portfolio / Penguin.

3. Hieatt, D. (2014). *Do purpose.* Do Book Company.

4. Mackay, H. (2013). *The good life.* Pan Macmillan.

5. Schultz, H. & Gordon, J. (2012). *Onward: How Starbucks fought for its life without losing its soul.* Rodale Publishing.

Chapter 1

1. Epistulae Morales ad Lucilium (Moral Letters to Lucilius). Letter LXXI: On the supreme good, line 3.

2. Dingle, C. (2000). *Memorable quotations: French writers of the past.* (p. 126).

3. Peters, T. J., & Waterman, R. H., Jr. (1984). *In search of excellence: Lessons from America's best-run companies.* New York: Harper & Row, Publishers.

4. Grant, A. (2013). *Give and take: Why helping others drives our success.* Weidenfeld & Nicolson.

5. Kierkegaard, S. (1974). *Concluding unscientific postscript.* (Swenson, D. F., & Lowrie, W., Trans.). Princeton, NJ: Princeton University Press.

6. Rogers, C. (1961). *On becoming a person: A therapist's view of psychotherapy.* London: Constable.

7. Rogers, C. (1961). *On becoming a person: A therapist's view of psychotherapy.* London: Constable.

8. Kierkegaard, S. (1974). *Concluding unscientific postscript.* (Swenson. D. F., & Lowrie, W., Trans.). Princeton, NJ: Princeton University Press.

9. Martin, R. (2011). *Fixing the game: Bubbles, crashes, and what capitalism can learn from the NFL.* Harvard Business Review Press.

10. Martin, R. (2011). *Fixing the game: Bubbles, crashes, and what capitalism can learn from the NFL.* Harvard Business Review Press.

11. Campbell, J. (2004). *Pathways to bliss.* New World Library.

12. Scharmer, C. O., & Kaeufer, K. (2013). *Leading from the emerging future: From ego-system to eco-system economies.* Berrett-Koehler Publishers.

13. Elangovan, A. R. (2014). Commencement Address, Gustavson School of Business. https://onlineacademiccommunity.uvic.ca/gustavson/2014/06/17/gustavson-2014-commencement-address/

14. *About The Work Foundation.* Retrieved from The Work Foundation website: http://www.theworkfoundation.com/Aboutus/Get-Involved

15. Elangovan, A. R., Pinder, C. C., and McLean, M. (2010). Callings and organizational behavior." *Journal of Vocational Behavior,* 76.3, 428-440.

16. *Culture of purpose – Building business confidence; driving growth: 2014 core beliefs & culture survey.* (2014). Deloitte Development LLC. Retrieved from the Deloitte website: http://www2.deloitte.com/us/en/pages/about-deloitte/articles/culture-of-purpose.html

17. *Culture of purpose – Building business confidence; driving growth: 2014 core beliefs & culture survey.* (2014). Deloitte Development LLC. Retrieved from the Deloitte website: http://www2.deloitte.com/content/dam/Deloitte/us/Documents/about-deloitte/us-leadership-2014-core-beliefs-culture-survey-040414.pdf

18. Bonini, S., & Görner, S. (2011). *The business of sustainability.* McKinsey & Company.

19. Economist Intelligence Unit. (2011). *"Gearing for growth: Future drivers of corporate productivity."*

20. Morgenson, G., & Story, L. (2010, February 6). Testy conflict with Goldman helped push A.I.G. to edge. *The New York Times.* Retrieved from *The New York Times* website: http://www.nytimes.com/2010/02/07/business/07goldman.html?pagewanted=all&_r=0

21. *GS Sustain: Focused on identifying the companies in each industry best positioned to deliver long-term outperformance through sustained industry leadership and profitability.* (2011, November). Goldman Sachs. Retrieved from the Goldman Sachs website: http://www.goldmansachs.com/our-thinking/archive/gs-sustain-2011/

22. Lois, G. (2012). *Damn good advice – for people with talent!* Phaidon Press.

23. Drucker, P. (1973). *Management: Tasks, responsibilities, practices.* New York: Harper & Row.

24. Quillen, R. (1923, April 6). Editorial Epigrams. *The Evening Repository* (Canton, OH), pg. 4, col. 3.

25. Tocqueville, A. de. (2000). *Democracy in America.* Chicago: The University of Chicago Press. ISBN 0-226-80532-8.

26. *United States Office of Personnel Management Planning and Policy Analysis.* (2014). Federal Employee Viewpoint Survey Results. Retrieved from the Federal Employee Viewpoint website: http://www.fedview.opm.gov/2014files/2014_Governmentwide_Management_Report.PDF

27. Maslow, A. (1954). *Motivation and personality.* New York, NY: Harper. p.236. ISBN0-06-041987-3.

28. Hurst, A. (2014, May). *The purpose economy: How your desire for impact, personal growth and community is changing the world.* Elevate Press.

29. In conversation with the author. (2014, May).

30. Ellsworth, R. R. (2002). *Leading with purpose: The new corporate realities.* Stanford University Press.

31. Drucker, P. (1970). *Management: Tasks, responsibilities, practices.*

32. Drucker, P. (1999). *Management for the 21st century.* HarperCollins.

33. Handy, C. (1998). *Beyond certainty: The changing worlds of organizations.* Harvard Business Review Press.

34. Drucker, P. (1970). *Management: Tasks, responsibilities, practices.*

35. Lincoln, A. (1859, September 30). *Address before the Wisconsin State Agricultural Society, in Milwaukee.* Retrieved from the Wikisource website: http://en.wikisource.org/wiki/Address_before_the_Wisconsin_State_Agricultural_Society

Chapter 2

1. Churchill, W., & James, R. R. (Ed.). (1922-1928). *Winston Churchill: His complete speeches, 1897-1963.* Chelsea House ed., vol. 4, p. 3706.

2. Douglas, F. (1845). *Narrative of the life of Frederick Douglass, an American slave.*

3. Hoffman, R., Casnocha, B., Yeh, C., (2013, June). Tours of duty: The new employer-employee compact. *Harvard Business Review.* Retrieved from the *Harvard Business Review* website: https://hbr.org/2013/06/tours-of-duty-the-new-employer-employee-compact

4. TELUS Annual Report. (2015).

5. TELUS Annual Report. (2014).

6. TELUS Annual Report. (2014).

7. TELUS continues to raise bar for telecom customer service in CCTS annual report. (2015, December 2). TELUS Media Release.

8. TELUS Annual Report. (2014).

9. TELUS Annual Report. (2014).

10. Hogue, W. (2013). *Elements of leaders of character: Attributes, practices, and principles.* WestBow Press. https://en.wikiquote.org/wiki/Heraclitus

Chapter 3

1. Rockefeller, J. (1906). *Random reminiscences of men and events.* Project Gutenberg.

2. Mieder, W. (1994). *The wisdom of many: Essays on the proverb.* University of Wisconsin Press.

3. Rucci, A. J., Kirn, S., & Quinn, R. T. (1998, January-February). The Employee-Customer-Profit Chain at Sears. *Harvard Business Review,* https://hbr.org/1998/01/the-employee-customer-profit-chain-at-sears

4. Edmans, A. (2010, January, 20). Does the stock market fully value intangibles? Employee satisfaction and equity prices. *Journal of Financial Economics,* 101(3), 621-640. http://papers.ssrn.com/sol3/papers.cfm?abstract_id=985735

5. Oswald., A. J., Proto, E., & Sgroi, D. (2009, December). *Happiness and Productivity.* IZA Discussion Paper No. 4645. Retrieved from the University of Warwick website: http://www2.warwick.ac.uk/fac/soc/economics/staff/academic/proto/workingpapers/happiness productivity.pdf

6. Pleiter, S. (2014, Winter). Engaging employees. *QSB Magazine.* Retrieved from the *QSB Magazine* website: http://qsb.ca/magazine/winter-2014/features/engaging-employees

7. Pryce-Jones, J. (2011, September 18). The five drivers of happiness at work. *The Wall Street Journal.* Retrieved from *The Wall Street Journal* website: http://blogs.wsj.com/source/2011/09/18/the-five-drivers-of-happiness-at-work/

8. *Trends: Global human capital trends* (2015). Deloitte Development LLC. Deloitte University Press. Retrieved from the Deloitte University Press website: http://dupress.com/periodical/trends/human-capital-trends-2015/?id=us:2el:3dc:dup1179:eng:cons:hct15

9. Ray, R., & Rizzacasa, T. (2012). *So we're slightly less miserable at work. Shall we break open the bubbly?* Job Satisfaction 2012 Edition.

10. *Gallup daily: U.S. employee engagement.* (2015). Gallup, Inc. Retrieved from the Gallup website: http://www.gallup.com/poll/180404/gallup-daily-employee-engagement.aspx

11. *State of the global workplace.* (2013). Gallup, Inc. Retrieved from the Gallup website: http://www.gallup.com/strategicconsulting/164735/state-global-workplace.aspx

12. Easterlin, R. (1974). *Does economic growth improve the human lot? Some empirical evidence.* University of Pennsylvania. Retrieved from The New York Times website: http://graphics8.nytimes.com/images/2008/04/16/business/Easterlin1974.pdf

13. Kahneman, D., & Deaton, A. (2010.) *High income improves evaluation of life but not emotional well-being.* PNAS Early Edition. Retrieved from the Princeton website: https://www.princeton.edu/~deaton/downloads/deaton_kahneman_high_income_improves_evaluation_August2010.pdf

14. Weise, K. (2015, December 1). The CEO paying everyone $70,000 salaries has something to hide. *Bloomberg Businessweek.* Retrieved from the Bloomberg website: http://www.bloomberg.com/features/2015-gravity-ceo-dan-price/

15. In conversation with the author. (2015, July)

16. Mishel, L., & Davis, A. (2015, June 21). *Top CEOs make 300 times more than typical workers.* Economic Pay Institute. Retrieved from the Economic Pay Institute website: http://www.epi.org/publication/top-ceos-make-300-times-more-than-workers-pay-growth-surpasses-market-gains-and-the-rest-of-the-0-1-percent/

17. Drucker, P. (1977, May 23). Is executive pay excessive? *Wall Street Journal.*

18. Hume, S. (2014, February 18). BC Ferries a bloated, inefficient and recessionary drag on the province. *The Vancouver Sun.*

19. Pontefract, D. (2013). *FLAT ARMY: Creating a Connected and Engaged Organization.* Elevate.

20. Keynes, J.M. (1930). *Economic possibilities for our grandchildren.*

21. Layard, R. (2006). *Happiness: Lessons from a new science.* Penguin Books.

22. Leigh, D., Igan, D., Simon, J., & Topalova, P. (2012, April). *Growth resuming, dangers remain.* World Economic Outlook. International

Monetary Fund. http://www.imf.org/external/pubs/ft/weo/2012/01/pdf/c3.pdf

23. Handy, C. (2010). *Speech on qualities of vision and leadership at the leadership all-stars conference.* Drucker Institute. https://www.youtube.com/watch?v=KrR-OUSCWjE

24. Foster, K., Meijer, E., Schuh, S., & Zabek, M. A. (2011). *The 2009 survey of consumer payment choice.* Federal Reserve Bank of Boston. Retrieved from the Bank of Boston website: http://www.bos.frb.org/economic/ppdp/2011/ppdp1101.pdf

25. *Consumer Credit.* (2015, November). Board of Governors of the Federal Reserve System. Retrieved from the Federal Reserve website: http://www.federalreserve.gov/releases/g19/current/

26. *Consumer Credit.* (2015, November). Board of Governors of the Federal Reserve System. Retrieved from the Federal Reserve website: http://www.federalreserve.gov/releases/g19/current/

27. Goldman, M. C. (2013, August, 23). Canadian consumer debt balloons to $27,131 in second quarter, study suggests. *Financial Post.* Retrieved from the Financial Post website: http://business.financialpost.com/2013/08/28/debt-canada-q2/?_lsa=0762-c938

28. *UK consumer credit in the eye of the storm: Precious Plastic 2011.* PricewaterhouseCoopers LLP. Retrieved from the PricewaterhouseCoopers website: http://www.pwc.lu/en/banking/docs/pwc-precious-plastic-2011.pdf

29. Dobbs, R., Lund, S., Woetzel, J., & Mutafchieva, M. (2015, February). *Debt and (not much) leveraging.* McKinsey Global Institute.

30. Smith, A. (1776). *The wealth of nations.* W. Strahan and T. Cadell, London.

31. Handy, C. (1995). *Beyond certainty.* Arrow Books Limited.

32. State of the Union address. December 2, 1902.

33. Bakan, J. (2003). *The corporation: The pathological pursuit of profit and power.* Simon & Schuster.

34. Friedman, M. (1962). *Capitalism and freedom.* University of Chicago Press.

35. Friedman, M. (1970, September 13). The social responsibility of business is to increase its profits. *The New York Times Magazine.*

36. Rajan, R. (2005). *Has financial development made the world riskier?* Proceedings – Economic Policy Symposium – Jackson Hole, Federal Reserve Bank of Kansas City, issue August, pages 313-369. Retrieved from the National Bureau of Economic Research website: http://www.nber.org/papers/w11728.pdf

37. *Employment Situation Summary.* (2015). Bureau of Labor and Statistics. Retrieved from the Bureau of Labor Statistics website: http://www.bls.gov/news.release/empsit.nr0.htm

38. *UK unemployment increases to 2.5 million.* (2010, April 21). BBC News. Retrieved from the BBC News website: http://news.bbc.co.uk/1/hi/8634241.stm

39. *Canadian Unemployment at 7.1%.* (2015). HRM Guide. Canadian Human resources. Retrieved from the HRM Guide website: http://www.hrmguide.net/canada/jobmarket/canadian-unemployment.htm

40. *"East Asia and Pacific Update: Battling the forces of global recession."* (2009). The World Bank.

41. Lazonick, W. (2014, September). Profits without prosperity. *Harvard Business Review.* Retrieved from the *Harvard Business Review* website: https://hbr.org/2014/09/profits-without-prosperity/ar/1

Chapter 4

1. Cordes, L. (1981). *The reflecting pond: Meditations for self-discovery.* Hazelden Meditations.

2. Wilson, W. (1913, September 21). From a letter to Mary A. Hulbert.

3. Redding. L. (n.d.)(2012, March 11). LinkedIn [Profile Page]. Retrieved from: https://nz.linkedin.com/pub/linds-redding/16/888/247

4. Redding, L. (2012, March 11). *A short lesson in perspective.* Retrieved from: http://www.lindsredding.com/2012/03/11/a-overdue-lesson-in-perspective/

5. Zak, P. (2013, October 6). This is your organization on oxytocin, part 1. *Psychology Today.* Retrieved from the Psychology Today website:

http://www.psychologytoday.com/blog/the-moral-molecule/201310/
is-your-organization-oxytocin-part-i

6. Festinger, L. (1957). *A theory of cognitive dissonance.* Stanford, CA: Stanford University Press.

7. *The workplace in 2014 – a disillusioned and unhappy workforce.* (2014, July 18). Kalixa Pro. Retrieved from the Kalixa Pro website: http://kalixapro.blogspot.ca/2014/07/the-workplace-in-2014-disillusioned-and.html?m=1

8. In conversation with the author. (2013).

9. Pfeffer, J. (2010). *Power: Why some people have it—and others don't.* HarperCollins Publishers.

10. Nortel 2001 Annual report page 22. https://bib.kuleuven.be/files/ebib/jaarverslagen/NortelNetworks_2001.pdf

11. Calof, J., Richards, G., Mirabeau, L., Mouftah, H., MacKinnon, P., Chapman, P., & Vasudev, P. M. (2014). *An overview of the demise of Nortel Networks and key lessons learned.* Telfer School of Management, University of Ottawa. Retrieved from the Telfer School of Management, University of Ottawa website: http://sites2.telfer.uottawa.ca/nortelstudy/

12. Calof, J. (2014, May 28). The strength of Nortel was its people. *Ottawa Citizen.* Retrieved from the *Ottawa Citizen* website: http://ottawacitizen.com/business/local-business/jonathan-calof-the-strength-of-nortel-was-its-people

13. Kanter, R. M. (1979, July–August) "Power failure in management circuits." *Harvard Business Review* 57, no. 4: 65–75.

14. Blundell, J. (2008). *Margaret Thatcher: A portrait of the iron lady.* Algora Publishing.

15. Trahair, R., & Kyle, B. (2012). *Human relations and management consulting: Elton Mayo and Eric Trist.* The Oxford handbook of Management Consulting, Wright, C., & Kipping, M., eds. Oxford University Press.

16. *The state of performance management.* (2007, July). A survey brief by WorldatWork and Sibson Consulting. Retrieved from

the WorldatWork website: http://www.worldatwork.org/waw/adimLink?id=20261

17. Culbert, S. A., & Rout, L. (2010) *Get rid of the performance review: How companies can stop intimidating, start managing – and focus on what really matters*. New York: Business Plus.

18. van der Pool, L. (2011, April 19). Survey: Majority hate performance reviews. *Boston Business Journal*. Retrieved from the Boston business Journal website: http://www.bizjournals.com/boston/news/2011/04/19/survey-majority-hate-performance.html

19. Stevenson, C. (2013, October 31). *Performance management: Sticking with what doesn't work*. I4cp. Retrieved from the i4cp website: http://www.i4cp.com/trendwatchers/2013/10/31/performance-management-sticking-with-what-doesn-t-work

20. Cunningham, L. (2015, July 23). Accenture CEO explains why he's overhauling performance reviews. *The Washington Post*. Retrieved from *The Washington Post* website: http://www.washingtonpost.com/news/on-leadership/wp/2015/07/23/accenture-ceo-explains-the-reasons-why-hes-overhauling-performance-reviews/

Chapter 5

1. Gibbs, L. (2002). *Aesop's fables*. A new translation by Laura Gibbs. Oxford University Press (World's Classics): Oxford.

2. *Epictetus*. Book III, ch. 23.

3. Terkel, Studs. (1974). *Working: People talk about what they do all day and how they feel about what they do*. NY: Pantheon/Random House.

4. Maslow, A. (1954). *Motivation and personality*. New York, NY: Harper.

5. Huxley, A. (1962). Island. Harper and Brothers.

6. Christensen, C. (2010, July). How will you measure your life. *Harvard Business Review*.

7. Henley, W. E. (2010). *Echoes of life and death*. Nabu Press.

Chapter 6

1. Ziglar, Z. (1985). *Steps to the top.* p. 16.

2. Les faux-monnayeurs [The Counterfeiters] (1925).

3. In conversation with the author. (2014, October).

4. Rehak, Judith. (2002, March 23). Tylenol made a hero of Johnson & Johnson: The recall that started them all. *The New York Times.* Retrieved from *The New York Times* website: http://www.nytimes.com/2002/03/23/your-money/23iht-mjj_ed3_.html

5. *Our credo values.* Johnson & Johnson. Retrieved from the Johnson & Johnson website: http://www.jnj.com/about-jnj/jnj-credo

6. *Investor Relations.* Johnson & Johnson. Retrieved from the Johnson & Johnson website: http://www.investor.jnj.com/investor-relations.cfm

7. Distefano, M., & Kurtzman, J. (2014, August 11). *Alan Mulally: The man who saved Ford.* Korn Ferry Institute. Retrieved from the Korn Ferry website: http://www.kornferry.com/institute/alan-mulally-man-who-saved-ford

8. *About Plum Creek.* Plumcreek. Retrieved from the Plum Creek website: http://www.plumcreek.com/about

9. *Plum Creek Mission Beliefs, Plum Creek.* Retrieved from the Plum Creek website: http://www.plumcreek.com/about/mission-beliefs

10. *Plum Creek Timber (PCL) Earnings Report: Q4 conference call transcript.* (2015, January 27). The Street transcripts. Retrieved from The Street website: (http://www.thestreet.com/story/13023740/10/plum-creek-timber-pcl-earnings-report-q4-2014-conference-call-transcript.html

11. Young, L., Chakroff, A., & Tom, J. (2012). Doing good leads to more good: The reinforcing power of a moral self-concept. *Review of Philosophy and Psychology,* 3(3), 325-334.

12. Grant, A. (2013). *Give and Take: A Revolutionary Approach to Success.* Penguin.

13. *Epictetus.* (2009). *The Golden Sayings of Epictetus.* Echo Library. Hastings Crossley (Translator).

14. *The IKEA Vision*, IKEA. http://www.ikea.com/ms/en_CA/the_ikea_ story/working_at_ikea/our_vision.html

15. Kamprad, I. (2007). *The Testament of a Furniture Dealer - A Little IKEA ° Dictionary.*

16. Drucker, P. (1954). *The practice of management.* HarperCollins.

17. Gagné, M., & Bhave, D. (2011). *Autonomy in the workplace: An essential ingredient to employee engagement and well-being in every culture.* Human Autonomy in Cross-Cultural Context. edited by Valery I. Chirkov, V., Ryan, R. M., & Sheldon, K.M. 163-187. Dordrecht: Springer. doi:10.1007/978-90-481-9667-8_8

18. Senge, P. (1990). *The fifth discipline: The art & practice of the learning organization.* New York: Doubleday.

19. *2012 Global workforce study.* (2012). Towers Watson. Retrieved from the Towers Watson website: https://www.towerswatson.com/Insights/ IC-Types/Survey-Research-Results/2012/07/2012-Towers-Watson-Global-Workforce-Study

20. In conversation with the author. (2014, May).

21. *2012 Global workforce study.* (2012). Towers Watson. Retrieved from the Towers Watson website: https://www.towerswatson.com/Insights/ IC-Types/Survey-Research-Results/2012/07/2012-Towers-Watson-Global-Workforce-Study

22. *National business ethics survey.* (2007). Ethics Resource Center. Retrieved from the ECI connects website: http://erc.webair.com/files/ u5/NBESResearchBrief2.pdf

23. Bogle, J. C. (2006). *The battle for the soul of capitalism.* Yale University Press.

24. Forest L. Reinhardt, F. L., Stavins, R. N., & Vietor, R. H. K. (2008, Summer). "Corporate social responsibility through an economic lens," *Review of Environmental Economics and Policy*, Oxford University Press for Association of Environmental and Resource Economists, vol. 2(2), pages 219-239.

25. Keyes, C. L. M. (2011). Authentic purpose: the spiritual infrastructure of life. *Journal of Management, Spirituality & Religion.* Vol. 8, Iss. 4.

26. *Chairmen's message.* BBVA. Retrieved from the BBVA website: http://

www.bbva.com/TLBB/tlbb/ing/informacion-corporativa/conozcanos/
carta-presidente/index.jsp

27. King, Rev. Dr. M. L. (1965, June). *Commencement address for Oberlin College*. Retrieved from the Oberlin College website: http://www.oberlin.edu/external/EOG/BlackHistoryMonth/MLK/MLK mainpage.html

28. Morrison, M. (2012, December 17). *McDonald's to franchisees: Merry Christmas. Now open your doors*. Advertising Age. Retrieved from the Advertising Age website: http://adage.com/article/news/mcdonald-s-pushes-franchisees-stay-open-christmas/238797/

29. *Restaurant employment, In-N-Out Burger*. Retrieved from the In-N-Out Burger website: http://www.in-n-out.com/employment/restaurant.aspx

30. *Quick service restaurants missing big opportunity in customer service*. (2013, July 25). Inmoment. Retrieved from the Inmoment website: http://www.inmoment.com/press/study-quick-service-restaurants-missing-big-opportunity-in-customer-service/

31. Jamieson, D. (2014, March 11). Obama's ambassador for raising the minimum wage makes his case for $10.10. *The Huffington Post*. Retrieved from *The Huffington Post* website: http://www.huffingtonpost.com/2014/02/11/obama-minimum-wage-tom-perez_n_4766219.html

32. Rogers, R. W. (2004). *Realizing the promise of performance management*. DDI Press.

33. Branson, R. (2014, August 14). *Why Business is about people, people and people*. Virgin Entrepreneur. Retrieved from the Virgin website: http://www.virgin.com/entrepreneur/richard-branson-why-business-is-about-people-people-and-people

34. *Letter to Gertrude Natkin*. (1906, March 2).

35. *SHRM survey findings: Employee recognition programs*. (2013, Spring). SHRM. Retrieved from the SHRM website: http://www.shrm.org/research/surveyfindings/documents/Globoforce_SHRM_Survey_Spring_2013_FINAL.pdf

36. *Psychometrics, A Study of Employee Engagement in the Canadian Workplace*. (2010).

37. Bradler, C., Dur, R., Neckermann, S., & Non, A. (2014, July). *Employee recognition and performance: A field experiment.* IZA DP No. 8311.

38. Mackey, J., & Sisodia, R. (2013). *Conscious capitalism: Liberating the heroic spirit of business.* Harvard Business Review Press.

39. Freeman, R. E. (2010) *Strategic Management: A Stakeholder Approach.* New York: Cambridge University Press.

40. Tapscott, D. (2015, January 22). Davos: What future do you want? *The Huffington Post.* Retrieved from *The Huffington Post* website: http://www.huffingtonpost.com/don-tapscott/davos-what-future-do-you-want_b_6525574.html

41. *You and BBVA E-Newsletter.* (2013, September). BBVA. Retrieved from the BBVA website: https://www.youand**bbva**.com/static/enewsletter/.../EnewsSeptember.pdf

42. *Corporation legal roadmap.* B Corporation. Retrieved from the B Corporation website: https://www.bcorporation.net/become-a-b-corp/how-to-become-a-b-corp/legal-roadmap/corporation-legal-roadmap

43. In conversation with the author. (2015, May).

44. King Arthur Flour. Retrieved from the King Arthur Flour website: http://www.kingarthurflour.com/

45. *Benefit Corporation Report.* (2014). King Arthur Flour. Retrieved from King Arthur Flour website: https://www.kingarthurflour.com/about/documents/King_Arthur_Flour_Benefit_Corporation_Report_for_Fiscal_Year_2014.pdf

46. *Buckminster Fuller: The estate of Buckminster R. Fuller.* Retrieved from the Buckminster Fuller website: http://buckminsterfuller.net/

Chapter 7

1. de Motteville, F. B. (1899). *Memoirs of Madame de Motteville.* Versailles Historical Society.

2. Steindl-Rast, D. (1984). *Gratefulness, the heart of prayer: An approach to life in fullness.* Paulist Press.

3. Pink, D. H. (2009). *Drive: The surprising truth about what motivates us.* New York, NY: Riverhead Books.

4. Joseph Campbell, J. (1988). *The power of myth*. Doubleday & Company, Incorporated.

5. Wrzesniewski, A., McCauley, C., Rozin, P., & Schwartz, B. (1997). Jobs, careers, and callings: People's relations to their work. *Journal of Research in Personality*. Vol. 31, 21–33.

6. Conley, C. (2007). *Peak: How great companies get their mojo from Maslow*. Wiley.

7. Hagel, J., Brown, J. S., Ranjan, A., Byler, D. (2014). *Passion at work: Cultivating worker passion as a cornerstone of talent development*. Deloitte University Press.

8. Scott-Jackson, W., Porteous, A., Gurel, O., Rushent, C. (2014). *Building GCC national talent for the strategic competitive advantage*. Oxford Strategic Consulting. http://www.oxfordstrategicconsulting.com/ new-research-shows-75-employees-committed-work/

9. Why making money is not enough. (2013, Summer). *MIT Sloan Magazine*.

10. Quinn, R. E. (1996). *Deep change: Discovering the leader within*. Jossey-Bass.

11. Dyke, L. S. and Duxbury, L. E. (2011). The implications of subjective career success. *Journal for Labour Market Research*, 43, 219-229.

12. Schwartz, B. (2015). *Why we work*. Simon & Schuster/ TED.

13. Baumeister, Vohs, Aaker, & Garbinsky. (2013). Some key differences between a happy life and a meaningful life. *Journal of Positive Psychology* 8.6. 505-516.

14. Grant, A. (2014). *Give and take: Why helping others drives our success*. New York: Penguin Books.

15. Ruiz-Quintanilla, S. A., & England, G. W. (1996). How working is defined: Structure and stability. *Journal of Organizational Behavior* 17. 515-540.

16. Humphrey, S. E., Nahrgang, J. D. and Morgeson, F. P. (2007). Integrating motivational, social, and contextual work design features: A meta-analytic summary and theoretical extension of the work design literature. *Journal of Applied Psychology* 92.5.1332-1356.

17. The George Washington University Commencement. (2015, May 17). Day of Rush Edition. https://commencement.gwu.edu/sites/commencement.gwu.edu/files/downloads/GW%20Commencement%20Transcript%205-17-15.pdf

Chapter 8

1. Nietzsche, F. W. (1996). *Human, all too human: A book for free spirits.* Trans. R. J. Hollingdale. Cambridge: Cambridge University Press.

2. Frost, R. (1999). *Mountain Interval.* New York: Henry Holt and Company, 1920; Bartleby.com.

3. Turner, V. (1975). *Dramas, fields, and metaphors: Symbolic action in human society.* Cornell University Press.

4. Newsham, J., & Duffy, J. (2014, August 28). As Arthur T. returns, Market Basket springs back to life. *Boston Globe.* Retrieved from the Boston Globe website: https://www.bostonglobe.com/business/2014/08/28/market-basket-employees-get-back-work/QvbKfUoSNubZdn7AhUameI/story.html

5. In conversation with the author. (2015, October).

6. In conversation with the author. (2015, October).

7. Ross, C. (2015, June 27). One year after walkout, Market Basket is thriving. *Boston Globe.* Retrieved from the *Boston Globe* website: https://www.bostonglobe.com/business/2015/06/27/year-later-market-basket-thriving-after-near-meltdown/EIePjTzCJYhgLWwRpBuoAI/story.html

8. In conversation with the author. (2015, August).

9. Frankl, V. E. (Viktor Emil, 1905-1997) (1955). *The doctor and the soul; an introduction to logotherapy.* New York, Knopf.

10. Harvard Business Staff. (2012, June). Captain planet. *Harvard Business Review.* Retrieved from the *Harvard Business Review* website: https://hbr.org/2012/06/captain-planet

11. Saunders, A. (2011, March). *The MT interview: Paul Polman of Unilever.* Management Today. Retrieved from the Management Today website: http://www.managementtoday.co.uk/features/1055793/MT-Interview-Paul-Polman-Unilever/

12. Unilever: Sustainable living, Unilever. (2014). Retrieved from the Unilever website: http://www.unilever.com/sustainable-living-2014/

13. Gunther, M. (2013, June 10). Unilever's CEO has a green thumb. *Fortune*, 00158259, Vol. 167, Issue 8.

14. Unilever's strategic response to sustainable development and its implications for public affairs professionals. (2012). *Journal of Public Affairs*. Volume 12 Number 3 pp 224– 229.

15. *Unilever: 2014 full year and fourth quarter results.* (2014, December 31). Retrieved from the Unilever website: http://www.unilever.com/images/ir_Q4-2014-full-announcement_tcm13-405226.pdf

16. *Unilever: Making sustainable living commonplace.* (2014). Annual report and accounts 2014, strategic report 2014. Retrieved from the Unilever website: https://www.unilever.com/Images/ARA-2014-Strategic-Report_tcm244-421153.pdf

17. *Missions & Values, Etsy.* Retrieved from the Etsy website: https://www.etsy.com/ca/mission

18. *Notes from Chad: Towards the New Year, Etsy News Blog.* (2014, December 18). Retrieved from the Etsy website: https://blog.etsy.com/news/2014/notes-from-chad-towards-the-new-year/

19. Rifkin, J. (2014). *The zero marginal cost society: The internet of things, the collaborative commons, and the eclipse of capitalism.* St. Martin's Press.

20. *Conscious capitalism: Q&A with Whole Foods CEO John Mackey.* (2013, March 1). *Forbes.* Retrieved from the Forbes website: http://www.forbes.com/sites/ashoka/2013/03/01/qa-with-whole-foods-ceo-john-mackey-about-conscious-capitalism/

21. Amabile, T., & Kramer, S. (2011). *The progress principle: Using small wins to ignite joy, engagement, and creativity at work.* Harvard Business Press.

Chapter 9

1. Mandela, N. & The Nelson Mandela Foundation. (2010). *Nelson Mandela by himself: The authorised book of quotations.*

2. Frankl, V. (2006). *Man's Search for Meaning.* Beacon Press.

3. McLuhan, M., & McLuhan, E. (1988). *Laws of media: The new science*. University of Toronto Press.

4. Drucker, P. (1954). *The practice of management: A study of the most important function in American society*. Harper & Row.

5. Mintzberg, H. (2015, October). We both need networks and communities. *Harvard Business Review*.

6. Martin, R. (2007, June). How successful leaders think. *Harvard Business Review*.

7. Handy, C. (2002, December). What's a business for? *Harvard Business Review*.

8. Craig, N., & Snook, S. (2014, May). From purpose to impact. *Harvard Business Review*.

9. *2015 Workforce Purpose Index*. Imperative and New York University.

10. In conversation with the author. (2015, November).

11. In conversation with the author. (2015, October).

12. In conversation with the author. (2015, September).

13. Vaillant, G. E. (2012). *Triumphs of experience: The men of the Harvard Grant Study*. Belknap Press.

14. In conversation with the author. (2014, April).

15. Moll, J., Krueger, F., Zahn, R., Pardini, M., de Oliveira-Souza, R., & Grafman, J. (2006, October 17). *Human fronto-mesolimbic networks guide decisions about charitable donation*. Proceedings of the National Academy of Sciences, Vol. 103(42), pp. 15623-15628.

16. In conversation with the author. (2015, October).

17. In conversation with the author. (2015, September).

18. Cage, J. (1974, May 2). *Oral history interview*. http://www.aaa.si.edu/collections/interviews/oral-history-interview-john-cage-12442

19. In conversation with the author. (2015, May).

20. Wartzman, R. (2015, January). What Unilever shares with Google and Apple. *Fortune Magazine*.

21. *Our vision, Unilever.* Retrieved from the Unilever website: https://www.unilever.com/about/who-we-are/our-vision/

22. *About us, Quicken Loans.* Retrieved from the Quicken Loans website: http://www.quickenloans.com/about

23. *John Deere: Our guiding principles.* (2012, September). Retrieved from the John Deere website: https://www.deere.com/en_US/docs/Corporate/investor_relations/pdf/corporategovernance/guidingprinciples/guidingprinciples_english.pdf

24. *Our values and mission, Whole Foods.* Retrieved from the Whole Foods website: http://www.wholefoodsmarket.com/careers/our-values-and-mission

25. *Our reason for being, Patagonia.* Retrieved from the Patagonia website: https://www.patagonia.com/ca/patagonia.go?assetid=2047

26. Tyler, G. R. (2013). *What went wrong: How the 1% hijacked the American middle class...and what other countries got right.* BenBella Books.

27. In conversation with the author. (2015, November).

28. In conversation with the author. (2015, November).

29. Matthews, A. (2015, August, 13). The environmental crisis in your closet. *Newsweek.* https://docs.google.com/document/d/1g_E4vqLlpQ96MgyCTRYNQgMhhDfeFwIzwNG_tZ0ILTU/edit

30. Stout, L. (2012). *The shareholder value myth: How putting shareholders first harms investors, corporations, and the public.* Berrett-Koehler Publishers.

31. Lazonick, W. (2014, June). *Taking stock: Why executive pay results in an unstable and inequitable economy.* Roosevelt Institute.

32. Koch, C. G. (2015). *Good profit: How creating value for others built one of the world's most successful companies.* Crown Business, an imprint of Penguin Random House LLC.

33. Murphy, M. (2015, June 22). *All great leadership styles begin by spending time with employees.* Leadership IQ. Retrieved

from Leadership IQ website: https://www.leadershipiq.com/
are-you-spending-enough-time-with-your-bossor-too-much/

34. Branson, R. (2014, August, 20). *Why business is about people, people and people.* Virgin Entrepreneur. Retrieved from the Virgin website: http://www.virgin.com/entrepreneur/ richard-branson-why-business-is-about-people-people-and-people

35. Bersin by Deloitte. *New Bersin & associates research shows organizations that excel at employee recognition are 12 times more likely to generate strong business results.* (2012, November 7). Bersin by Deloitte. Retrieved from the Bersin website: http://www.bersin.com/ News/Content.aspx?id=16023

36. *National Business Ethics Survey: The importance of ethical culture: Increasing trust and driving down risks. Ethics Resource Center.* (2009). http://www.ethics.org/files/u5/CultureSup4.pdf

37. The Grammar of English Grammars from Project Gutenberg. Public domain.

AUTHOR'S RELATED WORK

For more information and resources,
visit www.DanPontefract.com